The Lukan Transfiguration Account
The Exalted Lord in the Glory of the Kingdom of God

Centre for Pentecostal Theology Classics Series

THE LUKAN TRANSFIGURATION ACCOUNT

THE EXALTED LORD IN THE GLORY OF THE KINGDOM OF GOD

CENTRE FOR PENTECOSTAL THEOLOGY CLASSICS SERIES

R. HOLLIS GAUSE

CPT Press
Cleveland, Tennessee USA

The Lukan Transfiguration Account
The Exalted Lord in the Glory of the Kingdom of God
Centre for Pentecostal Theology Classics Series

Published by CPT Press
900 Walker ST NE
Cleveland, TN 37311
USA
email: cptpress@pentecostaltheology.org
website: www.cptpress.com

ISBN: 978-1953358035

Copyright ©2020 CPT Press

All rights reserved. No part of this book may be reproduced or transmitted in any form or by any means, electronic or mechanical, including photocopying, recording, or by any information storage or retrieval system, without permission in writing from the publisher. For information, contact us at CPT Press, 900 Walker ST NE, Cleveland, TN 37311, or online at www.cptpress.com.

Most CPT Press books are available at special quantity discounts when purchased in bulk by bookstores, organizations, and special-interest groups. For more information, please email cptpress@pentecostaltheology.org.

TABLE OF CONTENTS

SERIES PREFACE

The Centre for Pentecostal Theology Classics Series makes available to a wider audience monograph length studies from previous generations that are of special significance for Pentecostal scholarship. While the works included are not all written by Pentecostal scholars, they all address themes and issues that inform constructive Pentecostal theology and/or make special contributions to such by means of methodology or approach.

ACKNOWLEDGEMENTS

It is not possible to complete a project of this nature without the support of many people. Space will not allow me to name all those who have been helpful, but some have made contributions to this work who must be mentioned.

Professor William A. Beardslee, the director of my dissertation, has been most helpful. His perceptive criticism and many helpful suggestions have served as both guide and encouragement in this completion of this study. I am grateful for the contributions made by other readers of the dissertation and members of the thesis committee: Professors Leander Keck, Arthur Wainwright, John Lawson, and Frederick C. Prussner.

The assistance of a skillful and dedicated secretary is an invaluable asset in such a project as this. I am especially grateful to Miss Peggy Jane Bell for her help in typing, proofing, and editing this material. She has devoted many hours and great energy far beyond reasonable expectation.

My wife has given a great deal of time to this project; above all, however, her love and encouragement have been essential to its completion.

I express my appreciation to all of these people.

R. Hollis Gause

Abbreviations

AJT *American Journal of Theology*

BAG Bauer, Walter, *A Greek-English Lexicon of the New Testament and Other Early Christian Literature* (trans. and ed. W.F. Arndt and F.W. Gingrich; Chicago: University of Chicago Press, 1957).

BDF Blass, Friedrich, Albert Debrunner, and Robert Walter Funk, *A Greek Grammar of the New Testament and Other Early Christian Literature* (Chicago: University of Chicago Press, 1961).

HTR *Harvard Theological Review*

JBL *Journal of Biblical Literature*

JTS *Journal of Theological Studies*

NTS *New Testament Studies*

Vie Sp. *Vie Spirituelle*

TDNT Kittel, Gerhard, Geoffrey William Bromiley, and Gerhard Friedrich, *Theological Dictionary of the New Testament* (trans. G. Bromiley; 10 vols.; Grand Rapids, MI: Eerdmans, 1964-).

TSK *Theologische Studien und Kritiken*

ZNW *Zeitschrift für die Neutestamentliche Wissenschaft*

1

Review of the Literature

This study examines the Transfiguration narrative of Luke. As will be shown below, an understanding of the Transfiguration pericope itself requires also a careful consideration of the closing verse of the preceding section. Thus, this chapter will first consider this latter problem, the interpretation of Lk. 9.27, and will then examine the history of the interpretation of the Transfiguration narrative itself (Lk. 9.28-36).

Interpretations of Luke 9.27

On the basis of form-critical studies, a number of scholars separate the Markan parallel to Lk. 9.27 (Mk 9.1) from the account of the Transfiguration. They see the Transfiguration account in Mk 9.2-10 as an interruption of Mk 9.1 and 11.13.[1] The implication is that the discontinuity is still inherent in Luke, even though it may be more skillfully edited. The supposed discontinuity arises from the supposition that Mk 9.1 is a Parousia prediction and the Transfiguration is a resurrection account.[2] As a consequence, Lk. 9.27 is taken also as a Parousia prediction with some Lukan modification.[3] In this line of

---

[1] Rudolf Bultmann, *Theology of the New Testament* (trans. K. Grobel; New York: Scribner, 1951), pp. 26-30; Benjamin W. Bacon, 'The Transfiguration Story', *American Journal of Theology* 6 (1902), p. 241; T.A. Burkill, *Mysterious Revelation* (Ithaca, NY: Cornell University Press, 1963), p. 148; Karl Goetz, *Petrus als Gründer und Oberhaupt der alten Kirche* (Leipzig: Hinrichs, 1927), pp. 11, 12.

[2] Bultmann, *Theology of the New Testament*, pp. 26-30; Goetz, *Petrus*, pp. 11, 12.

[3] Hans Conzelmann, *The Theology of St. Luke* (trans. Geoffrey Buswell; London: Faber & Faber, 1960), p. 105.

interpretation, it is generally concluded that this statement does not refer to the Transfiguration.

Most scholars who interpret the Transfiguration as a historical event (of some sort) correctly recorded in the pre-crucifixion period of the gospel narrative see a predictive connection between Lk. 9.27 (and parallels) and the Transfiguration. This interpretation does not rule out the treatment of this verse and/or its parallels as a Parousia prediction.[4]

Plummer has brought together the various interpretations of the reference of Lk. 9.27 into a single list. His list is as follows:

> 1. The Transfiguration (most of the Fathers), 2. The Resurrection and Ascension (Cajetan, Calvin, Beza), 3. Pentecost and subsequent signs (Godet, Hahn), 4. The Spread of Christianity (Nösgen), 5. The internal development of the gospel (Erasmus, Klöstermann), 6. The testing of Jesus (Wetstein, Alford, Morison, Plumptre, Mansel), 7. The Second Advent (Meyer, Weisse, Holtzmann).[5]

There is a wide range of other interpretations: the destruction of Jerusalem,[6] Pentecost,[7] the resurrection,[8] a vision of the triumph of the kingdom,[9] and the church.[10] C.H. Dodd, in the development of his 'realized eschatology', proposes that Pentecost may be taken as 'the moment of perception' that the kingdom has come.[11]

One of the most significant interpretations is that of Hans Conzelmann. Conzelmann argues that Lk. 9.27 is the earliest attempt

---

[4] G.H. Boobyer, *St. Mark and the Transfiguration Story* (Edinburgh: T & T Clark, 1942), p. 57; G.B. Caird, 'The Transfiguration', *Expository Times* 67 (1955-56), p. 291; E. Earle Ellis, *The Gospel of Luke* (London: Nelson, 1966), p. 141; Edward Evans, 'The Transfiguration of Jesus', *Evangelical Quarterly* 26 (1954), p. 99.

[5] Alfred Plummer, *The Gospel According to St. Luke* (International Critical Commentary; New York: Scribner, 1896), p. 249.

[6] Norman Geldenhuys, *Commentary on the Gospel of St. Luke* (Grand Rapids: Eerdmans, 1951), p. 277.

[7] John Martin Creed, *The Gospel According to St. Luke* (London: Macmillan, 1957), p. 32.

[8] R.A. Cole, *The Gospel According to St. Mark* (Tyndale New Testament Commentary; Grand Rapids: Eerdmans, 1961), pp. 140, 141.

[9] Thomas M. Lindsay, *The Gospel According to St. Luke* (New York: Scribner, 1887), p. 140.

[10] Ned B. Stonehouse, *The Witness of St. Luke to Christ* (London: Tyndale Press, 1951), p. 156.

[11] C.H. Dodd, 'The Kingdom Has Come', *Expository Times* 48 (1936), p. 138.

to exegete Mk 9.1, which is a Parousia statement. Luke substitutes a 'timeless conception' of the kingdom for Mark's imminent Parousia.[12]

All of the views presented are in some sense eschatological. Some are eschatological only by accommodation; it is clear that the interpreters seek to find some historical event that occurred within Jesus' generation that will also suffice as a fulfillment of the promise. These events (such as the destruction of Jerusalem) are rendered eschatological by way of typology. Others seek a more direct eschatological interpretation and fulfillment.

The primary difficulty with most of these views is that they seek an interpretation and fulfillment from outside the literary context of Lk. 9.27. If one takes this context seriously, the choices are narrowed to two: the Parousia and the Transfiguration.[13]

Interpretations of Luke 9.28-36

Luke's account of the Transfiguration appears in Lk. 9.28-36; it opens with the time reference and closes with Luke's remark concerning the silence of the three disciples. Most of the exegetical and form-critical studies of the Transfiguration have been concentrated on Mark's account, with passing attention given to the peculiarities of Luke and Matthew.[14]

In the early nineteenth century, David Friedrich Strauss gave a summary of the interpretations of the Transfiguration; he listed three general categories: (1) 'the transfiguration of Jesus considered as a miraculous external event', (2) 'the natural explanation in various forms', and (3) 'the history of the transfiguration considered as mythus'.[15] he cites one scholar who supports the interpretation given in number 1 above.[16] Strauss places the visionary interpretation in

[12] Conzelmann, *The Theology of St. Luke*, p. 55.

[13] The presentation of arguments on each of these is more appropriately taken up in the exegesis of the passage in Chapter 3.

[14] On the Matthew account, however, see Thomas F. Best, 'Transfiguration and Discipleship in Matthew' (PhD dissertation, Graduate Theological Union, 1974).

[15] David Friedrich Strauss, *The Life of Jesus Critically Examined* (Lives of Jesus Series; Leander E. Keck [gen. ed.]; trans. George Eliot; ed. Peter C. Hodgson; Philadelphia: Fortress, 1972), pp. 535-46.

[16] Strauss, *The Life of Jesus Critically Examined*, pp. 535-36 nn. 3 and 4: Hermann Olshausen, *Biblical Commentary on the New Testament* (6 vols.; trans. David Fosdick, Jr.; New York: Blakeman and Co., 1857-1858), I, pp. 534-36

category 2 above and cites Johann Herder, Peter Gratz, Tertullian, and Marcion as favoring this interpretation.[17] Strauss acknowledges that this view is really not a natural explanation.[18] If the Transfiguration is to be treated in this way, he prefers 'to break this thread, and restore all to the external world: so that we now have a natural external occurrence before us …'[19]

Strauss himself favors the last of the three views; he does not regard the Transfiguration as historical (either as miracle, vision, or natural event) and attributes it to the construction of the church after the pattern of the Sinai theophany. It is mythological narrative; in addition to similarities with the Sinai tradition, he also sees similarities with other religious traditions.[20]

These categories of the interpretation of the Transfiguration generally fit the two antithetical interpretations presently identified with the historical view of the Transfiguration and the history of religious view of the Transfiguration. In contemporary scholarship, this subject is generally set within one or the other of these two schools of thought.

It is not possible to develop totally clear lines of separation between these two schools of interpretation as they deal with the Transfiguration. Generally, however, the following distinctions apply. Those who interpret this passage from the historical viewpoint understand that the synoptics record an event which took place in the life of Jesus prior to his crucifixion. These interpreters understand the record to be one of a miraculous change in the attire, appearance, and nature of Jesus which was also accompanied by a miraculous appearance of Moses and Elijah.[21] Such an interpretation is specifically

---

[17] Strauss, *The Life of Jesus Critically Examined*, p. 537 n. 1: 'Thus Tertull adv. Marcion, IV, 22; Herder, ut sup. 115f., with whom Gratz agrees. Comm. z Matth. 2, s. 163f., 169.'

[18] Strauss, *The Life of Jesus Critically Examined*, p. 538.

[19] Strauss, *The Life of Jesus Critically Examined*, p. 539: he cites Heinrich Paulus and Friedrich Schleiermacher as favoring this view (p. 540 nn. 7 and 8).

[20] Strauss, *The Life of Jesus Critically Examined*, pp. 540-46: On page 545 n. 18, he cites the following authors who concur that the Transfiguration is mythological: DeWette, Bertholdt, Credner, Schulz, and Fritzsche.

[21] Boobyer, *St. Mark and the Transfiguration Story*, pp. 65-67; A.E. Burn, 'The Transfiguration', *Expository Times* 14 (1902-03), pp. 442-47; Evans, 'The Transfiguration of Jesus'; Geldenhuys, *Commentary on the Gospel of St. Luke*, pp. 280-83; Frédéric Louis Godet, *Commentary on the Gospel of Luke* (trans. E.W. Shalders; Edinburgh: T & T Clark, 1887; reprinted, Grand Rapids: Zondervan, 1965), p. 135; William L. Groves, 'The Significance of the Transfiguration of Our Lord', *Theology*

historical and assumes no special experience of the three disciples except that of observing a miracle.

The methodology and conclusions of the history of religions school have had considerable impact on the interpretation of the Transfiguration historically as a pre-crucifixion event in the life of Jesus. Their conclusions are that there is a historical event lying behind the Transfiguration story, and that this event is properly understood by the methodology of history of religions study.

Representative of the conclusions drawn from this interpretative approach are the following. The Transfiguration is to be understood as a theophany.[22] The theophany concept is closely akin to Bernandin's description of the Transfiguration as a revelation of Christ's preexistent glory[23] and Burkill's description as a lifting of 'the veil of the flesh'.[24] The Transfiguration is frequently treated as a vision, which does not exclude the authors cited above; generally, however, the treatment of the experience as a vision centers on the spiritual experience of the disciples.[25]

These views generally have the following characteristics in common. They place the event historically in the life of Jesus. Though they may use a typology after the pattern of the history of religions school, they see in the event a transformation of Jesus' appearance (either by miraculous change of nature or by appearance in vision). Some of those who hold these views appeal to form-critical

---

11 (1925), pp. 86-92; E.F. Harrison, 'The Transfiguration', *Bibliotheca Sacra* 95 (1936), pp. 315-23; H.A.A. Kennedy, 'The Purpose of the Transfiguration', *JTS* 4 (1903), pp. 270-73; Arthur Michael Ramsey, *The Glory of God and the Transfiguration* (London: Longmans, Green & Co., 1949), pp. 106-109.

22 Benjamin W. Bacon, 'The Transfiguration Story', *American Journal of Theology* 6 (1903), pp. 230-65. A.M. Denis, 'Une theologie de la vie chretienne chez saint Marc (VI, 30-VIII, 27)', *Vie Sp.* 41 (1959), pp. 416-27; L.F. Rivera, 'El misterio del Hijo del Hombre en la Transfiguracion', *Revista Biblica* 28 (1966), pp. 79-89; L.F. Rivera, 'Interpretatio Transfiguracionis Jesu in redactione evangelii Marci', *Ver Con* 46 (1968), pp. 99-104. The entries of Denis and Rivera are based on research in *New Testament Abstracts* 4 (1960), pp. 134, 135; 11 (1967), pp. 210, 211; 11 (1967), p. 323; the original materials are not available to me.

23 Joseph B. Bernardin, 'The Transfiguration', *JBL* 52 (1933), pp. 181-89.

24 T.A. Burkill, *Mysterious Revelation*, p. 156.

25 Bacon, 'The Transfiguration Story'; F.J. Babcock, 'The Transfiguration', *JTS* 22 (1921), pp. 321-26; Adolf von Harnack, *Die Verklärungsgeschichte Jesu, der Bericht des Paulus (1 Kor. 15, 3ff) und die beiden Christusvisionen des Petrus* (Sitzungsberichte der Königlich Preussischen Akademie der Wissenschaften zu Berlin 7; Berlin: Walter de Gruyter, 1922), pp. 62-80; Eduard Meyer, *Ursprung und Anfänge des Christentums* (Stuttgart and Berlin: J.G. Cotta, 1923), pp. 153, 154.

categories, but the consciousness of an actual event dominates the interpretation. Generally, these interpretations develop ethical and pietistic exhortations from the account. The Transfiguration, though an event distinct from the resurrection and ascension, is interpreted to have predictive significance. There is little uniformity in the conclusions concerning the relationship between Lk. 9.27 (and parallels) and 9.28-36 (and parallels).

The history of religions school seeks to understand the Transfiguration (and other religious experiences) in the light of comparative studies with other religious traditions. As we have noted earlier, such a methodology does not preclude historical interpretation; however, this discipline does not presuppose the historicity of the particular event under study. So, in relation to the Transfiguration, a number of scholars that are identified (in varying degrees) with this school understand the Transfiguration as a religious experience of the early Christian community. Its *Sitz im Leben* is in the life of the church.

The Transfiguration is, in this discipline, most often compared with the Sinai tradition; however, appeal to traditions from outside Judaism is not uncommon.[26]

Within the framework of this mode of interpretation, the historicity of the event is generally not considered necessary to the account, although many who interpret the Scriptures by these principles do conclude that a historical event is in the background of the account.[27]

Among the earlier writers who treated the Transfiguration as unhistorical and as mythological are DeWette, Bertholdt, Credner,

---

[26] Strauss, *The Life of Jesus Critically Examined*, p. 545 n. 19: 'Plato also in the Symposion (p. 223, B. ff. Steph.), glorifies his Socrates by arranging in a natural manner, and in a comic spirit, a similar group to that which the Evangelists here present in a supernatural manner, and in tragic spirit'. Peter Jensen, 'Die Verlärungsberg-Szene und Nachbarepisoden in einem chinesischen Märchen?', *Theologische Studien und Kritiken* 104 (1932), pp. 229-37; 105 (1933), pp. 330-36: Cited by Boobyer, *St. Mark and the Transfiguration Story*, p. 2 n. 1. Jensen relates the Transfiguration to a Chinese fairy tale that is as old as Mark, to the Gilgamesh Epic, and to the Sinai tradition; Hans-Peter Müller, 'Die Verlärung Jesu, eine motivgeschichtliche Studie', *ZNW* 51 (1960), pp. 56-64: There are two motifs and originally two stories here. Jesus changes into a Lichtgestalt (Mk 9.2c-6, 8); Jesus' appearance changes in the pattern of the Sinai tradition (vv. 2a, b, 7, 9); Ernst Lohmeyer, 'Die Verlärung Jesu nach dem Markus Evangelium', *ZNW* 21 (1922), pp. 185-215; in this article, he attributes the Transfiguration motif to a Hellenistic origin; subsequently, in his commentary on Mark, he attributes it to a Jewish source.

[27] See n. 22.

Scholz, and Fritsche.[28] Bruno Bauer is also to be placed here;[29] so also are von Soden[30] and Wrede.[31]

Probably the best known of the interpretations in this line of thought is the view that the Transfiguration was 'originally a resurrection appearance ... (that) was eventually transferred to the life of Jesus as a transfiguration story'.[32] This conclusion does not regard the Transfiguration as historically distinct from the resurrection. Historicity is unnecessary in either event, though not necessarily denied.

The views expressed by scholars in the history of religions school generally have the following in common. The typology for this event is sought in a comparison with other religious experiences; hence the account is taken to have mythological elements (if it is not entirely mythological). The *Sitz im Leben* is sought in the experience of the primitive church; this episode is placed by the synoptic authors (as they reflect the various traditions of the early church) in the record of Jesus' life; it thus represents one aspect of the kerygma. The Transfiguration is included in the gospel records as a representation of the exaltation of Jesus; consequently, it is often taken to be a misplaced resurrection account.

Form-critical studies of the Transfiguration have not been precise in identifying a genre for this record in the synoptics. It is designated as a 'formless story' by Redlich; he concludes that this and other such stories 'stand outside the purview of Form Criticism'.[33] Dibelius

---

28 See n. 20.

29 The Transfiguration is the literary invention of Mark.

30 Hermann Freiherr von Soden, *Die wichtigsten Fragen im Leben Jesu* (Berlin: Alexander Duncker, 1904), p. 24. It is of secondary origin and is derived from the theology of the early Christian community.

31 William Wrede, *The Messianic Secret* (trans. J.C.G. Greig; Cambridge and London: James Clarke & Co., 1971), The Transfiguration is 'something supramundane which has no place in the earthly life of Jesus' (p. 68); the reference to the Transfiguration, the predictive reference to Jesus' death and reference to the resurrection are 'not that of material presenting us with the actual life of Jesus' (pp. 89, 90).

32 Charles Edwin Carlston, 'Transfiguration and Resurrection', *JBL* 80 (1961), p. 233; Julius Wellhausen, *Das Evangelium Marci* (Berlin: G. Reiner, 1909), p. 71; Wilhelm Boussett, *Jesus* (trans. J.P. Trevelyan; London: Williams & Norgate, 1911); Alfred F. Loisy, *The Birth of the Christian Religion* (trans. L.P. Jacks; New Hyde Park, NY: University Books, 1962), p. 101; Müller, 'Die Verlärung Jesu'; Bultmann, *Theology of the New Testament*, p. 27; Erich Klöstermann, *Das Lukas Evangelium* (Tübingen: J.C.B. Mohr, 1929), pp. 107, 108; Goetz, *Petrus*; there are a number of recent writers (in addition to those listed above) who hold this view; some of these will be cited in other portions of this paper, especially in the exegesis of Lk. 9.27-36.

33 Edwin Basil Redlich, *Form Criticism* (New York: Scribner, 1939), p. 184.

designates the Transfiguration account as legend.[34] Such a designation generally classifies the Transfiguration as in the broad category of romantic literature, but this helps little in formal analysis.

The literary form that comes closest to this literary genre is the epiphany form.[35] The most frequently applied form motif of this nature is the parallel with the Sinai theophany. The parallels deal more with content than with literary forms. The characteristics of the Sinai theophany are frequently combined with the vision of the appearance of the Son of man (Dan. 7.13, 14).[36] Parallels are frequently drawn between the Transfiguration and other events in NT literature. The most frequently cited events are the voice from heaven at the baptism of Jesus, the resurrection, the ascension, and the appearances of the risen Lord in Acts.

We turn our attention now to the interpretations that are drawn from the Transfiguration accounts. Here our review will not attempt to reflect the interpretation of each detail of the Transfiguration. Instead, we shall note the broad significance attached to the Transfiguration. As early as Wellhausen, the Transfiguration is treated as a post-resurrection defense by the church of the divine sonship of Jesus and is thus considered to be a resurrection story.[37] It is plainly and simply a resurrection story.[38] Somewhat related to this view is the interpretation that sees in the Transfiguration a prefiguring of resurrection glory.[39]

---

34 Martin Dibelius, *A Fresh Approach to the New Testament* (trans. D.S. Noel and G. Abbott; New York: Scribner, 1936), pp. 38-42; Rudolf Bultmann, *The History of the Synoptic Tradition* (trans. John Marsh; New York and Evanston: Harper & Row, 1963), p. 286; Müller, 'Die Verlärung Jesu': the mythical 'light-form'; Jensen, 'Die Verlärungsberg-Szene und Nachbarepisoden in einem chinesischen Märchen?, the Chinese fairy tale.

35 E. Kautsch, 'Theophany', in *The New Schaff-Herzog Encyclopedia of Religious Knowledge* (New York: Funk and Wagnalls, 1911), II, pp. 403-405.

36 Rivera, 'El misterio del Hijo del Hombre en la Transfiguracion', pp. 79-89; G.B. Caird, *The Gospel According to St. Luke* (Baltimore: Penguin, 1963), p. 132; Caird, 'The Transfiguration', pp. 291, 292; Wallace Eugene Rollins and Marion Benedict Rollins, *Jesus and his Ministry* (New York: Seabury Press, 1954), p. 196.

37 Wellhausen, *Das Evangelium Marci*, p. 71.

38 Loisy, *The Birth of the Christian Religion*; Bultmann, *The History of the Synoptic Tradition*; Goetz, *Petrus*; Carlston, 'Transfiguration and Resurrection'.

39 Harnack, *Die Verklärungsgeschichte Jesu*; Harrison, 'The Transfiguration', p. 317; Kennedy, 'The Purpose of the Transfiguration', pp. 271, 272; Margaret E. Thrall, 'Elijah and Moses in Mark's Account of the Transfiguration', *NTS* 16 (1970), p. 310.

Probably the majority of students see a broader prefigurement. It embraces the whole exaltation concept inclusive of Jesus' death, resurrection and ascension.[40] This view is frequently extended to embrace also the heavenly estate of Jesus.[41] This heavenly estate relates not only to the future glory, but to the preincarnate glory of the Son of God.[42] The application of the Transfiguration to the glory of the Parousia appears frequently in the literature.[43]

A related but considerably different interpretation is the one chiefly associated with Frédéric Louis Godet. In the Transfiguration, Jesus stepped into the realm of glory, which is the Father's reward for a perfect life in accordance with the law and justice of God.[44] A.E. Burn incorporates this view and adds to it the application that the Transfiguration teaches the secret of progress.[45] One of the most recent authors to take this position is Edward Evans. The Transfiguration is 'a natural event in the life of a perfect man'; it is the glory intended for humanity had they not sinned and the glory in which Christ shall reign.[46] Hence, Evans argues that Jesus passed through judgement and by miraculous Transfiguration stepped into the glory of his reward. Similar views are also expressed by William C. Brathwaite[47] and William L. Groves.[48]

The common denominator of all of these interpretations is eschatology. The fashion in which Jesus is seen in the Transfiguration

---

40 Caird, 'The Transfiguration' pp. 291, 292; Walter E. Pilgrim, 'The Death of Christ in Lukan Soteriology' (PhD dissertation, Princeton Theological Seminary, 1971), pp. 195, 196; S. Lewis Johnson, 'The Transfiguration of Christ', *Bibliotheca Sacra* 124 (1967), pp. 135-36.

41 Babcock, 'The Transfiguration', p. 326; Burkill, *Mysterious Revelation*, p. 156; Ramsey, *The Glory of God and the Transfiguration*, p. 109.

42 Bernardin, 'The Transfiguration', pp. 182-84, 187; Julius Schniewind, *Das Evangelium nach Markus* (Göttingen: Vandenhoeck and Ruprecht, 1949), pp. 116, 117; B.H. Branscomb, *The Gospel of Mark* (London: Hodder & Stoughton, 1937), p. 160.

43 Boobyer, *St. Mark and the Transfiguration Story*, p. 29; Rivera, 'El misterio del Hijo del Hombre en la Transfiguracion', pp. 79-89; James Moffatt, *The General Epistles* (New Testament Commentary; New York and London: Harper & Bros., 1938), p. 186.

44 Godet, *Commentary on the Gospel of Luke*, p. 275.

45 A.E. Burn, 'The Transfiguration', *Expository Times* 14 (1902-1903), p. 444.

46 Evans, 'The Transfiguration of Jesus', pp. 97-104.

47 William C. Braithwaite, 'The Teaching of the Transfiguration', *Expository Times* 17 (1905-1906), pp. 372-75.

48 William L. Groves, 'The Significance of the Transfiguration of Our Lord', *Theology* 11 (1925), pp. 86-92.

is representative of the Parousia or some other aspect of the future manifestation of the kingdom of God.

Most exegetes take particular note that there are two groups of witnesses of the Transfiguration: the three disciples and the two OT characters. Separate interpretational significance is attached to each group. For the most part the presence of Peter, John, and James is accounted for in the interests of the church. They witness the Transfiguration in order to establish it for the later church,[49] in order to make the resurrected Christ recognizable[50] and to correct false notions about the person of Jesus.[51] The Transfiguration confirmed to the disciples the confession made at Caesarea Philippi.[52] Peter, John, and James represent the concentration of apostolic power, and to them is entrusted the mystery of the kingdom of God.[53] Peter, John, and James were present as the subjects of the kingdom being revealed.[54]

The two witnesses from the OT are usually taken as eschatological symbols in the Transfiguration. Apocalyptic books place a number of OT heroes at the coming of the Messiah and there is a special interest in those who according to tradition were translated: Enoch, Elijah, Ezra, Baruch, Jeremiah, and perhaps Job.[55]

Most of the interpretations of Moses' and Elijah's presence depend on their identification with the law and prophets respectively. The law and prophets foretell the passion of the Messiah.[56] Babcock adds other interpretations. Moses is the commencement of prophecy and all Scripture. Elijah fulfills the concept of his own coming in the flesh; he is John the Baptist. He also represents the end prophecy as Moses represents its beginning.[57]

The significance of Moses and Elijah is made especially important by their removal at the point of the heavenly command, 'Hear him'.

---

49 Groves, 'The Significance of the Transfiguration of Our Lord', p. 86.

50 H.A.A. Kennedy, 'The Purpose of the Transfiguration', *JTS* 4 (1903), p. 271.

51 R. Holmes, 'The Purpose of the Transfiguration', *JTS* 4 (1903), p. 546.

52 E.J. Martin, 'The Transfiguration', *Expository Times* 38 (1926-27), p. 189.

53 Rivera, 'El misterio del Hijo del Hombre en la Transfiguracion', pp. 79-89.

54 G. Stringer Rowe, 'The Transfiguration', *Expository Times* 15 (1903-04), p. 336.

55 H.L. Strack and Paul Billerbeck, *Kommentar zum Neuen Testament und Midrasch* (Munchen: C.H. Beck'she Verlagsbuchhandlung; 1924), I, pp. 753-58.

56 F.J. Babcock, 'The Transfiguration', *JTS* 22 (1921), pp. 323, 324; Burn, 'The Transfiguration', p. 444; Harrison, 'The Transfiguration', pp. 319, 320.

57 Babcock, 'The Transfiguration', pp. 321-26.

The disciples are to hear Jesus as superseding Moses and Elijah.[58] Others, without emphasizing the removal, make the same point: Moses and Elijah point to Jesus as superseding them.[59]

The proposal of Peter to build three tabernacles to commemorate the Transfiguration is frequently interpreted in relation to the feast of tabernacles. Some see in this proposal an evidence that the Transfiguration took place at the time of the feast.[60] MacMillan relates the proposal to his claim that the villagers in the area of Mt. Hermon build little tabernacles to escape the heat.[61]

Many who do not emphasize the season of this occurrence do see in the proposal to build 'tabernacles' an eschatological symbol based on the interpretation of the feast of tabernacles.[62] It represents God's presence among the people. Lohmeyer applies this 'tabernacle' concept to the resurrection concept.[63]

There are three foci of interest in the voice of witness: the words of witness and their origin, the cloud and the meaning of the witness.

There is general recognition of the obvious: the parallel with the voice of witness at the baptism of Jesus and the divine and heavenly origin of the voice.

The cloud carries further the concept of the divine and heavenly origin of the witness. This is further enforced by the identification of the cloud as the Shekinah.[64] It answers to the cloud at Sinai and promises that God will dwell among us.[65] There is a specific application of these symbols to eschatological expectation.

The words of witness are of particular interest. The witness specifically affirms Jesus' supersession of Moses and Elijah. Israel should now hear Jesus as they once heard Moses.[66] This is a divine

---

58 Thrall, 'Elijah and Moses', p. 309.

59 C.F.D. Moule, 'The Christology of Luke–Acts', in D.E. Nineham (ed.), *Studies in Luke–Acts* (Oxford: Basil Blackwell, 1955), pp. 162-63.

60 W.M. Ramsay, 'The Time of the Transfiguration', *The Expositor* 6 (1908), pp. 560, 561; Walter Roehrs, 'God's Tabernacles Among Men: A Study of the Transfiguration', *Concordia Theological Monthly* 35 (1965), p. 18.

61 Hugh MacMillan, 'Water-Marks in the Narratives of Our Lord's Transfiguration', *Expository Times* 7 (1895-96), pp. 25-27.

62 Ernst Lohmeyer, 'Die Verklärung Jesu', *ZNW* 21 (1922), pp. 191-92; Ramsay, 'The Time of the Transfiguration', pp. 560-61.

63 Ramsay, 'The Time of the Transfiguration', pp. 560, 561.

64 Boobyer, *St. Mark and the Transfiguration Story*, pp. 78, 81; G.C. Montefiore, *The Synoptic Gospels* (London: Macmillan, 1927), I, p. 208.

65 Rivera, 'El misterio del Hijo del Hombre en la Transfiguracion', pp. 79-89.

66 Rivera, 'El misterio del Hijo del Hombre en la Transfiguracion', pp. 79-89.

witness to Jesus as prophet, but more – a prophet (in the fulfillment of Deut. 15.15, 18) who is Son.[67]

The specific interpretations of the Lukan account have been reserved for discussion in Chapters 3 and 4. In this connection, it may be observed that most of the exegetical critical work on the Transfiguration is based on Mark.

Our review of this literature seems to justify the following conclusions concerning the Transfiguration studies. The literature seems to fall into three categories: devotional, form-critical, and redaction critical.

The devotional literature tends to be non-critical. Its exegetical work is not very rewarding. The applications made from this type of study are primarily personal and subjective. They call for the imitation of Jesus' experience through prayer, obedience, etc. They offer comfort in tribulation by the promise of glory after the cross. They give assurance of the resurrection and the foreshadowing of its glory. These applications are frequent in the older liberal authors and not infrequent among conservative authors. The former is the result of the attempt to discover the historical Jesus and to make direct ethical and spiritual paradigms of every aspect of his life. The latter seems to be the result of the conservative preoccupation with the death, resurrection, and return of Jesus. The Transfiguration is an 'extra' that conservative theology has not involved in its structure.

In form-critical studies, the investigation of the Transfiguration is usually reserved for the study of Mark. This procedure is based on the assumption of the priority of Mark. The conclusion seems to be that the questions of origin and literary form are adequately answered at this point of inquiry. Certainly, such inquiry must begin at this point, but the inadequacy shows up in the following ways. The peculiarities of Luke are passed over superficially. Inadequate attention is given to the possibility of 'seams' in the Lukan account and the manner in which the Lukan account came together for him. Little attention is given the question of the priority of traditions lying behind the individual accounts.

The school of thought that associates the Transfiguration with the resurrection (either as resurrection appearance thrust back into the life of Jesus or as a foreshadowing of the resurrection) has tended to

---

[67] Moule, 'The Christology of Luke–Acts', pp. 162, 163.

consider the meaning of the Transfiguration settled. Little additional study is given the Transfiguration.

A new direction needs to be taken here. A comparison of the Transfiguration appearance with the ascension–exaltation motif in Acts will show greater parallels in symbolism (and perhaps in literary form). Perhaps it is the Luke–Acts body of literature that will provide the most fruitful basis of study here.

Special Transfiguration Studies

Four books represent special studies of the Transfiguration: Joseph Blinzler, *Die neutestamentlichen Berichte über die Verklärung Jesu* (Münster: Verlag der Aschendorffschen Verlagsbuchhandlung, 1937); G.H. Boobyer, *St. Mark and the Transfiguration Story* (Edinburg: T & T Clark, 1942); Harald Riesenfeld, *Jésus Transfiguré* (Copenhagen: Ejwar Munksgaard, 1947); and Heinrich Baltensweiler, *Die Verklärung Jesu* (Zurich: Zwingli Verlag, 1959). There are doubtless others, but these are at least representative of the major views of scholarship in the area. Because they are of a special nature, these books have been reserved for brief individual attention.

Joseph Blinzler

The presuppositions of Blinzler's book represent the traditional Roman Catholic position. Blinzler discusses virtually every viewpoint of the Transfiguration that has been seriously maintained in the scholarly world. The critiques which he offers of these positions are those of the Roman Catholic tradition.

The first chapter of the book consists of a meticulous analysis of the accounts of the Transfiguration, both canonical and apocryphal. There follows a statistical analysis of the vocabulary of the synoptic accounts. He recognizes the distinctive elements in each of the accounts. He concludes that the Transfiguration account in Mark is from Peter, an eyewitness, and he also concludes that Mark is the earliest gospel. Second Peter 1.16-18 represents a true Petrine tradition. Blinzler's explanation of the uniqueness of the Lukan account is that Luke wrote from a special source: the eyewitness accounts provided him by John and James. This is also the explanation for John's omission of a Transfiguration account.

Blinzler states and examines all of the positions on the Transfiguration usually set forth in the history of religions school: natural occurrence, allegorical, poetic doublet, mythical, dream, resurrection account, and so forth. He rejects them all. His own position is that the synoptic accounts are based on eyewitness reports of a historical event in the pre-crucifixion life of Jesus. It was a supernatural event and cannot be adequately explained by any of the hypotheses of the history of religions school.

The chief value of Blinzler's book is that it represents in one compilation a virtually complete list of the interpretations of the Transfiguration. The chief weakness here is that the criticism of the positions which he enumerates is carried out from a set of unexamined presuppositions. A weakness of the book from the interpretation standpoint is that it offers little new insight into the meaning of the Transfiguration.

G.H. Boobyer

G.H. Boobyer, by the title of his book, limits his study predominantly to the Markan account. He does, however, deal with most of the issues that are raised by the subject of the Transfiguration.

His review of the literature probably represents the most comprehensive review in English. The first section of the book traces the interpretation of the Transfiguration from the canonical accounts to the present. His analysis of the Ethiopic text of the Apocalypse of Peter is particularly informative.

The review of contemporary scholarship also contains a critique of these positions. He is particularly interested in the view that the Transfiguration was originally a resurrection account.[68] The heart of Boobyer's critique of this position is his contention that the Transfiguration is an ascension-exaltation story which the church distinguished from the resurrection stories.

Boobyer takes Mk 9.1 to relate to the Parousia; it is, therefore, a promise that some of Jesus' audience would see the coming of the kingdom in some sense. The Transfiguration naturally follows in Mark's mind and development. The transfigured appearance of Jesus is his 'parousia body' and not his resurrection body. He enforces his

---

68 For the purposes of statement and critique he deals especially with the statement of this issue in Karl Gerhold Goetz, *Petrus* (Leipzig: J.C. Hinrichs'she Buchhandlung, 1927), pp. 76-89.

identification of the Transfiguration in this way by interpreting various elements in the Transfiguration as evidence of eschatological motifs: the presence of Moses and Elijah, the tabernacles, the cloud (Shekinah), and the voice. Boobyer's citation of the Ethiopic text of the Apocalypse of Peter is highly significant for him. This apocalypse presents an account of the Transfiguration that combines both the Parousia and ascension motifs. Boobyer comes to a similar conclusion. The Transfiguration is a Transfiguration-ascension account and it also maintains the Parousia element.

Harald Riesenfeld

The most ambitious of the recent works is Harold Riesenfeld's *Jésus Transfiguré*. It is ambitious from the standpoint of the task Riesenfeld set for himself – an intensive review of cult in Israel, the development of a motif study of the Transfiguration based on these cultic elements – and from the standpoint of offering a new direction for Transfiguration studies. This new direction represented by his argument that the Transfiguration was cast in the form of a Jewish enthronement festival.

In these interests, he rejects rationalistic and mythological interpretations of the Transfiguration, though the nature of his work is in the discipline of the history of religions school. He also rejects Boobyer's interpretation of the Transfiguration from the standpoint of the Parousia.

Riesenfeld's thesis is developed as follows. He has a long and detailed study of motifs as they developed in the history of Judaism – by way of worship, feasts, messianism, and symbols. These are interpreted from an eschatological standpoint.

These motifs are to be found in the Transfiguration. Of special importance for Riesenfeld's interpretation of the Transfiguration is the Jewish enthronement festival. He argues that the feast of tabernacles had become an eschatological feast that anticipated the enthronement of the Messiah. This enthronement is in the pattern of the festival for the enthronement of Yahweh in Israel.

The eschatological elements in the Transfiguration that he uses to argue for this view are the mountain (as the place of enthronement), the glory (as Messiah's enduement with divine glory), the cloud (as representative of God's presence and an impending consummation of the kingdom), the voice (as the proclamation of Jesus' sonship and messianic kingship), and Moses and Elijah (as those who are precursors of the Messiah-king).

The most serious weakness of Riesenfeld's work is that he fails to show that there was a Jewish enthronement festival or that the feast of tabernacles had become such an enthronement festival. With this weakness, his arguments become arguments by analogy.

This weakness, however, does not destroy the value of this work. It is possible that his enthronement interpretation of the Transfiguration may stand without being based on an enthronement festival. His development of eschatological and enthronement motifs appears to have strength on other bases.

Heinrich Baltensweiler

Baltensweiler's work was originally presented to the Theological Faculty at the University of Basel as his doctoral dissertation (1958) and was published in 1959. Baltensweiler's methodology is that of the history of religions school. He feels, however, that the question of the historicity of the event of the Transfiguration has been neglected.

The outline of his study follows generally what we have seen in Blinzler and Boobyer – resumê of the interpretation of the Transfiguration, and of the apocryphal and canonical accounts of the Transfiguration. He accepts the priority of Mark.

As for the nature of the Transfiguration, Baltensweiler concludes that some event in the life of Jesus stands behind the Transfiguration. On the basis of the time reference in Mk 9.2, he concludes that the Transfiguration took place at the time of the feast of tabernacles. The six days relate to the span of time from the beginning of the feast to the sixth day. The occasion in Jesus' life was an experience of crisis such as the crisis in Gethsemane, which is evidenced by the element of suffering in the Transfiguration.

The synoptic accounts apply the Transfiguration both in relation to Jesus and the disciples. In relation to Jesus it was his assurance of sonship; it showed the nature of his messiahship and its identification with suffering; it strengthened him against the temptation to take the Zealot's route of messiahship. It was the rejection of political messiahship. As a result of the Markan redaction of this crisis event, the narrative in Mark is also turned toward the disciples. This is especially evident in the testimony of the divine Voice declaring Jesus' sonship.

There is also in Mark an enthronement motif. The disciples see the Son of man as he will come as Messiah-king.

The review of the literature on the subject of the Transfiguration shows that most studies follow one of two lines of investigation. They deal almost entirely with the Markan account or they deal with all of the synoptic accounts as if they were one document. In either case, Mark, as the oldest gospel and as the gospel that provides the framework of both Matthew and Luke, receives most of the attention in study. Consequently, there has been a dearth of study of the Lukan account of the Transfiguration as an individual account. Luke's account differs from Mark's in significant details. These differences merit the special investigation of this study and will be discussed in the subsequent chapters.

2

THE TEXT: ITS FORM AND HISTORY

The context of the Transfiguration account in Luke is a very closely bound unit. The relationship between the pericope containing the predictions of Jesus' death and resurrection (Lk. 9.21-27), the pericope containing the predictions of Jesus' death and resurrection (Lk. 9.21-27), and the pericope which describes the Transfiguration (9.28-36) is particularly close. It is apparently the intention of Luke to show that the first of these leads to the others.

This connection is particularly shown by vv. 27 and 28. Luke 9.27 is correctly taken as the climactic statement of vv. 21-27, and in that sense, it belongs to the pericope usually represented by vv. 21-27. Luke has unified v. 27 with v. 28 in such a way as to show that these two pericopes, in their entirety, are integral to each other. Verse 27 is the bridge between these two pericopes. This conclusion is supported by Luke's 'Εγένετο δὲ μετὰ τοὺς λόγους τούτους (v. 28a). This clause has as its antecedent the words of v. 27.

One of the aims of this study is to show that Luke understood that the words recorded in v. 27 were predictive of the Transfiguration.

The Greek Text

From the standpoint of text critical studies, the text has relatively few variants, and only one of special significance.[1] This one problem calls for particular attention.

---

[1] The text as given in Kurt Aland *et al.* (eds.), *The Greek New Testament* (New York: American Bible Society, 1966), will be used as the basis of this study.

Verse 35b reads as follows: Οὗτός ἐστιν ὁ υἱός μου ὁ ἐκλελεγμένος. The word ἐκλελεγμένος is supported by 𝔓45, 𝔓75, ℵ, B, L, Ξ, 892 and 1241. A related word ἐκλεκτός is witnessed to in θ, Family 1 and 1365. Either one or the other of these words is supported by the Old Latin, Syriac (Sinaitic and marginal reading of the Harclean), and the Coptic (Sahidic and Bohairic).

Ἀγαπητός in the place of ἐκλελεγμένος is supported by A, C (original hand), K, Π, Family 13, and a host of minuscules. It is supported by some of the Byzantine lectionaries, the Old Latin, the Vulgate, and Syriac versions. A number of the Fathers support the reading.

The decision here must take the following considerations into account: (1) Ἀγαπητός has a great amount of support in the number of witnesses to it; most of these are not manuscripts of Luke, but citations of Luke; (2) this reading agrees with Mark, which makes it suspect as an attempt to harmonize or as a tendency of a scribe to write from memory of a more familiar quotation; (3) the most impressive evidence supports ἐκλελεγμένος. The evidence is as follows: (a) the earliest evidence and the most trustworthy witnesses support it; (b) a variant of this word appears in a significant number of other witnesses; and (c) a host of other witnesses support one or the other of these words. There is little question but that ἐκλελεγμένος is the correct reading in this instance.[2]

A Comparison of Mark 9.1-10 and Luke 9.27-36

A comparison of the accounts of Mark and Luke will show what is common to both and where Luke differs from Mark. Those elements that are represented by all the synoptic authors became inseparable from the story, even if the individual author fails to make any interpretational use of a specific element in the story. The individual author's viewpoint will emerge in the story in the form of some particular emphasis or application that is distinctively his own.

---

[2] Bruce M. Metzger, *A Textual Commentary on the Greek New Testament* (London and New York: United Bible Societies, 1971), p. 148: 'The original Lukan reading is undoubtedly ἐκλελεγμένος, which occurs in a quasi-technical sense only here in the NT. The other readings, involving more usual expressions, are due to scribal assimilation (ἐκλεκτός Lk. 23.35; ἀγαπητός Mk 9.7; Lk. 3.22; ἀγαπητός ἐν ᾧ εὐδόκησα Mt. 17.5)'.

In order to investigate these factors, it is necessary first to list those fundamental elements shared by Mark and Luke. We will then be prepared to take note of the material unique to Luke and to study his interpretative use of this material.

The following parallel accounts are designed to show the areas of difference between Mark and Luke. For purposes of making this presentation Mark is treated as the 'original'. His account provides the outline of the story in Luke.

In the parallel below, the following symbols will be used:

(1) Identity of vocabulary will appear side by side.

(2) Identity of thought but different words will be underlined as a change by Luke.

(3) Non-parallel items will appear on separate lines.

(4) Inversions will be enclosed by slash marks / /

(5) Omission will be indicated by a line ———

Mk 9.1	Lk. 9.27
καὶ ἔλεγεν αὐτοῖς,	———
Ἀμὴν λέγω ὑμῖν ὅτι	λέγω δὲ ὑμῖν ἀληθῶς ———
εἰσίν τινες ὧδε τῶν	εἰσίν τινες τῶν αὐτοῦ
ἑστηκότων	ἑστηκότων
οἵτινες οὐ μὴ	οἳ οὐ μὴ
γεύσωνται θανάτου	γεύσωνται θανάτου
ἕως ἂν ἴδωσιν	ἕως ἂν ἴδωσιν
τὴν βασιλείαν τοῦ θεοῦ	τὴν βασιλείαν τοῦ θεοῦ.
ἐληλυθυῖαν ἐν δυνάμει.	———
9.2	9.28
Καὶ	———
	Ἐγένετο δὲ μετὰ τοὺς
	λόγους τούτους
μετὰ ἡμέρας ἓξ	ὡσεὶ ἡμέραι ὀκτὼ
	(καὶ)
παραλαμβάνει	παραλαβὼν
ὁ Ἰησοῦς	———
τὸν	———
Πέτρον καὶ	Πέτρον καὶ
τὸν	———
Ἰάκωβον καὶ τὸν Ἰωάννην,	/Ἰωάννην καὶ Ἰάκωβον/
καὶ	———
ἀναφέρει	ἀνέβη
αὐτοὺς	———

εἰς ὄρος	εἰς τὸ ὄρος
ὑψηλὸν	———
κατ' ἰδίαν μόνους.	———
	προσεύξασθαι.
	9.29
καὶ	καὶ
	ἐγένετο ἐν τῷ
	προσεύχεσθαι αὐτὸν
μετεμορφώθη	τὸ εἶδος τοῦ προσώπου
	αὐτοῦ ἕτερον
ἔμπροσθεν αὐτῶν,	———
9.3	
καὶ τὰ ἱμάτια αὐτοῦ	καὶ ὁ ἱματισμὸς αὐτοῦ
ἐγένετο στίλβοντα	———
λευκὰ λίαν	λευκὸς ἐξαστράπτων.
οἷα γναφεὺς ἐπὶ τῆς	———
γῆς οὐ δύναται οὕτως	———
λευκᾶναι,	———
9.4	9.30
καὶ ὤφθη αὐτοῖς	καὶ ———
	ἰδοὺ
Ἠλίας σὺν Μωυσεῖ, καὶ	ἄνδρες δύο συνελάλουν
ἦσαν συλλαλοῦντες τῷ	αὐτῷ, οἵτινες ἦσαν
Ἰησοῦ.	/Μωυσῆς καὶ Ἠλίας/
	9.31
	οἳ ὀφθέντες ἐν δόξῃ ἔλεγον
	τὴν ἔξοδον αὐτοῦ ἣν ἤμελλεν
	πληροῦν ἐν Ἰερουσαλήμ.
	9.32
	ὁ δὲ Πέτρος καὶ οἱ σὺν αὐτῷ
	ἦσαν βεβαρημένοι ὕπνῳ·
	διαγρηγορήσαντες δὲ εἶδον τὴν
	δόξαν αὐτοῦ καὶ τοὺς δύο
	ἄνδρας τοὺς συνεστῶτας αὐτῷ.
	9.33
	καὶ ἐγένετο ἐν τῷ διαχωρίζεσθαι
9.5	αὐτοὺς ἀπ' αὐτοῦ
καὶ ἀποκριθεὶς ὁ Πέτρος	εἶπεν ὁ Πέτρος πρὸς
λέγει τῷ Ἰησοῦ	τὸν Ἰησοῦν
Ῥαββί,	Ἐπιστάτα,
καλόν ἐστιν ἡμᾶς ὧδε	καλόν ἐστιν ἡμᾶς ὧδε
εἶναι, καὶ ποιήσωμεν	εἶναι, καὶ ποιήσωμεν

τρεῖς σκηνάς,	/σκηνὰς τρεῖς,/
σοὶ μίαν καὶ	/μίαν σοὶ/ καὶ
Μωυσεῖ μίαν.	/μίαν Μωυσεῖ/
καὶ Ἠλίᾳ μίαν,	καὶ /μίαν Ἠλίᾳ,/
9.6	
οὐ γὰρ ᾔδει τί ἀποκριθῇ,	μὴ εἰδὼς ὃ λέγει.
ἔκφοβοι γὰρ ἐγένοντο.	———
9.7	9.34
	ταῦτα δὲ αὐτοῦ λέγοντος
καὶ	———
ἐγένετο νεφέλη	ἐγένετο νεφέλη
	καὶ
ἐπισκιάζουσα αὐτοῖς,	ἐπεσκίαζεν αὐτούς ἐφοβήθησαν
	δὲ ἐν τῷ εἰσελθεῖν αὐτοὺς εἰς
	τὴν νεφέλην.
	9.35
καὶ ἐγένετο φωνὴ ἐκ τῆς	καὶ /φωνὴ ἐγένετο/ ἐκ τῆς
νεφέλης	νεφέλης
	λέγουσα
Οὗτός ἐστιν	Οὗτός ἐστιν
ὁ υἱός μου ὁ ἀγαπητός,	ὁ υἱός μου ὁ ἐκλελεγμένος,
ἀκούετε αὐτοῦ.	/αὐτοῦ ἀκούετε./
9.8	9.36
	καὶ ἐν τῷ γενέσθαι τὴν φωνὴν
καὶ ἐξάπινα περιβλεψάμενοι	———
οὐκέτι οὐδένα εἶδον	εὑρέθη Ἰησοῦς μόνος.
ἀλλὰ τὸν Ἰησοῦν	———
μόνον μεθ' ἑαυτῶν.	———
	καὶ αὐτοὶ ἐσίγησαν καὶ οὐδενὶ
	ἀπήγγειλαν ἐν ἐκείναις ταῖς
	ἡμέραις οὐδὲν ὧν ἑώρακαν.
9.9	
Καὶ καταβαινόντων αὐτῶν ἐκ	
τοῦ ὄρους διεστείλατο αὐτοῖς	
ἵνα μηδενὶ ἃ εἶδον διηγήσωνται,	
εἰ μὴ ὅταν ὁ υἱὸς τοῦ ἀνθρώπου	
ἐκ νεκρῶν ἀναστῇ.	
9.10	
καὶ τὸν λόγον ἐκράτησαν πρὸς	
ἑαυτοὺς συζητοῦντες τί ἐστιν	
τὸ ἐκ νεκρῶν ἀναστῆναι.	

The Divergencies of Luke 9.27-36 From Mark 9.1-10

The Greek texts presented in parallel above show the manner in which these two accounts relate to each other. Luke's dependence on the framework of Mark[3] is shown by the similarity of contexts, the similarity of vocabulary and in some cases verbatim agreement.

There are important points of difference between Mark and Luke. Some of these differences may be accounted for as stylistic preferences of a specific author. These are significant for literary study, but they do not necessarily represent significant interpretational differences between the two authors.[4] Closely related to these, however, are differences that seem to reflect a specific redactional bias of the individual author – in this case Luke. Luke calls attention to such differences by his omissions and additions.

---

3 I am assuming the priority of Mark, as is common to most biblical scholarship.

4 The stylistic differences may be noted and set aside. In 9.27 Luke uses λέγω δὲ for Mark's καὶ ἔλεγεν and ἀληθῶς as the equivalent of Ἀμὴν. In the same verse, Luke uses a rarity in biblical Greek when he uses the adverbial τῶν αὐτοῦ for Mark's ὧδε following τινες (BDF, §103). Ἐγένετο δὲ (9.28) appears frequently in Luke; in this clause he apparently writes under the stylistic influence of the Septuagint. E.P. Sanders, *The Tendencies of the Synoptic Tradition* (Cambridge: The University Press, 1969), p. 200, writes,

> The New Testament writer who is most frequently mentioned as imitating the Septuagint is Luke. We may take as an example a sentence pattern with which Luke introduces many of his gospel narratives ... The pattern is ἐγένετο (introduced by either καὶ or δέ) and adverbial phrase indicating time ..., and the main verb, usually, but not always, introduced by καὶ.

In the designation of the mountain on which the Transfiguration took place, Luke is simpler; in Luke it is simply 'the mountain' and not a 'high mountain' (H.J. Cadbury, *The Style and Literary Method of Luke* (Harvard Theological Studies 6; Cambridge: Harvard University Press, 1970), p. 118). This same simplicity and directness of Luke appears in the description of the ascent into the mountain and his description of the Transfiguration of Jesus.

In 9.33b Luke uses his own peculiar address of Jesus (Ἐπιστάτα) in Peter's response to the Transfiguration experience. This word is peculiar to Luke. He uses it exclusively for addresses of Jesus; it is found in the following places: Lk. 5.5; 8.24, 45; 9.33, 49; 17.13.

The adverbial clause in Lk. 9.34a, ταῦτα δὲ αὐτοῦ λέγοντος (for Mark's abrupt transition) is doubtless stylistic.

There is a minor change from Mark's order in 9.35 in the command of the Voice from heaven αὐτοῦ ἀκούετε; it is probably reflective of the Septuagint order in Deut. 18.15.

There is a significant abbreviation of Mk 9.1 in Lk. 9.27. Luke does not include the phrase ἐν δυνάμει in the prediction of 9.27. We have separated it from the main listing of the possible stylistic differences because it is in fact especially significant. Conzelmann calls it exegetical, but he claims too much for his position.[5] In expressing this view, Conzelmann assumes that Mk 9.1 is a Parousia prediction and that Lk. 9.27 is not.[6]

It appears that Luke has already anticipated the ἐν δυνάμει in v. 26 when he refers to the glory of the Son of man in his coming. In looking ahead, Luke expected to demonstrate this quality of the kingdom in the Transfiguration. So, it seems reasonable to conclude that Luke drops the phrase ἐν δυνάμει in order to remove a redundancy.[7] There is a stylistic characteristic at work here, and that is Luke's general tendency to abbreviate Mark.[8]

There are other instances where Luke has abbreviated the account of the Transfiguration.[9] These, however, do not imply an interpretational purpose; they reflect Luke's editorial and stylistic tendencies.

At the end of the Transfiguration narrative, Luke closes the account abruptly, and does not at all reflect Mk 9.9, 10 except to observe that the three disciples were silent about these events 'in those days'. This change does not directly affect Luke's interpretation of the Transfiguration.[10]

---

[5] Conzelmann, *The Theology of St. Luke*, p. 104: 'This verse is of central importance for determining the concept of the kingdom and for the idea of the postponement of the parousia ... Luke offers the earliest example of an exegesis of the difficult Markan saying which takes account of the problem it presents'.

[6] Contra: A.L. Moore, *The Parousia of the New Testament* (London: Brill, 1966), pp. 125-31; he applies Mk 9.1 to the Transfiguration; E. Earle Ellis, 'Present and Future Eschatology in Luke', *NTS* 12 (1965-66), pp. 27-41; he questions whether 'until' in Mk 9.1 does not militate against a direct Parousia application.

[7] Ellis, 'Present and Future Eschatology in Luke', p. 34.

[8] Sanders, *The Tendencies of the Synoptic Tradition*, pp. 86, 87: 'We may note that Luke is shorter than Mark much more consistently than is Matthew. Since his relation to Matthew is not the same, however, it is somewhat difficult to argue that Luke was a consistent abbreviator. Nevertheless, the hypothesis of abbreviation is more likely in the case of Luke than of Matthew.'

[9] Luke 9.28 (par. Mk 9.2) omission of ὑψηλὸν κατ' ἰδίαν μόνους; 9.29 (par. Mk 9.2) omission of ἔμπροσθεν αὐτῶν; 9.29 (par. Mk 9.3) omission of οἷα γναφεὺς ἐπὶ τῆς γῆς οὐ δύναται οὕτως λευκᾶναι.

[10] It may indeed imply something of Luke's concept of Elijah and John the Baptist. This statement seems to be Luke's representation of the disciples' obedience to Jesus' charge, though he does not record the charge.

Though personal literary style often results in non-substantive changes in a tradition, it is sometimes an instrument of redactional bias; hence the observations which follow are subject to identification from either standpoint. It seems clear in each of these instances that Luke's style is especially used to aid his interpretation of the event.

Luke's temporal reference is a specific departure from Mark. There is a careful and deliberate effort on Luke's part to associate 9.27 with Jesus' taking his three intimate disciples up the mountain.[11] Specifically, it may be said that Luke intends to establish it that the antecedent of the phrase μετὰ τοὺς λόγους (9.28a) is the statement of Jesus in 9.27. He thus specifies more precisely the relation seen between Mk 9.1 and 9.2.

The second temporal connection that Luke establishes here is the general time reference to 'about eight days'. Mark's reference, Καὶ μετὰ ἡμέρας ἓξ, is probably a semitism[12] which Luke avoids quite uncharacteristically. Luke either was not aware of this nuance of Mark's phrase or he chose to eliminate it from his account of the Transfiguration. In the light of the frequency of Luke's use of semitisms, it is not likely that he would have deliberately eliminated a semitism unless the elimination served a definite purpose. The symbolism in Mark is apparently a Sinai motif, which is also compatible with Luke's purpose. So, it would seem that Luke here chose to follow a generalized tradition that did not emphasize the 'after six days' = 'on the seventh day'[13] cultic formula.

Luke's failure to use the word μεταμορφόω in describing the Transfiguration (9.29) probably reflects his difficulties with the word itself because of its gnostic implication[14] and the pattern of the metamorphosis of the gods in heathen religions.[15] Luke takes pains to

---

[11] Burton Scott Easton, *The Gospel According to St. Luke* (New York: Scribner, 1926), p. 146: 'But L has an independent dating of the vision'. Easton here is presupposing the existence of L and draws the conclusion stated.

[12] Foster R. McCurley, Jr., '"And After Six Days" (Mk 9.2) A Semitic Literary Device', *JBL* 93 (1974), pp. 67-91: This author suggests that Mark's expression reflects a background as a literary device, common to Semitic literature generally and the OT specifically. He asserts that the phrase is the equivalent of 'on the seventh day' and that it has a ceremonial or cultic background.

[13] McCurley, '"And After Six Days" (Mk 9.2) A Semitic Literary Device'.

[14] There is evidence of an anti-gnostic tendency in Lukan literature: Charles H. Talbert, *Luke and the Gnostics* (Nashville: Abingdon, 1965).

[15] Plummer, *The Gospel According to St. Luke*, p. 251: 'The Gentile Luke writing for Gentiles avoids the word μεταμορφώθη (Mt. 17.2; Mk 9.2) which might be

describe as full a change in the appearance and nature of Jesus as Mark does; so he preserves the nature of the change, but he avoids what was probably an offensive word to him.

One of the most significant differences between Luke and Mark lies in the word of witness from the cloud (Lk. 9.35; Mk 9.7) – Luke's use of ἐκλελεγμένος where Mark has ἀγαπητός. This difference is emphasized by the fact that Mark and Luke agree exactly in this announcement to this point.[16]

Jeremias in his study of παῖς θεοῦ has proposed that ἀγαπητός and ἐκλελεγμένος represent alternative readings of Isa. 42.1. These alternate readings were preserved in the various traditions lying behind the synoptic accounts. The two forms of witness represent messianic titles derived from these alternate readings of Isa. 42.1.[17] If this assessment is correct, this peculiarity of Luke's account of the Transfiguration represents his editorial choice between two forms of the tradition. He may have understood both words to represent messianic titles, but he chose ἐκλελεγμένος because it brings together the themes of election and sonship.

There are two segments in Luke's Transfiguration account that have no parallel in Mark: the element of prayer (9.28, 29) and the subject of the conversation between Jesus and Moses and Elijah (9.30, 31).

Luke introduces the element of prayer in v. 28 by stating that Jesus' purpose in ascending the mountain was to pray. This is a clear departure from Mark; he continues this theme by observing that Jesus was engaged in prayer at the time that the change of appearance

---

understood of the metamorphosis of heathen deities'; P.M.J. LaGrange, *Evangile Selon Saint Luc* (Paris: Librairie Victor Le Coffre, 1921), p. 272.

16 Though the word is not unique to Luke in the NT, he uses it more frequently than any' other writer. It appears eleven times in Luke–Acts; it does not appear in the baptismal witness of Jesus, which is the closest parallel to the text before us. In five of the instances of its use it is used of divine election: Lk. 6.13; 9.35; Acts 1.2, 24; 13.17; 15.7.

17 Walther Zimmerli and Joachim Jeremias, 'παῖς θεοῦ', *TDNT*; Paul G. Bretscher, 'Exodus 4.22-23 and the Voice from Heaven', *Journal of Biblical Literature* 30 (1968), p. 290: 'In his argument concerning the origin of this statement, Jeremias takes Isa. 42.1 as best accounting for Luke's use of ἐκλελεγμένος'. Bretscher also recognizes Isa. 42.1 as the background of this word.

took place. There is a thematic use of prayer in Luke,[18] and the introduction of prayer here serves that purpose. The most consistently appearing association with prayer in Luke is eschatology. The question of the source of this material naturally rises in the face of these observations. Because of the brevity of the passage, this question cannot be resolved on the basis of linguistic and vocabulary studies. This material is fully integrated to Luke's style and thought. This does not justify the conclusion that the element of prayer is a Lukan editorial conjecture.

The second body of material unique to Luke in this pericope is the description of the conversation between Jesus and Moses and Elijah (9.31-33a). The most distinctive aspect of this material is its general content: the 'exodus' which Jesus must fulfill in Jerusalem. This passage also ascribes glory to the appearance of Moses and Elijah.

This material represents a wide departure from Mark.[19] It is such a departure that we could hardly attribute it to Luke's creation, unless we assume that Luke subjected the traditions at hand almost totally to his own editorial purposes. It would seem that Luke considered this element necessary either to the completeness of the record of the Transfiguration or to the theology of the Transfiguration. Conceivably, he felt the necessity of both. In the light of these considerations, it would seem a reasonable conclusion that Luke here used a tradition which was not known to Mark or was not used and preserved by Mark. The reasons for using this material are his sense of its necessity for accuracy and his own redactional aims.[20]

An Assessment of the Priority of Sources

The use of Mark as the framework of comparison and literary form presupposes the priority of Mark; hence, the changes from the Markan pattern indicate a composition that is secondary to Mark, or at

---

[18] The following references to prayer are unique to Luke: 3.21 22; 5.16; 6.12; 9.18; 9.28, 29; 11.1; 22.31, 32; 23.34 (of doubtful reading), the following are not unique to Luke: 10.21; 22.41, 42.

[19] Three words appear in this passage that have come to be taken as characteristic of L by those who support the hypothesis of such a written source: δόξα, Ἰηρουσάλημ, and ἤμελλεν.

[20] On the subject of a written source L, see Burton Scott Easton, 'Linguistic Evidence for the Lukan Source L', *JBL* 24 (1910), pp. 169, 170: '... the supposition lies close at hand that L contained a Transfiguration account which Luke here has combined with that in Mark'.

least subsequent to Mark. This does not necessarily say that the sources used by the later editor were subsequent to Mark. The points of difference from Mark belong to the subsequent author (in this case Luke); the changes may be attributed to his own speculation, redactional bias, personal style, or to a source whose authority he accepts as a basis of differing from Mark.

Burton has given some points in helping to determine whether an addition is to be attributed to an individual author: (1) lengthening that interrupts the line of thought is probably personal addition; (2) omission that destroys a line of thought may be individual; (3) if a motive (doctrinal, etc.) can be shown in the author's tendency, an expansion or an omission in the interest of that motive may be the author's own addition.[21]

The axiom of many literary critics that detail indicates material of later origin is not universally applicable. There is some evidence that detail sometimes indicates priority. So, each investigation calls for the individual examination of the literature. Detail in literature seems to be cyclical. Sanders summarizes the position of H.J. Cadbury: 'The earliest tradition, then, was detailed, but the details were lost quite rapidly, and the material was passed down in isolated pericopes. Details were once more added at a late stage when novelistic interest led to the filling out of the material.'[22]

From these opinions, it appears that we cannot on the basis of the general characteristics of individual synoptic authors establish a priority of sources for individual pericopes. We may be able to use this information as one of the arguments concerning the priority of one book over another, as we do in concluding that Mark is the earliest gospel. However, when an individual pericope in a book runs contrary to the general tendency of that book the question of priority (or independence) of sources in this one unit of study needs to be raised again. This would seem to be the case in Luke's Transfiguration account.

---

21 Ernst DeWitt Burton, *Principles of Literary Criticism and the Synoptic Problem* (Chicago: University of Chicago Press, 1904), p. 198.

22 Sanders, *The Tendencies of the Synoptic Tradition*, p. 95; Cadbury, *The Style and Literary Method of Luke*, pp. 34, 35: Wilhelm Bussmann 'was of the opinion that details tended to be added. Luke, the least detailed of the Gospels, represents the earliest form of the narrative', Cited from *Synoptische Studien*, I, pp. 85-86.

In this pericope there are a number of details in which Luke differs from Mark. Not all of them contribute to the answering of the questions before us. Those details that do seem to contribute to our investigation are: (1) the element of prayer, (2) the content of the conversation between Jesus, Moses and Elijah, and (3) the explanation which Luke gives of the fear of the disciples.

In comparing the length of Mark's and Luke's material, Luke's general tendency is to abbreviate Mark.[23] In the Transfiguration, however, Luke's tendency is toward expansion. By word count, Luke's Transfiguration account is 53% longer than Mark's. This is a significant point because Luke generally abbreviates Mark.[24]

Some of these expansions fit Burton's tests which illustrate individual author contribution cited earlier. The expansions do not interrupt thought; they do pick up the special interests of Luke. This means that in the immediate circumstance of the writing of this piece of literature, these changes are to be attributed to Luke. Does this mean that he added these details out of his own speculation or that he added them without the authority of some form of tradition (whether written or oral)? Certainly, this information standing alone does not supply a self-evident answer to this question.

In addressing this question, we may observe that Luke's Transfiguration account shows evidence of the following layers. First, his outline is in agreement with Mark's.[25] Second, there are evidences of detail in this pericope that tend to support the conclusion that Luke used a tradition that Mark did not have or did not choose to use.[26]

---

[23] Luke is not always consistent here; even within the Transfiguration pericope, Luke varies from abbreviation to expansion. There is the long expansion of the conversation and the dropping of the charge of silence; there is the dropping of the phrase 'in power' (v. 27) and the more elaborate description of the glory of Jesus' appearance (v. 29).

[24] Sanders, *The Tendencies of the Synoptic Tradition*, pp. 86, 87.

[25] Robert H. Stein, 'What is *Redactionsgeschichte*?', *JBL* 88 (1969), p. 49: 'The writing of the gospels proved a major step in the transmission of the gospel materials. It gave a definite pattern to the materials, so that from the time of Mark the gospel materials had received a definite framework. The writing of the first gospel therefore marked the twilight of the oral period.'

[26] In his prologue, Luke has said one of his provocations for writing was the existence in his time of many attempts to 'reproduce a narrative' (BAG, p. 61) of the things believed in the Christian community. The process of Luke's writing did involve selection from traditions. One would make these selections on the same basis that he would use for speculation; that is, his selections would be governed by his special interests. Ellis, 'Present and Future Eschatology in Luke', p. 31 n. 4,

The allusion to Deut. 18.15 is a pre-Lukan[27] and perhaps pre-synoptic element. It seems to reflect traditions that are preserved in the pseudepigrapha (Sirach 44.23 – 45.5; Wisdom of Solomon 10.16; 11.1; Assumption of Moses 11.16). The Moses-Elijah-Messiah typology appears in the Damascus Document and in Josephus.[28] It is widely held that the concept of a suffering servant was already present in Judaism among the contemporaries of Jesus.[29] The details that are here are not the sort that prove lateness of origin. It may be agreed that the introduction of prayer into this account is Lukan because of Luke's special interest in this subject throughout the book.[30] This observation does not require that we conclude that Luke acted and wrote without using any tradition. The introduction of the 'exodus' of Jesus is hardly novelistic.[31] It seems that a novelistic tendency here would have resulted in a more explicit description of the crucifixion. Instead the symbolic and somewhat oblique word 'exodus' is used to fill in the content of the conversation. At the same time this is a rather bold departure from Mark; it is such a step that it is difficult to conclude that Luke introduced this element on his own conjecture. It would seem to me that Luke had at his disposal a very early Christian

---

suggests that there is a block of Q material that pre-dates Mark in the background of his account:

> It appears likely that the agreement of Matthew and Luke against Mark as well as other textual phenomena point to a 'Q' tradition of this pericope (v. 27). Dodd and Brunsly … have so argued for Mark viii 38 … If in the pre-Markan tradition this pericope was already joined to the Transfiguration episode, the case is strengthened for a parallel 'Q' tradition of the whole.

27 J. Jeremias, 'Μωυσῆς', *TDNT*; Howard Clark Kee, 'The Transfiguration in Mark: Epiphany or Apocalyptic Vision?', in John Reumann (ed.), *Understanding the Sacred Text* (Valley Forge, PA: Judson Press, 1972), p. 146.

28 Jeremias, 'Μωυσῆς'.

29 Jeremias, 'Μωυσῆς'.

30 Oscar Gerald Harris, 'Prayer in Luke–Acts: A Study in the Theology of St. Luke' (PhD dissertation, Vanderbilt University, 1966), p. 116.

31 The identification of 'novelistic detail' by Bultmann, *The History of the Synoptic Tradition*, is so sweeping that any detail is treated as novelistic; the giving of any name is the basis for imagining a period of growth of the tradition as if the early records of Jesus were preserved completely without the identification of any of his associates. According to him circumstances of place 'belong to the editorial stage' (p. 242). Dates and times are also secondary. Bultmann identifies Mk 9.2 as 'part of a legendary story' (p. 243). Novelistic detail may be better understood as the kind of insertions that are the product of curiosity created by lack of detail. These kinds of insertions are amply illustrated in the apocryphal gospels. Names are given where none appears in any NT record; trades are assigned to characters; magical elements are added to the miracle stories.

tradition that included this material; he did not feel the liberty of excluding it from the Transfiguration story, and it confirmed to him the particular redactional motif that is evident in his writings.[32]

The omission of the charge of silence (Mk 9.9, 10) is probably Lukan; we know that he had the account of Mark before him; so, his decision to cut short the entire account was a redactional decision. His purpose probably lay in his understanding of the mission of John the Baptist.

An Assessment of the Formal Structure of the Text

The Transfiguration does not have a form sufficiently in common with other stories in biblical literature to be designated by form.[33] The

---

32 It is not necessary to claim a written source L. It does seem, however, that there is a source that may be identified by such a symbol in order to distinguish it from Mark, M, or Q, and in order to attribute it to a tradition of authority for Luke other than his own conjecture or doctrinal motivation. Easton concludes that the independent dating of the Transfiguration argues for the L tradition ('Linguistic Evidence for the Lukan Source L', pp. 169, 170). Vincent Taylor lists the Transfiguration as one of the four pericopes in Luke that may give evidence of a second written source for Luke in addition to Mark. The percentage of word agreement with Mark is the next to the lowest of the four pericopes that he groups with it (*Behind the Third Gospel* (Oxford: Clarendon Press, 1926), p. 84, cf. p. 16 n. 2; p. 89). It should be noted that Taylor argues predominantly for Proto-Luke, not L as such.

The literary data here offer us the options or raise the questions. If Luke invented material (whether by outright invention or by a speculative extension of the context), the material would be harmonious in theme, vocabulary, and style with the rest of his literature. If he drew from a source (whether written or unwritten), and if he had thoroughly integrated that material to his own aims (or if his own aims were governed or strongly influenced by that material), it would still be harmonious with his usual style and theology. If this new material were significantly different from the rest of Luke's literature, this situation could be evidence for concluding that the new material had been taken over from another source. If he has taken over material that runs contrary to his aims, or that is simply included without any integration (as if Luke felt an obligation to record it but did not know what to do with it), we may safely conclude that he is drawing from another source. This answer comes from the literary data. The first two options offered above cannot be decided from literary data. In such cases there is no difference between what is presented as invention and what is presented from another source. The interpreter's presuppositions will affect the choice between these options. My own theological orientation leads me to favor the conclusion that Luke wrote from a tradition of authority to him and he did not create the substantive differences from Mark.

This decision does not change the interpretation of the form in which we are studying this account. Our primary task is to interpret the document as it now stands in its most accurate textual form.

33 Contra: Carlston, 'Transfiguration and Resurrection', p. 234: This author defends the position that the Transfiguration does fit within the formal characteristics of the resurrection stories.

Transfiguration story is frequently designated as a legend,[34] but this helps little in literary analysis because the term 'legend' itself is imprecise, and the Transfiguration does not fit the classical marks of a true legend.[35]

The most frequently suggested formal identification of the Transfiguration is with the resurrection appearances of Jesus. There are two forms in which the resurrected Jesus appears in the NT: the pre-ascension appearance and the heavenly (post-ascension) appearance. The appearance of the resurrected Jesus prior to the ascension is not accompanied by angels (though they do appear in the empty tomb), does not occur in the mountain (with one exception – Mt. 28.16-20), is not ever described as in a body of glory, is not accompanied by Moses and Elijah,[36] and does not receive the verbal witness of sonship from the Shekinah.[37] The kerygmatic interpretation of the resurrection was that it was itself the declaration of sonship. Paul cites an early Christian tradition in Rom. 1.4 which affirms this understanding of the resurrection. The resurrection testimony to Christ's divine sonship needed no vocal augmentation. It is difficult to see how stories of such diversity from the Transfiguration account can be used to supply the form for the Transfiguration.

The objections that we listed above in relation to the pre-ascension appearance of Jesus prevail in the consideration of Jesus' post-ascension appearance, with the exception of the element of glory. It is consistent with all of the appearances of Jesus from heaven that he appears in glory (Acts 7.54-60; 9.3-9; Paul uses the term 'glory' in describing this vision [Acts 22.11]; the resurrection body of Jesus and of believers are bodies of glory [1 Cor. 15.43]). These references help us in seeing the appearance of Jesus, but they still do not help in the

---

34 Bultmann, *The History of the Synoptic Tradition,* p. 259.

35 Bultmann, *The History of the Synoptic Tradition,* p. 259, cites H. Gunkel in *Zum religionsgeschichtlichen Verstaendnis des N.T.*, p. 71: 'Christ appears here (in the walk to Emmaus) as the unknown traveler – in the way that God of old liked to walk among men, in simple human form dressed as a traveler – and revealed his secret divine nature by peculiar characteristics; but as soon as he was recognized, he disappeared'. Contra: It is clear that the Transfiguration does not fit any of these marks of the legend which Gunkel and Bultmann draw from the Emmaus story.

36 It cannot be argued that Moses and Elijah are the angels of the empty tomb appearances, because the angels do not accompany the resurrected Jesus in his appearances.

37 For the contrary argument see Carlston, 'Transfiguration and Resurrection', pp. 223-40.

determination of a specific literary form that is identifiable with the Transfiguration.

The theophany (or epiphany) form seems to have had some influence on the Transfiguration presentation.[38] It is clear that the description of the Transfiguration has a number of parallels with the elements of the theophany. Luke may offer more parallels here than the other synoptics. The event occurred at night and on a mountain. Jesus appeared in brilliant light (though we must also observe that glory was ascribed to Moses and Elijah). God spoke out of the cloud, and the disciples reacted in fear, though Jesus (the 'chosen Son') did not. Peter proposed to perpetuate this event in the cultic symbols of the three tabernacles. The authority of Jesus as the prophet of God is affirmed by the command 'Hear him' (Deut. 18.15).

The opening of the heavens is an important element in theophanies; we see this element in the following events of revelation: Luke 3.21 (καὶ προσευχομένου ἀνεῳχθῆναι τὸν οὐρανὸν); Acts 7.56 (θεωρῶ τοὺς οὐρανοὺς διηνοιγμένους); Acts 10.11 (καὶ θεωρεῖ τὸν οὐρανὸν ἀνεῳγμένον); note also the following references outside Lukan literature (Mt. 3.16; Jn 1.51; Rev. 9.11). All of these instances (except the references to Jesus' baptism) may be more precisely designated as Christophanies, described in the pattern of a theophany. It is significant that the Transfiguration does not have this element. Probably the reason for this is the fact that the Transfiguration is not a revelation from heaven; that is, the revelation does not originate in heaven and descend from the opened heaven to become visible to human sight. This revelation originates on the mountain from which Jesus 'ascends' into the estate of glory.

The most profitable formal comparison of the Transfiguration is with the two ascension accounts both of which are given in Lukan literature (Luke 24.50-52 and Acts 1.3-11).

---

38 This form is not a sufficiently developed form in the NT to use in the assessment of the form of the Transfiguration story. There are formal characteristics that may be noted from the OT theophanies. The formal characteristics of the theophany that appear consistently are clouds, darkness, fire, thunder, and lightning. The storm seems to be a symbol of God's power. The mountain is a frequent symbol; it is used as the place where God descends to make himself known and not the place of his dwelling. The appearance of God is central to the cultic act or response. On the basis of Psalm 90 and Isaiah 6, prophetic utterance is directly linked to the theophany. The normal response to the appearance of God is fear except in the case of God's chosen representative.

In terms of literary form, there is common ground between the Transfiguration account and the ascension account under the designation of narrative. These two pericopes are short forms and may more appropriately be designated as episodes, which is the basic unit of the narrative form. In the process of the development of the longer narrative units, the early Christian community edited the episodes into a single plot. This process and product are illustrated in the passion narrative.[39] The episode is short, 'has a clearly marked beginning and ending',[40] stands out from its context and can 'stand alone'.[41]

Such narrative units were the instruments of cultic experiences: the affirmation of faith,[42] reenactment of experience and anticipation of the future.[43]

This literary form is an instrument of worship very much in evidence in the OT,[44] which is doubtless the source of its use and development in certain sectors of the early Christian community. We have here two formulae that may be used for comparative studies of the Transfiguration account and the ascension account: the literary narrative form and the cultic form. In a subsequent chapter we will return to these formulae under the designation of 'cultic narrative'.

The following parallels between Lk. 9.28-36 and 24.50-52 are to be noted. Jesus led the disciples to Bethany (a mountain site). It is a private appearance in that only the disciples are led there. Jesus was lifted up while he was in the act of blessing the disciples. From this mountain the disciples went into Jerusalem. This account is Luke's skeletal description to the Ascension.

---

39 Thomas Eugene Boomershine, 'Mark, the Storyteller: A Rhetorical-Critical Investigation of Mark's Passion and Resurrection Narrative' (PhD dissertation, Union Theological Seminary, 1974), p. 41: 'The content unit of the story is the description of a whole event at a particular time or place ... The story ... is the content unit of the narrative within which the episodes have their place.'

40 Boomershine, 'Mark, the Storyteller', p. 41.

41 Gerhard von Rad, *Old Testament Theology* (trans. D.M.G. Stalker; New York: Harper & Bros., 1962), I, p. 50.

42 von Rad, *Old Testament Theology*, II, p. 422.

43 William A. Beardslee, *Literary Criticism of the New Testament* (Philadelphia: Fortress, 1970), p. 21. Narrative is the mode par excellence of religious experience. Cf. John R. Donahue, 'The Narrative Structure of Religious Experience in the Markan Passion Narrative', an unpublished paper read at the Southern Section of the Society of Biblical Literature, March 15, 1974.

44 von Rad, *Old Testament Theology*, II, p. 422.

In Acts 1.1-11, the ascension story is introduced as a resurrection appearance (v. 4). It is then turned to a commission story commanding the disciples to receive the Holy Spirit. The ascension is characterized by the following features: The ascension took place while the disciples were looking at Jesus. Jesus was taken up and received from the sight of the disciples by a cloud. As the disciples looked into heaven, two men in white clothing appeared to them. The character of the ascension is projected as the form of the Parousia by the words of the men: 'This Jesus who has been taken up from you, thus he shall come in the manner that you have seen him going into heaven' (v. 11). It occurred in a mountain (the Mt. of Olives) (v. 12).

It is not uncommon to observe the parallels between the Lukan Transfiguration account and the ascension. Our question here is the form-critical question.

Neither of these stories manifest a particular literary form. There are, however, some areas of investigation in form-critical study that we may suggest. The Transfiguration suggests a pattern of revelatory stories. Specifically, there is a pattern of prayer – ecstasy – revelation (vision) in Luke–Acts. There is an exaltation pattern in Luke–Acts consisting of 'exodus' (ἔξοδος – ἀνάλημψις) and appearance in glory. The appearance in glory is consistently described as a brilliant appearance of Jesus (as Son of man, Messiah or Lord).

It can also be shown that the Lukan Transfiguration and ascension accounts have some form and redactional affinities. A comparison of Luke 9 and Acts 1.1-2 shows basic parallels in vocabulary: power (δύναμις and ἐξουσία), kingdom of God, witness (μαρτύριον, μάρτυρες) ὑποστρέφω, looking (ἀναβλέπω, βλέπω) into heaven, mountain (ὄρος), white garments (ἱματισμὸς λευκός, ἐσθήσεσι λευκαῖς, two men (καὶ ἰδοὺ ἄνδρες δύο), and cloud (νεφέλη).[45]

There are also common themes between the two accounts. These themes do not necessarily repeat vocabulary, but they do show Luke's thematic use of tradition. The disciples are given an eschatological preaching mission in both chapters (Lk. 9.1; Acts 1.8). Both chapters recognize the distinctive roles of Jesus and John the Baptist (Lk. 9.18-20; Acts 1.5). Jerusalem is central to both chapters (Lk. 9.31, 51; Acts 1.4, 12). Jesus' eating with his disciples is common to both chapters;

---

45 J.G. Davies, 'The Prefigurement of the Ascension in the Third Gospel', *JTS* 6 (1955), p. 230.

in each case the meal is associated with the mission of Jesus (Lk. 9.10-17; Acts 1.4 – συναλιζόμενος). The relationship of Jesus' death to his exaltation is shown in both (Lk. 9.22, 31, 51; Acts 1.2, 3). Both give a promise of the coming of the kingdom of God (Lk. 9.27; Acts 1.11).

From an overall viewpoint both these passages are eschatological. The vocabulary has a high concentration of words that have become in biblical literature eschatological symbols.

The manner in which these two passages are constructed shows a common redactional pattern. Both the Transfiguration and the ascension are placed in a context of Jesus' talking to the apostles about the 'things of the kingdom of God' (Lk. 9.23-27; Acts 1.3-8). In each case these instructions are antecedent to the event recorded. The Transfiguration is Jesus' presentation in glory (Lk. 9.29-32); the ascension is Jesus' way into heaven from which he hereafter appears in glory (Acts 1.9, 10). Each event is related to a specific eschatological promise. The Transfiguration is related to the promise of Lk. 9.27. The ascension is related to Acts 1.11. Each of the passages is a collage of eschatological terms and symbols which appear and are explained throughout the two books of Luke.

These similarities have led to the conclusion by some that the Transfiguration and the ascension are both anticipations of the Parousia.[46] A close examination of the two accounts reveal differences worthy of note.

In the ascension Jesus does not appear in glory but ascends into heaven where he takes on the appearance of glory. The cloud is the vehicle of his ascension and by application of his Parousia. In the ascension, he is accompanied by two unnamed men; this also seems to be a part of the Parousia symbolism. The ascension took place on the Mt. of Olives with its specific symbolism and not a mountain.

In the Transfiguration Jesus appears in glorified form. He is accompanied by two men specifically named. The cloud functions here to envelop Jesus and the three intimates and is not the vehicle of translation. In the exegesis we will attempt to show that these are patterns appropriate to the form of the kingdom after the Parousia,

---

[46] Davies, 'The Prefigurement of the Ascension in the Third Gospel', pp. 229-333; Boobyer, *St. Mark and the Transfiguration Story*; Ramsay, 'The Time of the Transfiguration', pp. 560-61.

when the kingdom is gathered around the Messiah as the company of the redeemed.

Summary

Luke has tied together the context of the Transfiguration in such a way as to indicate that he understood the Transfiguration to be the fulfillment of Jesus' promise in Lk. 9.27.

The correspondence between Mk 9.1-10 and Lk. 9.27-36 suggests that Luke accepted the order of events in Mark for the presentation of his own account. Luke does, however, introduce some significant differences from Mark. The most significant of these are (1) the omission of ἐν δυνάμει in 9.27, (2) the introduction of the element of prayer in 9.28, 29, (3) the introduction of the 'exodus' concept in the conversation of Jesus with Moses and Elijah in 9.31, (4) the introduction of the word δόξα as the description of the transfigured appearance in 9.31, 32 and (5) the use of ἐκλελεγμένος where Mark has ἀγαπητός in 9.35. We concluded that the dropping of ἐν δυνάμει may be accounted for as Luke's dropping of a redundancy as he presented the account. The introduction of prayer and the 'exodus' concept are best accounted for as Luke's adaptation of material from another source which Mark did not have and/or use. The introduction of the word δόξα represents Luke's peculiar interpretation of the appearance of Jesus, Moses, and Elijah. Luke's use of ἐκλελεγμένος instead of ἀγαπητός may be accounted for on the basis of the development of two strands of interpretation from a common source – Isa. 42.1.

From the form-critical standpoint, the Transfiguration account has some affinities with the literary forms of theophany and legend. The comparisons are not exact; this is particularly true of the legend-form. The narrative form is significant for this study. There is an important union of narrative and cultic activity that will be investigated in Chapter 4.

There are close parallels between the Transfiguration account and Luke's two ascension accounts. All three of these passages have specific parallels in vocabulary and themes. Luke 9.28-36 and Acts 1.12 are definitely eschatological. There are significant contrasts, which suggest that Luke intended to record two different events and intended to draw two specific and distinct eschatological analogies.

3

An Exegesis of Luke 9.27-36

Annotated Translation of Luke 9.27-36

The following annotated translation of Lk. 9.27-36 represents the exegetical orientation of this study. In this sense, it is the basis of the exegesis to follow.

(9.27) But[1] I say to you, truly[2] there are some standing here[3] who will not taste of death until they see the kingdom of God.

(28) And about eight days[4] after these words[5] when he had taken Peter and James and John, he went up the mountain to pray.[6]

---

1 δέ has the adversative effect here. This statement stands in contrast to the material in vv. 21-26. It is the culmination of this pericope, but it achieves this peak by contrast.

2 ἀληθῶς is a classical form (BDF, §243) and appears in Luke–Acts in the following places: 9.27 (this text); 12.44 (parallel, Mt. 24.47); 21.3 (parallel, Mt. 12.43); Acts 12.11. Luke employs this term for ἀμὴν in the citation of the words of Jesus.

3 τινες τῶν αὐτοῦ ἑστηκότων. The use of the genitive neuter of αὐτός as an adverb of place is the same as Mark's ὧδε τῶν ἑστηκότων (BDF, §103).

4 ἡμέραι ὀκτὼ: a nominative of the designation of time (BDF, §144; James Hope Moulton, *A Grammar of New Testament Greek* (Edinburg: T & T Clark, 1957, reprint of 3rd edn), I, pp 69, 70; III, p. 231.

5 μετὰ τοὺς λόγους τούτους: Jesus' words are the antecedent: 'After these sayings …' (J. Reiling and J.L. Swellengrebel, *A Translator's Handbook on the Gospel of Luke* [Leiden: Brill, 1971], p. 380).

6 εἰς … προσεύξασθαι: infinitive of purpose (BDF, §390).

(29) And while he was praying[7] the appearance of his face (became) another and his clothing was shining white.[8]

(30) And behold[9] two men were talking[10] with him who were Moses and Elijah.

(31) The men who were seen in glory were speaking[11] of his exodos[12] which he was about to fulfill[13] in Jerusalem.

(32) And Peter and the men who were with him were burdened down with sleep; but[14] when they had remained awake,[15] they saw his glory and the two men who were standing with him.

(33) And while they were departing from him, Peter said to Jesus, 'Master,[16] it is good for us to be here; so, let us make three

---

7 προσεύχεσθαι: The present infinitive (with αὐτὸν as subject) has durative force. The change took place while Jesus was praying. 'The aspect is durative, "during his prayer," "there he prayed for a time, then …"' (Reiling and Swellengrebel, *A Translator's Handbook on the Gospel of Luke*, p. 380).

8 ἐξαστράπτω: 'to flash, or, gleam like lightning' (Reiling and Swellengrebel, *A Translator's Handbook on the Gospel of Luke*, p. 380).

9 A septuagentism (BDF, §4.2).

10 συνελάλουν: durative imperfect (Reiling and Swellengrebel, *A Translator's Handbook on the Gospel of Luke*, p. 381).

11 ἐλέγον: This imperfect takes up the durative force of συνελάλουν (Reiling and Swellengrebel, *A Translator's Handbook on the Gospel of Luke*, p. 381).

12 ἔξοδος appears in the NT only in this text, in Heb. 11.22 (of the exit of Israel from Egypt) and in 2 Pet. 1.15 (of the anticipated death of Peter). Compare Luke's use of ἀναλήμψεως (Lk. 9.51; Acts 1.2, 11, 22).

13 ἦν ἤμελλεν πληροῦν. ἤμελλεν: 'means here "he was destined"' (Reiling and Swellengrebel, *A Translator's Handbook on the Gospel of Luke*, p. 381). πληρόω: 'Its use here implies that Jesus' death is in some way a fulfillment of his mission' (Reiling and Swellengrebel, *A Translator's Handbook on the Gospel of Luke*, p. 381).

14 δέ here has the adversative effect in order to contrast the sleepiness of the three intimates and their remaining awake.

15 διαγρηγορέω means to remain awake (cf. RSV). '… for διαγρηγορήσαντες εἶδαν Lk. 9.32. This would give the meaning "since they had kept awake" they saw' (BAG, p. 181). Reiling and Swellengrebel regard this translation as 'less probable' than 'after waking up' (*A Translator's Handbook on the Gospel of Luke*, p. 382).

16 'Επιστάτα: An address which emphasizes authority, hence here translated 'Master'. Luke is the only NT writer to use the term (Lk. 5.5; 8.24, 45; 9.33 (this text), 49; 17.13). In all cases except 17.13 it is a word found only on the lips of disciples. It is the equivalent of the Hebrew רבי. 'Several commentators think that *epistata* carries a note of special authority but as shown by the parallels quoted in Moulton and Milligan the emphasis is rather on an intimate, though respectful relationship than on authority' (Reiling and Swellengrebel, *A Translator's Handbook on the Gospel of Luke*, p. 228).

tabernacles:[17] one for you, and one for Moses and one for Elijah', not knowing what he was saying.

(34) And while he was saying these things, a cloud came and was overshadowing them.[18] And they were afraid when they entered into[19] the cloud.

(35) And a voice came out of the cloud saying, 'This is my Son, the chosen One; hear him'.

(36) And when the voice had come (spoken), Jesus was found alone. And they were silent and reported to no one in those days any thing of that which they saw.[20]

Exegesis

1. The announcement and setting of the Transfiguration (9.27-28).

Although 9.27 is formally the climax of its own pericope (9.21-27), it is integral to the Transfiguration account. The unity of this context is seen by the manner in which Luke establishes the words of Jesus (v. 27) as the antecedent of τοὺς λόγους τούτους. This editorial structure is also reflected in the other synoptic accounts, which may, in turn, reflect a pre-canonical union of these traditions.[21] Luke has tied together the confession (Lk. 9.18-20), the announcement of the

---

[17] σκηνὰς: An infrequent word in Luke–Acts, and doubtless used under the influence of the Septuagint. It is used chiefly for the Hebrew אהל in the Septuagint. In Luke–Acts it appears in the following places: this text; Lk. 16.9 (of 'eternal tabernacles'); Acts 7.43 (of the 'tabernacles of Moloch'); 7.44 (of the 'tabernacle of witness'); 15.16 (of the 'tabernacle of David' which had fallen). In a note on Jn 1.14, Raymond E. Brown observes: 'The radicals *skn* which underlie the Greek word "to tent" resemble the Hebrew *skn* which also means "to dwell" and from which the noun *shekinah* is derived. In rabbinic theology *shekinah* was a technical term for God's presence dwelling among people' (*The Gospel According to St. John I-XII* [The Anchor Bible; Garden City; NY: Doubleday, 1966], p. 33).

[18] BAG, p. 298: 'Of the cloud that indicates the presence of God (cf. Exodus 40.35; Odes of Solomon, 35.1; Mt. 17.5; Lk. 9.34 … (Ps 90 (91).4); Mk 9.7'.

[19] ἐν τῷ εἰσελθεῖν αὐτοὺς εἰς τὴν νεφέλην: The aorist articular infinitive (with αὐτοὺς as subject) should carry the meaning 'after that' (BDF, §404.2). 'Εἰσελθεῖν tends to confirm the translation of ἐπεσκίαζεν given above. 'Luke distinguishes carefully between the present and the aorist infinitive, the latter being used only of completed action' (Creed, *The Gospel According to St. Luke*, p. xxix).

[20] ἑώρακαν: an aorist perfect (BDF, §343.3; Moulton, *A Grammar of New Testament Greek*, I, p. 144).

[21] Ellis, 'Present and Future Eschatology', p. 31; Werner Georg Kümmel, *Promise and Fulfillment* (trans. Dorothea M. Barton; London: SCM Press, 1957), p. 27.

passion of the Son of man (Lk. 9.21, 22), the definition and call to discipleship (Lk. 9.23-25), the warning of judgement (Lk. 9.26, 27), the promise of the seeing of the kingdom of God (Lk. 9.27), and the Transfiguration.[22]

It is the contention of this study that the object of v. 27 is to be supplied in the immediate literary context.

The editorial unification of this entire cycle of material (see note 22) and the particularly close relationship of v. 27 with v. 28[23] point to the Transfiguration as the object of v. 27.[24] This is also consistent with Luke's scheme by which he places the Transfiguration at the heading of Jesus' journey to Jerusalem.[25] The problematic nature of this verse is apparent from the number of interpretations that have developed over its prediction and fulfillment.[26] One of the difficulties of most of these interpretations is that they seek to impose interpretations from outside the literary context of the passage. Certain form-critical studies have attempted to show that in Mark there is a discontinuity between Mk 9.1 and 9.2 (Lk. 9.27, 28 parallel). If that

---

22 Conzelmann, *The Theology of St. Luke*, p. 56: 'It is clear that the Feeding, the Confession, the Prediction of the Passion and the Transfiguration form a complete cycle, to which Luke assigns a prominent function in his whole structure'. Frederick H. Borsch, *The Son of Man in Myth and History* (Philadelphia: Westminster, 1967), p. 37: 'in the synoptic section which begins with the confession at Caesarea Philippi and closes with the discussion regarding the suffering of the Son of Man and Elijah following the transfiguration we are dealing with a primitive cycle of materials fully dominated by concern with the Son of Man'. Additionally, Tödt's judgement of the Markan order that there 'is a soteriological continuity between the fellowship with Jesus on earth and fellowship with the Son of Man in the kingdom of God' would seem to be valid for all of the synoptics (H.E. Tödt, *The Son of Man in the Synoptic Tradition* (trans. Dorothea M. Barton; London: SCM Press, 1973), pp. 146, 147).

23 Hobert Kenneth Farrell, 'The Eschatological Perspective of Luke–Acts' (PhD dissertation, Boston University, 1972), p. 26.

24 J.W.C. Wand, *Transfiguration* (London: Faith Press, 1967), p. 15; Ellis, 'Present and Future Eschatology', p. 31 n. 4.

25 Conzelmann, *The Theology of St. Luke*, pp. 180, 196.

26 Plummer has given an equate summarization of the views on the fulfillment of this promise. The summary is as follows:

1. The Transfiguration (most of the Fathers),
2. The Resurrection and Ascension (Cajetan, Calvin, Beza),
3. Pentecost and subsequent signs (Godet, Hahn),
4. The spread of Christianity (Nosgen),
5. The internal development of the gospel (Erasmus, Klostermann),
6. The destiny of Jesus (Wetstein, Alford, Morison, Plumptre, Mansel),
7. The second advent (Meyer, Weisse, Holtzmann)

Plummer, *The Gospel According to St. Luke*, pp. 249, 250.

discontinuity can be shown in Mark, it is not apparent in Luke. Luke has unified his context; this is generally true for this author.[27] We will attempt to demonstrate the unity of context between 9.27 and the Transfiguration account in the process of the exegesis of the passage.

The promise extended is a restrictive promise. The first restriction is that it is addressed to 'some of those standing here'. The 'some' refers to a distinction within the immediate audience of Jesus as Luke presents it. Some of those standing before Jesus will see the kingdom before their death; others will not see the kingdom before their death. 'No interpretation can be correct that does not explain εἰσίν τινες which implies the exceptional privilege of some, as distinct from the common experience of all'.[28]

This promise is restricted also by the implication in the reference to death. Those who will see the kingdom in the sense promised here are not by this promise exempted from the prospect of death.[29] The inference cannot be drawn that such persons will not die or that seeing the kingdom is an experience that substitutes for or fulfills the necessity of death.[30] It should be noted that the term 'death' here is

---

27 Conzelmann, *The Theology of St. Luke*, pp. 57, 58.

28 Plummer, *The Gospel According to St. Luke*, p. 249.

29 Ellis, 'Present and Future Eschatology', p. 30 n. 3. Additionally, this view interprets 9.27 as a promise of the Parousia, yet there are no clear Parousia symbols in the verse, though they are in the context (p. 34). Contra G.B. Caird, *The Gospel According to St. Luke*, p. 130: Jesus 'was promising that although some of them (i.e. the disciples) will share with him in the death which God had decreed for the Son of man, others will survive to see the triumph of God's kingdom which that death will secure'. The difficulty with this view is that it makes the recording of this promise in Luke's time meaningless.

30 Ellis, 'Present and Future Eschatology', p. 32 n. 2: 'When modifying a negative main clause, the conjunction, ἕως, regularly signifies that the event in the main clause will in fact occur when the statement of the dependent clause is fulfilled'. Plummer, *The Gospel According to St. Luke*, p. 250, writes 'Moreover, the οὐ μὴ γεύσωνται θανάτου ἕως implies that the τινες will experience death after seeing the βασιλεία which would not be true of those who live to see the παρουσία'. Kümmel acknowledges this from a grammatical point of view, but denies it for other considerations in his own thesis (*Promise and Fulfillment*, p. 26 n. 23): 'It is correct that the wording of the saying does not exclude the idea that the τινες will yet die later … ; but it is only possible to understand it in this way by wrongly referring the arrival of the βασιλεία with power to historical events'. In the text relating to this passage, Kümmel states 'they are not to die because the kingdom of God will previously have been made known to them' (*Promise and Fulfillment*, p. 26 n. 23).

understood in the usual sense of physical death.[31]

In addition to the specific reference to death, the term also reflects an eschatological meaning: i.e. it describes a route for seeing the kingdom.[32] The interpretation reflected in 2 Esdras 6.26-28 (note 31) probably derived from such an eschatological understanding of the expression γεύεσθαι θανάτου. It does, however, seem to show that the critical terminology of this verse consists of eschatological symbols. Perrin understands that those who do not 'taste of death' are translated prior to death.[33] This evidence combined with the citation earlier from Kummel (note 30) does reveal here an eschatological saying.

The third restriction placed on this promise is that it promises an experience of 'seeing' the Kingdom of God. This restriction lies in the terminology (βασιλεία τοῦ θεοῦ) itself.

The term 'seeing' the kingdom specifically does not promise that these 'some' τινες will be able to observe the kingdom of God in a temporal, historical, and spatial establishment of it. This is not a promise that they will see Jesus reigning from Jerusalem and restoring the kingdom to Israel. Instead the term 'see' (ἰδεῖν) is used in the sense of seeing by revelatory experience.[34] This is not a restriction

---

31 This conclusion is supported in a number of sources (BAG, p. 56; Strack-Billerbeck, I, pp. 751-52; 2 Esdras 6.26; Anthologia Palatina, 662; Mt. 16.28; Mk 9.1; Jn 8.52; Heb. 2.9; BAG, p. 156). The verb usually takes the genitive object and carries the meaning to partake or to experience a thing (its object in the genitive). 'The formula γεύεσθαι – θανάτου Mk 9.1 and parallels: Jn 8.52 (of the Logion P. Oxy., 654, 5), Heb. 2.9 ('to experience death as what it is'), like ἰδεῖν or θεορεῖν (Heb. 11.5; Lk. 2.26; Jn 8.51), is a graphic expression of the hard and painful reality of dying which is experienced by man and which was suffered also by Jesus (cf. Heb. 2.9: τὸ πάθημα τοῦ θανάτου)' (Behm, 'γεύμαι', *TDNT*).

32 Benjamin W. Bacon, 'After Six Days: A New Clue for Gospel Critics', *HTR* 8 (1935), p. 255:

> We have seen that the rare and peculiar 'taste of death' (γεύεσθαι θανάτου) of Mark 9.1 = Matt 16.28 = Luke 9.27 is distinctive of this peculiar eschatological tenet. Now in 2 Esdras 6.26, we read that those who survive the great tribulation 'shall see the men that have been taken up, who have not tasted death from their birth'.

33 Norman Perrin, *Rediscovering the Teaching of Jesus* (Philadelphia: Westminster, 1963), p. 199.

34 Conzelmann, *The Theology of St. Luke*, p. 105: 'The expression "to see the Kingdom" means that although the kingdom cannot actually be seen, it can in the interpretation of the life of Jesus be perceived'. The thesis which is being pursued in this study is specifically contrary to Conzelmann's view that the kingdom is 'seen'

based in the meaning of the word ἰδεῖν but drawn from the sentence and its context, and certainly allowed by the word ἰδεῖν. By seeing the fulfillment of this word in a revelatory experience, the meaning of the 'some' is made clear. It is a seeing that is restricted to some: namely those chosen for such an experience.

This restriction is determined by Luke's concept of the kingdom of God. This will determine what is seen as the kingdom and hence the most important restriction in this promise. What follows is a summary answer to the question, What is the kingdom of God according to Luke?

The kingdom is identified by the presence of Jesus and/or his Spirit and through the preaching of Jesus.[35] It is manifested by the blessings of the kingdom. At the same time, Luke maintains a concept of the kingdom which is to be manifested in the future. This manifestation of the kingdom, he identifies by certain eschatological and apocalyptic symbols.

A more extensive discussion of the nature of the kingdom of God will appear in Chapter 4.

The final restriction of this promise is that in its present form and context it anticipates verification by a foreseeable event. The editorial purpose of Luke is to place this promise in proximity to its fulfillment. So, the question is raised: Is there an event or experience alluded to or recorded that will satisfy the demands of this fulfillment?

This question may be put to all of the synoptics,[36] but our special interest is Luke's record in its present form.

The interpretations of the fulfillment of Lk. 9.27 may be grouped under the following categories: (1) those who see a spiritualized fulfillment; (2) those who see a historical fulfillment within Jesus' generation, (3) those who see an eschatological fulfillment, and (4) those who see an especially provided fulfillment in the Transfiguration.

Of the first category attention may be called to C.H. Dodd, who argued that the prediction would be fulfilled if it (i.e. the kingdom) came at any time between the utterance of the saying and the moment of perception whenever that might be. But it is consistent with

---

in the 'interpretation of the life of Jesus'; however, the verb ἰδεῖν is adaptable to both interpretations. To see is to experience or to perceive the kingdom.

35 I. Howard Marshall, *Luke: Historian and Theologian* (Grand Rapids: Zondervan, 1970), p. 134.

36 Evans, 'The Transfiguration of Jesus', p. 99.

the view that the Kingdom of God actually came in the complex of events ending with the resurrection of Christ, and that the disciples shortly afterwards perceived that this was the case. The story of Pentecost may in my view be taken to represent the moment of perception.[37] Creed proposed that the

> omission of ἐληλυθυῖαν ἐν δυνάμει is significant. The first generation must have almost if not quite died out, and Luke and his contemporaries still looked for a 'coming in power'. But Acts i.ii suggests that he would have been able to recognize a fulfillment of the coming of the kingdom in the coming of the Spirit. The omission makes it easier to adopt such a spiritualized interpretation for the present text.[38]

Both Dodd and Creed see the fulfillment related to the Pentecostal experience.

Others project other spiritualized interpretations. Caird, for example, states that Jesus 'was promising that although some of them (i.e. the disciples) will share with him in the death which God has decreed for the Son of man, others will survive to see the triumph of God's kingdom which that death will secure'.[39] Lindsay writes that 'what Christ promised was such a vision as would produce assurance of the triumph of his kingdom in the future'.[40] Stonehouse suggests that the church may be included in the kingdom as a demonstration of the rule of God's grace.[41]

Of those who see a historical fulfillment occurring within Jesus' generation we take note of Geldenhuys, who concludes that 'the destruction of Jerusalem and the downfall of the Jewish nation' reveal God's 'kingly dominion over the unbelieving Jewish nation'.[42] In this way the kingdom of God is revealed to some of those to whom Jesus spoke.

Those who see an eschatological fulfillment of this verse tend to be in one of two extremes of interpretation. Some treat the verse as a statement of an expectation of imminent Parousia. On the other end of the scale are those who see the Parousia in this verse but see

---

[37] Dodd, 'The Kingdom Has Come', p. 138.
[38] Creed, *The Gospel According to St. Luke*, p. 32.
[39] Caird, *The Gospel According to St. Luke*, p. 130.
[40] Lindsay, *The Gospel According to St. Luke*, p. 140.
[41] Stonehouse, *The Witness of St. Luke to Christ*, p. 156:
[42] Geldenhuys, *Commentary on the Gospel of St. Luke*, p. 277:

a symbolical fulfillment of Parousia in the Transfiguration. Most, however, recognize on the first extreme that this sense is not in Luke, though they may see it in Mark or Matthew. If this is the assumption concerning this promise, it is treated as having been de-eschatologized as in Conzelmann's 'timeless conception' of the kingdom of God.[43]

On the other end of the continuum, there are a number who do see a Parousia prediction here but assume that it at first reflects a proleptic fulfillment of the kingdom in the Transfiguration. Ellis writes, 'The connection with the transfiguration, implicit in the order of the episodes, creates a second reference to the parousia. For the transfiguration reveals privately what will be publicly manifested at the last day.'[44] Conzelmann sees Luke's transmission of this passage as 'the earliest example of an exegesis of the difficult Markan saying'.[45] According to Conzelmann, then, Luke here de-eschatologized the kingdom of God: 'The idea of the coming of the kingdom of God is replaced by a timeless conception of it'. And he concludes that 'it is from the life of Jesus that we can see what the kingdom of God is like'.[46]

The final group of interpretations is that group that sees this verse to be fulfilled in the Transfiguration. Among those authors who embrace this view are J. Dillersberger, E. Evans, H.K. Farrell, A.R.C. Leany, and G.S. Rowe.[47] It seems that this interpretation leaves the fewest questions unanswered. It provides a special event for the fulfillment. It is such an event that does not fall within Luke's terms of the time-space limitations that pertain to a kingdom that 'comes with observation' (17.20, 21). It provides a picture of the kingdom and Jesus in his kingly glory that Luke is just now beginning to introduce.

---

43 Conzelmann, *The Theology of St. Luke*, p. 105.

44 Ellis, *Luke*, p. 141. I acknowledge here some confusion in Ellis' position because in his article on 'Present and Future Eschatology' he seems to deny Parousia elements in 9.27. He does, however, make clear his opinion that there is a connection between 9.27 and 9.28-36.

45 Conzelmann, *The Theology of St. Luke*, p. 105.

46 Conzelmann, *The Theology of St. Luke*, p. 105.

47 Joseph Dillersberger, *The Gospel of St. Luke* (Westminster, MD: Newman Press, 1958), p. 254; Evans, 'The Transfiguration of Jesus', pp. 98, 99; Farrell, 'The Eschatological Perspective of Luke–Acts', p. 32; A.R.C. Leaney, *A Commentary on the Gospel of St. Luke* (New York: Harper, 1958), p. 166; Rowe, 'The Transfiguration', p. 336.

This picture of Jesus is consistent with the description of Jesus when he appears after his ascension.

In what form can the kingdom of God be seen? This is critical to our thesis. If the kingdom of God can be seen in such a way that it can be said, 'Lo here, or Lo there', it is a temporally-realized kingdom. This verse will stand, in that case, in contradiction to Lk. 17.20, 21. This is the primary difficulty with those interpretations of this verse that see its fulfillment in such temporal events as the destruction of Jerusalem, Pentecost, and even the resurrection. It does not seem reasonable to postulate a fulfillment of this promise by means of any strictly time-space event. All such events would allow a 'pointing to' the kingdom as 'there and not here'. Its fulfillment must be realized in a supramundane event: that is an event that is not identifiable in the time-space relation of 'Lo here, Lo there'.

The projection of this study is that the Transfiguration supplies the essentials for the fulfillment of this promise. Is there a basis in the language of this verse to justify our conclusion? First, it is to be observed that the term kingdom of God is used without qualifying terms; even Mark's 'in power' is dropped by Luke here. So, the concept of the kingdom to be seen is left open to whatever definition the rest of Luke–Acts literature provides. The kingdom in its present reality can be seen now by any who can perceive that the preaching of the gospel, the deliverance of the captives, and the remission of sins represent the reign of God. Hence, we judge that this kind of seeing the kingdom is not what is anticipated in 9.27.

The seeing of the kingdom in its apocalyptic nature can be experienced by death and/or by the in breaking of that kingdom in the new age. This, however, is in its order a universal experience, which puts it beyond what is anticipated here.

There is a third possible route for seeing the kingdom: a special experience provided for a selected group of the disciples. It is consistent with the content of Luke–Acts to expect specially granted experiences or particular purposes.[48] If Luke conceives of Jesus'

---

[48] There are examples in Acts that illustrate this principle of revelation: certain of the resurrection appearances (10.41), Stephen's experience at his stoning (7.55, 56; only Stephen was witness to the opened heavens), the revelation at the conversion of Saul (9.3-7; note especially v. 7), and the revelation to Peter (10.9-16). Though these instances of revelation are not designated as the kingdom of God, they do show that the witnesses to God's revelations are chosen by him.

promise as envisioning a special experience, we can expect Luke to provide a story that will meet the terms of this expectation.

It would seem that these considerations are such that the interpretation is open to fulfillment by such an event as the Transfiguration.

One final problem remains in the consideration of this verse and this is Luke's omission of ἐν δυνάμει (Mk 9.1).[49] In an attempt to answer this question, it is important to notice again the difference between Mark and Luke. Mark 9.1 describes the kingdom in this way: τὴν βασιλείαν τοῦ θεοῦ ἐληλυθυῖαν ἐν δυνάμει; Lk. 9.27 in this way: τὴν βασιλείαν τοῦ θεοῦ.

There are two important considerations: Mark's ἐληλυθυῖαν[50] and Luke's omission ἐν δυνάμει. By his omissions, Luke is certainly interpreting Mark; therefore, it is necessary to understand each one in the light of the other.

The promise as given in Mk 9.1 is 'there are some standing here who shall not taste death until they have seen the kingdom of God come in power'. It is the kingdom that is to be seen.[51] Mark describes this kingdom as being seen 'having come in power'. The pluperfect participle of ἔρχομαι emphasizes the consummated character of the kingdom when it is seen. Whenever the kingdom is seen it will have come in power. By the use of ἔρχομαι Mark implies the Parousia,[52] but it is not the Parousia singularly. What is seen is the Parousia

---

49 Conzelmann treats this omission as a part of Luke's exegesis of Mark and takes the omission to be critical to the de-eschatologizing of the kingdom concept in Luke (*The Theology of St. Luke*, p. 105). Creed understands this omission to represent a spiritualized meaning of the promise realized in Pentecost as distinct from the Parousia (*The Gospel According to St. Luke*, p. 132). Ellis treats the omission as the removal of 'a redundancy. For Luke the presence of the kingdom is always ἐν δυνάμει' ('Present and Future Eschatology', p. 105).

50 BDF, §347: The fact that this is a pluperfect verb emphasizes both the aoristic and the perfect implications of this verb form.

51 A specific interpretation of Mark would call for a summary of his presentation of the kingdom. Because of the limitations of this paper, this cannot be done here. Its salient characteristics are as follows. The kingdom is imminent, and its gateway is repentance. It comes in the Person, presence, and preaching of Jesus (C.F.D. Moule, *The Gospel According to Mark* [Cambridge: The University Press, 1965], p. 14). It is a mystery and knowledge of it is by revelation (James M. Robinson, *The Problem of History in Mark* [Naperville, IL: Alec R. Allenson, 1957], p. 51). The kingdom is eschatological and redemptive in nature.

52 The word ἔρχομαι is a verb of arrival; so, this verse does relate to the event of the kingdom's appearance, the Parousia.

completed and the kingdom established (hence ἐληλυθυῖαν)[53] having come in power.

Luke, as distinct from Mark, does not emphasize the Parousia aspect of the promise; hence, he does not use either the verb form or the phrase ἐν δυνάμει. His emphasis is that some will see the kingdom, but he speaks more of the presence of the kingdom than he does of the process and character of its arrival.

Consistent with the other synoptics, Luke notes the time span between the two pericopes 9.21-27 and 9.28-36.

The time reference in Luke is more general ('about 8 days') than in Mark. In fact, Luke seems deliberately to avoid the specific statement of Mark. This leads to the conclusion that Luke is not attaching a special meaning to this designation of time.[54]

---

[53] This participle (ἐληλυθυῖαν) emphasizes both the aoristic and the perfect implications of this verb form. BDF, §347.

[54] Quite a few commentators see the evidence of a Sinai motif in Mark's 6 days. J.A. Ziesler, 'The Transfiguration Story and the Markan Soteriology', *Expository Times*, 81 (June 1970), p. 265: 'Six days (9.2) cf. Exod. 24.16. This very odd giving of exact time ... refers at least as readily to Mount Sinai, as to the days between the Day of Atonement and the Feast of Tabernacles'. Eduard Schweizer, *The Good News According to Mark* (trans. Donald H. Madvig; Richmond: John Knox Press, 1970), pp. 181, 182: 'There is a link between the scene of Moses receiving the Law on Mount Sinai (Exod. 24) and Jesus' confirmation as Son on the unnamed mountain in Palestine'. McCurley, '"And After Six Days" (Mk 9.2) A Semitic Literary Device', p. 68:

> It is the purpose of this study to demonstrate that the Marcan-Matthean phrase 'and after six days', is related directly to the Sinai narrative at Exod. 24.15b-18 and that the phrase derives from a common Semitic literary pattern, an understanding of which sheds particular light on the interpretation of the Transfiguration story as a whole.

This author goes on to claim that this literary pattern was not only in the OT ('after 6 days' = 'on the seventh day'), but that it existed until at least the end of the second century BCE and that it is entirely possible that 'the originator of the Transfiguration story, as well as the author of Mark, was familiar with the scheme' (McCurley, '"And After Six Days" [Mk 9.2] A Semitic Literary Device', p. 75). If Luke is aware of the Sinai motif, he chooses here not to emphasize it. This would seem to be enforced by the fact that semitisms and Septuagintisms are frequent in Luke; in this one instance, he chooses to avoid such. He inserts in its place an approximation. This is not to deny the presence of the Sinai motif elsewhere in Luke's Transfiguration account.

Luke does not make anything of a possible liturgical allusion (Bacon, 'After Six Days', pp. 111, 112); the assumption of Bacon is that reference to lapses of time are aetiological. He applies this assumption to the worship periods of the ancient church as they were read back into the narratives in the gospels. 'Is it unreasonable to trace a connection between the "six days" of "teaching" which according to Mk 9.2 and Mt. 17.1 separate the self-declaration of Jesus as the Christ to the disciples

Luke's expression seems deliberately general; it may be expressed in the phrase 'about a week'.[55] Luke's generalization prohibits a symbolic interpretation of this verse; it is not consistent with symbolism to use approximations. Approximation may lie in the historical background of a term; but whenever the symbol has developed (such as a place, a day or a number), it becomes specific.

The best interpretation of this alteration by Luke would appear to be that it represents Luke's concern for accuracy of detail. He avoids the specific reference.

Luke's reference to Jesus' and the intimates' ascent into the mountain is simply put: 'When he had taken Peter and John and James, he ascended into the mountain'. The only special attention given the 'mountain' is the use of the definite article, which could hardly be pressed interpretationally. Conzelmann claims that Luke intensifies Mark's symbolism of the mountain.[56] This conclusion does not seem

---

at Caesarea Philippi from the "theophany" of the Transfiguration … ?' (Bacon, 'After Six Days', pp. 111, 112). Bacon's aetiological scheme for explaining Luke's 'about a week' suggests 'the backward instead of the forward look; as the later church spoke of "the octave" of epiphany' ('After Six Days', pp. 111, 112). Even though there are liturgical allusions in the gospels, evidence for them is lacking here.

Furthermore, it does not seem reasonable to take E. Earle Ellis' interpretation that Luke's 'eight days' probably represent a symbolic alteration of Mk 9.2. He concludes that Luke's expression represents an entering into a 'new age of reality'. Ellis seeks support for this symbolism in Lk. 24.1, 13, 33: 'That very day: each of the resurrection episodes opens with a time reference to the "eighth day" … The symbolism identifies Jesus' resurrection as the beginning of a new creation' (*Luke*, p. 275). There is no precedent for the use of 8 days as such a symbolism in either the OT or the NT. Ellis forces the 8-day symbolism on Lk. 24.1, 13, 33. It is Ellis who coins the phrase 'eighth day'.

55 Reiling and Swellengrebel, *A Translator's Handbook on the Gospel of Luke*; Creed, *The Gospel According to St. Luke*, p. 134.

56 Contra: Conzelmann, *Theology of St. Luke*: 'It is the place of prayer, the scene of secret revelations, of communication with the unseen world. No temptation can take place on it nor any public preaching' (p. 29); 'In both cases (the mountain and the lake) Jesus is alone with his closest associates. In both settings manifestations take place, although of a different kind. The mountain reaches up to Heaven, the lake down to the abyss (vii, 26ff, especially 31ff.). The significance of the mountain is more fully brought out by means of contrast. The divine messengers descend upon it, and Jesus ascends it for the purpose of secret disclosure to his disciples' (pp. 44, 45).

Boobyer: '… it may be noted that the "mountain" has prominence both in the New Testament, and in other Christian or Jewish literature, as the place specially fitted far eschatological teaching or revelation' (Boobyer, *St. Mark and the Transfiguration Story*, pp. 64, 65). Here of course Boobyer appeals beyond Mark (his special study of the Transfiguration) and beyond Luke for his symbolism. It does not seem to be justified by Luke's use of the term. Of the ten times that Luke used the word 'mountain' there is no special stylized function in his literature. The mountain is by nature a place of seclusion; therefore, the references to Jesus' prayer there and his esoteric discourses with the disciples are natural. From a review of the use of the word ὄρος

---

to me that the symbolism can be supported in Luke. There is a special symbolism in Luke's use of the Mt. of Olives.

The word ὄρος appears in Luke–Acts in the following instances: Lk. 3.5 ('every mountain and hill shall be made low'); 4.29 ('they led him to the brow of the mountain'); 6.12 ('And it was in those days Jesus went out into a mountain to pray'); 8.32 ('a herd of swine on the mountain'); 9.28 ('he went up into the mountain to pray'); 9.37 ('when they descended from the mountain'; i.e. the mountain of the Transfiguration); 19.29, 37 (The triumphal entry begins at the foot (κατάβασις) of the Mt. of Olives.); 21.21 ('Then let the ones who are in Judea escape to the mountains'); 21.37 (during Passion Week 'at night when he went out, he passed the night in the mount called Olivet') 22.39-42, 45, 46 (The customary place of prayer (Gethsemane) and the prayer on the Mt. of Olives); 23.30 ('Then they-will begin to say to the mountains, "Fall on us", and to the hills "Hide us".' (Hosea 10.8); Acts 1.12 ('Then they returned to Jerusalem from the mount called Olivet'); 7.30 ('the desert of mount Sinai' – the place of the appearance of the Angel in a flame of fire in a bush); 7.38 (The Angel spoke to Moses in Mt. Sinai).

In three of the instances above the mountain is a place of prayer for Jesus (Lk. 6.12; 9.28; 22.39-42, 45, 46). Luke does not limit Jesus' praying to the mountain. Note Lk. 3.21 (at the river Jordan); 5.16 (in the wilderness); 9.18 (Jesus was alone praying); and 11.1 (praying 'in a certain place').

In four instances special revelations or experiences are given on a mountain: Lk. 9.28, 37 (the Transfiguration); Acts 1.6-12 (the ascension); 7.30 (the 'burning bush' in the wilderness of Mt. Sinai); 7.38 (The Angel spoke in Mt. Sinai). Luke, however, does not limit special visitation to the mountain. The appearance of the heavenly messengers to Zacharias (Lk. 1.5-25) and Mary (Lk. 1.26-38) did not occur in a mountain, though the appearance to Zacharias was in the temple. The manifestation of the Holy Spirit upon Jesus following his baptism and during his praying did not occur in a mountain (Lk. 3.21, 22). Two appearances of the resurrected Jesus (prior to the ascension) are not in a mountain setting: the Emmaus appearance (Lk. 24.13-31) and the appearance in Jerusalem (Lk. 24.36-48). Luke speaks of visions and trances separate from any mountain reference. He uses the ward ὀπτασία in the following places: Lk. 1.22 (the congregation's understanding of Zacharias' experience in the temple); 24.23 (the Emmaus disciples' description of the appearance of the angels to the women at the tomb); Acts 26.19 (Paul's reference to his Damascus Road experience as the 'heavenly vision'). Ὅραμα is never used by Luke of a mountain experience. Note the following instances of Luke's use of the word: Acts 9.10 (Ananias' vision concerning Saul); 9.12 (Saul's vision concerning Ananias); 10.3-6 (Cornelius' vision concerning Peter); 10.10-19 (Peter's vision at Joppa); 11.5 (Peter's relating of his vision at Joppa); 12.7-11 (the appearance of the angel to Peter in Prison and Peter's confusing the experience with a vision [v. 9]); 16.9, 10 (a night vision to Paul of the Macedonian); 18.9 (a night vision to Paul prior to the shipwreck). Ὅρασις is used in Acts 2.17 to cite Joel 2.28. Luke uses the word ἔκστασις (trance) of Peter's Joppa vision in Acts 10.10 and 11.15. Paul is quoted as describing a temple experience as a 'trance' (Acts 22.17).

in Luke–Acts, it appears that the mountain is not a special symbol for Luke.

The relationship that the mountain of the Transfiguration has with the Mt. of Olives rests on the special symbolism of the latter mountain. The relationship with Mt. Sinai also depends on the special symbolism of Sinai and not a general mountain symbolism.

There are specific similarities with the Sinai tradition that suggest the Sinai motif: the prominence of Moses, the use of the term 'exodus',[57] the appearance of the glory of the Lord in the cloud, and the command 'Hear him'.

The most important emphasis of 9.28 (and one that is peculiar to Luke) is the statement of purpose; Jesus ascended the mountain in order to pray. This purpose is also taken up in v. 29 and is integrated with the Transfiguration of Jesus. Prayer is a special emphasis of Luke; though the other synoptics mention the prayers of Jesus, neither of them develop this element in Jesus' life as Luke does.[58] The references to prayer in Luke which are listed in note 48 indicate that Luke thinks of it as Jesus' pattern to seek privacy when he prayed; hence no special symbolism need be attached to the mountain setting of prayer. 'There is much evidence, especially in Luke, that he liked to be alone to pray.'[59]

2. The Transfiguration (9.29-36).

The change in Jesus' appearance (v. 29).

The integration of the act of praying (9.29) with the change of appearance (the Transfiguration) is stated clearly by the language of this verse: 'and while he was praying the image of his face was changed'.

---

[57] The 'exodus' theme will be developed in Chapter 4. Note C.F. Evans, 'The Central Section of Luke's Gospel', *in Studies in the Gospels*, in D.E. Nineham (ed.), *Studies in Luke–Acts* (Oxford: Basil Blackwell, 1955), pp. 37-53.

[58] Jesus is pictured as praying publicly at his baptism prior to the descent of the Holy Spirit on him (3.21) and from the cross (23.34, 46). He prays in seclusion after the healing of the leper before the calling of the twelve (6.12), before the confession of Peter (9.28, 29), when the disciples asked him to teach them to pray (11.1), and in Gethsemane before his arrest (22.39-46). He is apparently alone with the seventy (two) upon their return when 'He rejoiced in the Holy Spirit'. Reference is made in Lk. 22.31, 32 to Jesus' prayer for Peter, with the implication that until that time it had been a secret prayer.

[59] Greeven, 'προσεύχομαι', *TDNT*; Harris, 'Prayer in Luke–Acts', p. 50: 'Apparently Luke wanted his readers to understand that Jesus withdrew for prayer on many occasions.'

'The verb is repeated to bring out the connection between Jesus' communion with God in prayer and his transfiguration. The aspect durative, "during his prayer", "there he prayed for a time, then ..." .'[60]

It is consistent with Luke's use of prayer in the gospel and in Acts to connect prayer with extraordinary religious experience.[61]

There is a consistent introduction of the element of prayer in Luke in circumstances of this nature.[62] Three events mark the main stages of the ministry of Jesus: baptism, Transfiguration, and Gethsemane. These 'are assimilated to each other. On each of the three occasions a heavenly revelation is depicted as the answer to prayer.'[63] In the first of these two instances, the 'revelation' is eschatological in nature and in each there is a divine witness of Jesus' unique sonship.

If, as we hope to show later, this manifestation of glory is the kingdom of God in consummation, this is a very significant relationship. Prayer is the route of Jesus' entrance into the Transfiguration and his experience of kingdom glory.

The language that Luke uses to describe the change in Jesus' appearance avoids the use of μεταμορφόω but at the same time it is interpretative of that word, which certainly was before Luke in his sources (Mark in particular). In his statement that the 'image of his face (became) another',[64] Luke has expressed not simply a change in appearance but a change in nature.[65] Here I take issue with the

---

60 Reiling and Swellengrebel, *A Translator's Handbook on the Gospel of Luke*, p. 380.

61 This is a pattern that Luke continues in his record of the early Christian community. The Holy Spirit fell on the congregation while they were praying (Acts 4.32; δέομαι is used here for prayer). Ananias was told in a vision that Saul of Tarsus was praying and had seen a vision (Acts 9.10-12). Cornelius' vision is supposed to have been about the ninth hour – the hour of prayer (Acts 10.9-16; 11.5). Paul describes his experience of prayer in the temple; as he was praying, he went into a trance (Acts 22.17). There are certainly instances of revelation in Acts not associated with prayer, but the above references show a significant pattern.

62 Conzelmann, *The Theology of St. Luke*, p. 180; Conzelmann apparently takes Lk. 25.34a to be original.

63 Conzelmann does not here take note of the omission of Lk. 22.43, 44 by many witnesses. He apparently assumes its authenticity (*The Theology of St. Luke*, p. 180).

64 Reiling and Swellengrebel, *A Translator's Handbook on the Gospel of Luke*, p. 380: 'The appearance of his face took another form'.

65 Of the various views of the Transfiguration that were presented in the introductory chapter we may now concern ourselves with the understanding of this event from the perspective of the text itself. From whatever sources Luke draws his material and by whatever route it came to him, his language expresses an

representation of this as a visionary experience of the three disciples. This, at least, is not what Luke understood of his record. He does not use the language of vision to describe the event. Luke's language ascribes the change to Jesus and does not attribute it to a special subjective religious experience of the disciples. They are, in fact, dissociated from Jesus' experience by their drowsiness and are drawn into it only at the startling nature of the appearance.[66]

For Luke, this was a miraculous translation of Jesus into his glorified form – the form of immortality – in which he would be seen in his reign at God's right hand. The absoluteness of this change in nature is represented by the fact that this appearance of Jesus is described as being 'in glory' (vv. 31, 32). This glory is also reflected in the appearance of Jesus' garments; they became white like flashing lightning. In this description of Jesus there are two special terms of symbolic significance: δόξα and the white flashing garments.

The term δόξα is particularly important in our inquiry[67] because Luke alone of the synoptics uses it in the Transfiguration story. Luke

---

extraordinary change in the appearance of Jesus. That this change in appearance reflected a change in nature seems clear from the language of this pericope. The kind of change and its significance is the subject of this inquiry.

The following suggestions have been made in the literature on the subject. Here I limit the citation to those that represent interpretation of the language and do not investigate the question of origin in form-critical studies.

Several interpreters conclude that Jesus' change was a translation into the heavenly glorious estate. It is his translation into the glory of human immortality: Evans, 'The Transfiguration of Jesus', pp. 97-104; Godet, *Commentary on the Gospel of Luke*, p. 426; Groves, 'The Significance of the Transfiguration of Our Lord', pp. 86-92; Kennedy, 'The Purpose of the Transfiguration', pp. 270-73. In this view, the Transfiguration was Jesus' entrance into immortality as the reward for his obedience to God – the just and normal end of 'the perfect man.

W.R.F. Browning reaches the same conclusions on the significance of the Transfiguration, but ascribes the disciples' experience to a vision (*The Gospel According to St. Luke* [New York: Macmillan, 1960], pp. 291, 292); cf. Ellis, *The Gospel of Luke*, pp. 141-42; Farrell, 'The Eschatological Perspective of Luke–Acts', pp. 42-43; Harrison, 'The Transfiguration', p. 318; Johnson, 'The Transfiguration of Christ', pp. 133-44; Kee, 'The Transfiguration in Mark', pp. 135-52.

Yet another interpretation of this change is that it represented the shining through of the glory of the preexistent Son of God (Bernardin, 'The Transfiguration', pp. 181-89).

66 To the contrary, see: Kee, 'The Transfiguration in Mark', pp. 136-52.

67 BAG, pp. 202, 203: 'Everything in heaven has this radiance … especially God' (p. 202). It is applied to those 'who appear before God – Moses (2 Cor. 3.7-10); believers in the life to come (1 Cor. 15.34; Col. 3.4)'. It is also applied 'to those who stand in judgement, Rom. 3.23; 5.2' (p. 202). It is applied to Jesus' 'body of glory' (Phil. 3.21). Christ is the Lord of glory (1 Cor. 2.8). He is raised from the dead

uses the word in a number of other places in such a way that its meaning is heightened in this instance of its use.[68]

Luke's use of the term δόξα reflects the Septuagint use of the word as the 'true and dominant equivalent of כבוד'.[69] Luke uses δόξα in relation to Jesus primarily in an eschatological sense. It is in this sense that glory is used in the Transfiguration. The glory in which Jesus is translated here is his presentation in the apocalyptic kingdom setting. The symbols of this apocalypticism are the glory appearing in Jesus' face and the brilliance of his garments. This is the estate of Jesus in the new age.[70]

The personal identification of Jesus with the kingdom – his declaration of its presence in his person (Lk. 17.20, 21) – shows this scene to be a portrayal of the kingdom. The fact that he appears in apocalyptic glory gives to the kingdom itself apocalyptic identity.

The glory that is represented here is the kingdom glory, the glory in which Jesus is seen in all post-ascension manifestations, and the glory in which the Son of man reigns. Glory becomes synonymous with kingdom so that 'when the three saw Jesus' glory they saw the kingdom of God. Therefore, for Luke the saying in 9.27 is fulfilled in the Transfiguration'.[71]

This apocalyptic and eschatological symbolism is continued by the representation of Jesus' garments as brilliant. They possess the glory that is ascribed to the Son of man in his day (Lk. 17.24).[72]

The total appearance of Jesus – his face and his clothing is appropriate to the eschatological and apocalyptic expectation of Luke.

---

through the glory of the Father; here the concept of 'power' is attached to δόξα. 'The state of being in the next life is thus described as participation in the radiance or glory – a. w. ref. to Christ: … enter into his glory. Luke 24.26; cf. 1 Pt. 1.11 … Also of Christ's preexistence: Jn 17.5, 22, 24' (p. 203). It is used of the reflection of the glory of God.

68 We note in passing Luke's uses of the term in the following passages: The giving of praise to God in worship (Lk. 2.14; 17.18; Acts 12.23 (in the latter for the refusal of worship); the giving of praise among men (Lk. 14.10), the representation of the glory of a man (Lk. 12.27); of the kingdoms of the earth (Lk. 4.6). Other instances of this word in Luke–Acts will be noted in the body of this study.

69 G. Kittel and G. von Rad, 'Δόξα', *TDNT*.

70 Ellis, *Luke*, p. 142.

71 Farrell, 'The Eschatological Perspective of Luke–Acts', p. 43.

72 The closing phrase of this verse ἐν τῇ ἡμέραι αὐτοῦ has the greatest degree of manuscript support as the correct ending of the verse. The following witnesses support it: ℵ, A, K, L, W, X, Δ , θ, Π and Ψ. It is supported by many minuscules.

The heavenly messengers (vv. 30, 31).

The appearance of Moses and Elijah talking with Jesus is common to all of the synoptics.[73] Two aspects of their appearance are peculiar to Luke: namely, that they appeared in glory as Jesus did and that they talked with Jesus concerning his 'exodus'.

There are three areas of investigation to be pursued here: (1) the significance of Moses and Elijah's appearance, (2) the glory that is ascribed to them, and (3) the significance of Jesus' 'exodus' and their discussion of it with Jesus.

The significance of Moses and Elijah in this appearance must be drawn from the Moses and Elijah traditions and from the use of Moses and Elijah in the NT generally and Luke specifically.

Moses is the most frequently mentioned OT figure in the NT and he is most frequently mentioned as the lawgiver.[74] The appearance of

---

[73] There are insignificant inversions of the two names to Luke's order. It is probably best accounted for by the greater prominence of Moses in Luke–Acts than Elijah.

Neither Luke nor the other synoptics explain how the disciples knew Moses and Elijah. This is an unimportant issue to the gospel writer and may reflect an early characteristic of such stories. Heavenly personages are simply known by the nature of a revelation. A process of identification may appear in later forms of the story.

Attempts have been made to show that the original form of this story did not name the heavenly messengers. As the story developed in the early Christian tradition, names were added.

Hans-Peter Müller, 'Die Verlärung Jesu, Eine motivgeschichtliche Studie', *ZNW* 51.1-2 (1960), p. 56: There are two motifs: Jesus' change into a *Lichtgestalt* and the appearance of the cloud and the coming of the heavenly voice. Both of these have independent histories. The former is represented in the Markan narrative in Mark 9.2c-6 and 8, the latter in 2a, band 7 (and 9). Moses and Elijah belong in the tradition of the *Lichtgestalt*. They come into the full Transfiguration story only when these two traditions come together. C. Masson proposes that the original account mentioned only Elijah ('La Transfiguration de Jesus [Marc 9:2-13]', *Rev Theol Phil* 97 [1964], pp. 1-14).

Bultmann, *History of the Synoptic Tradition*, p. 260: 'The two figures that appear beside Jesus we may suppose to have been originally two unidentified heavenly beings ... The figures were then (by Mark?), following a law of folklore, identified and differentiated ...' Contra: The fact that names (or other details) appear in a story is not prima facie evidence of the secondary nature of these details. As we have seen the presence of detail may be a characteristic of a very early form of a story.

It seems, however, that regardless of the route by which this story developed, Luke had before him two fully-developed Transfiguration traditions, one of which was Mark. In the form in which Luke received the tradition, Moses and Elijah were recognized as a normal consequence in such experience.

[74] Jeremias, 'Μωυσῆς'.

the lawgiver (Moses) in a messianic setting is appropriate to the Moses tradition. It was expected that the messianic age would be the age of renewal of the law. This was true in mainstream Judaism and among the Covenanters at Qumran.[75] Some rabbinical schools expected a new Torah in the messianic age.[76] Moses has a place in a messianic scene as the lawgiver and by application as the representative of all of the law and the prophets.[77] Moses' relationship to the law and the expectation of the fulfillment of Deut. 18.15, 18 come together under the common banner of the prophetical office as it was occupied by Moses.[78]

---

[75] Howard M. Teeple, *The Mosaic Eschatological Prophet* (Philadelphia: Society of Biblical Literature, 1957), pp. 18, 20.

[76] Teeple, *The Mosaic Eschatological Prophet*, p. 23.

[77] Babcock, 'The Transfiguration', pp. 323-24; Moses as a person became idealized in the tradition. This led to a Moses-Messiah typology cast in the mold of 'first redeemer-last redeemer' which arose prior to the New Testament period and is attested by the Damascus document, Josephus and the NT (Jeremias, 'Μωυσῆς'). There was an expectation of Moses' return in the messianic age, and the further expectation 'that he would be an eschatological prophet' (Teeple, *The Mosaic Eschatological Prophet*, p. 43). This was at times interpreted as being fulfilled in Moses redivivus and in other places it is interpreted of a prophet like Moses (Teeple, *The Mosaic Eschatological Prophet*, p. 1). 'The emphasis on "signs and wonders" in Moses' mission led to a similar emphasis in the expectation of the "prophet like Moses" or of a Moses redivivus' (Wayne A. Meeks, *The Prophet-King* [Leiden: Brill, 1967], p. 163).

Two aspects of the Moses tradition appear which seem to be aberrational and late. The first is the identification of Moses and Messiah. The second is the bodily translation of Moses to heaven (Jeremias, 'Μωυσῆς'). The first reference to the bodily assumption of Moses appears in Josephus, which suggests a hellenistic origin and not a Palestinian origin of the thought. 'In the *Assumption of Moses* death and translation are combined, for while Michael is commissioned to bury Moses, Joshua sees 'the double Moses being taken up …' (Meeks, *The Prophet-King*, p. 159). Given that such references appear in only a few rabbinical passages (Jeremias, 'Μωυσῆς'), it does not seem likely that either of these notions affected the Transfiguration tradition.

[78] Moses' prophetic role is based in the OT and it is continued in the traditions of the Jews. The Spirit rests on him (Num. 11.17). 'He speaks the words that God teaches him' (T.R. Carruth, 'The Jesus-as-Prophet Motif in Luke–Acts' [PhD Dissertation, Baylor University, 1973], p. 45). God speaks to Moses in a unique way (Num. 12.6-8), and there is no prophet like him whom God knows face to face (Deut. 34.10, 11). The stature of Moses as prophet continues in the pseudepigrapha. Miracles are attributed to him (Sirach 44.23 – 45.5). The Wisdom-of Solomon 10.16 and 11.1 'claim the σοφία entered into Moses' soul' (Carruth, 'The Jesus-as-Prophet Motif in Luke–Acts'). Eupolemus has the 'concept of a succession of prophetic leaders after the type of Moses' (Carruth, 'The Jesus-as-Prophet Motif in Luke–Acts', p. 46). In the *Assumption of Moses*, Moses is God's chief prophet (11.16). According to 2 Baruch 84.5 Moses predicts Israel's history and he receives

The prophetical role is not a role in distinction from the law, but is a role that serves the purpose of the law. Moses' role as 'lawgiver' is a prophetic role;[79] these are drawn together under the motif of the messenger of God.[80]

The typology of Deut. 18.15, 18[81] appears in Jewish tradition as Moses redivivus or as a prophet like Moses. In either case, an eschatological prophet is expected.[82] This typology is further strengthened by the heavenly witness and command αὐτοῦ ἀκούετε (Lk. 9.35). From this command and the allusion to Deut. 18.15 we may conclude that Moses' relation to the Transfiguration is in part typological: 'in one passage at least the pre-Lukan tradition is shaped by the Moses/Messiah typology, namely in the account of the transfiguration in Mk 9.2-8 and par. The heavenly voice with its ἀκούετε αὐτοῦ (Mk 9.7) contains an allusion to Deut. 18.15 …'[83]

Moses' role as prophet (and so all other prophets) embraces 'the content of the O.T. (Lk. 16.29, 31; 24.27)'.[84] his presence here epitomizes the confirmation of all of the Scriptures upon the presentation of Jesus in the Transfiguration.

---

special revelation. 'The superiority of Moses to other prophets is emphasized by the tradition that God revealed all secrets to him, even that of the end of the ages' (Meeks, *The Prophet-King*, p. 156).

79 Meeks, *The Prophet-King*, p. 126 n. 9.

80 Meeks, *The Prophet-King*, p. 156 n. 5.

81 The Moses typology is particularly developed in Acts 7. It was in the wilderness of Mt. Sinai that an angel was seen in the burning bush from which Moses heard the voice of God (vv. 30, 31). Moses is the servant of God who is 'validated by miracles (Acts 7.36)' (Jeremias, 'Μωυσῆς'). Luke cites Deut. 18.15 as God's confirmation of Moses and as the promise of a prophet 'like Moses' (v. 37). He is the prophet of Messiah (v. 37); he is cast in the role of the suffering messenger of God (vv. 17, 44). He is powerful in his words and works. Lampe writes, 'It is … of little use for us to read the speech attributed to St. Stephen in the seventh chapter of the Acts of the Apostles, if we fail to recognize the typological correspondence which it presupposes between Christ and Moses'. G.W.H. Lampe, 'The Reasonableness of Typology', in T.W. Manson *et al.* (eds.), *Essays on Typology* (Naperville, IL: Alec R. Allenson, 1957), p. 19.

82 Teeple, *The Mosaic Eschatological Prophet*, p. 1.

83 Jeremias, 'Μωυσῆς'; Kee, 'The Transfiguration in Mark', p. 146: 'one can only conclude that Mark wants to present Jesus as the eschatological prophet whose coming Moses had announced'. This use and implication of Deut. 18.15 goes beyond rabbinic use: 'Deut. 18.15 and 18 are not interpreted eschatologically in extant rabbinic literature' (Meeks, *The Prophet-King*, p. 215).

84 Jeremias, 'Μωυσῆς'.

In the typological role what has been foreshadowed in Moses as type is now realized in the manner and the circumstances in which Jesus appears in Transfiguration.

Such a conclusion is appropriate to the eschatological nature of the Transfiguration scene. Both prophecy (as written and spoken) and typology (which is also prophetical) converge on the single point that fulfills them both – the kingdom glory of the Christ. This scene, then, is in the fullest sense eschatological.

Elijah's role in Mal. 3.1-4 and 4.4-6 is as an eschatological figure. Malachi 'sees in him a Messianic figure. He prepares the divine way for the heavenly king (3.1).'[85] Both of these passages describe this forerunner function. In addition to his preparing the way of the heavenly king, Elijah also is to purify the priesthood (3.2-4) and to establish peace (4.6).[86]

The forerunner function that is attributed to Elijah is variously interpreted as forerunner of the Messiah,[87] forerunner of God,[88] and forerunner of the day of the Lord.[89]

The manner in which the life of Elijah is recorded in the OT has contributed to the eschatological expectation related to him in Judaism and Christianity. His ministry is characterized by a following – a discipleship, especially Elisha. Miracles are significant in his ministry. Acts of divine retribution are prominent in his ministry both for their frequency and severity. The most significant event in this typology is the translation of Elijah and the descent of his mantle and power (2 Kgs 2.1-12). These and other events in the life of Elijah suggest an Elijah-Christ typology.

Jewish Elijah-traditions outside the canon of Scripture have early dating. There is a pre-Christian tradition that makes Elijah the 'high-priest of the last time'.[90] Sirach 48.1-12 (180 BCE) assigns Elijah (as the 'forerunner of God')[91] the task of restoring the tribes of Israel

---

85 J. Jeremias, 'Ἡλίας', *TDNT*.

86 Carruth, 'The Jesus-as-Prophet Motif in Luke–Acts', p. 39.

87 Jeremias, 'Ἡλίας'.

88 Carruth, 'The Jesus-as-Prophet Motif in Luke–Acts', p. 39.

89 Teeple, *The Mosaic Eschatological Prophet*, p. 4.

90 Jeremias, 'Ἡλίας'; Carruth, 'The Jesus-as-Prophet Motif in Luke–Acts', p. 40: Elijah became associated with this concept by combining Mal. 3.1; 4.9 with 2.4, 5, Test. XII.

91 Jeremias, 'Ἡλίας'; Carruth, 'The Jesus-as-Prophet Motif in Luke–Acts', p. 39.

to their original condition. 1 Maccabees 4.46 and 16.41 (125-100 BCE) anticipate a future prophet who would by the Spirit of Yahweh reveal the will of Yahweh. The expectation that prophecy would not be renewed until the messianic times leads to the conclusion that this would be an eschatological figure. According to Klausner these two references point to Elijah. He makes this claim on the basis of the rabbinic thought that Elijah would appear in the messianic age and that he would render judgement in difficult issues.[92] This conclusion is doubtful because of the lateness of the rabbinic literature. 'It is true that Elijah in rabbinic literature will make legal decisions when he returns, but up to the time that 1 Maccabees was written (125-100 BCE) this function is absent.'[93]

There may be some reference to the return of Elijah as the forerunner of the Messiah in the Damascus document, but this is not clear.[94]

Elijah is a key figure in the synoptic records; however, Luke uses his reference to Elijah in a specifically different way from Mark and Matthew.[95]

Probably the most significant commentary on Luke's use of Elijah is his omission of the conversation concerning Elijah as Jesus and the disciples descended from the mountain of Transfiguration.

In Matthew the conversation concerning Elijah may be taken as a commentary on the appearance of Elijah in the Transfiguration (Mt. 17.10-13). Matthew seemed to feel the necessity of adding the

---

92 Joseph Klausner, *The Messianic Idea in Israel* (trans. W.F. Stinespring; New York: Macmillan, 1955), p. 260.

93 Teeple, *The Mosaic Eschatological Prophet*, p. 3.

94 Jeremias, 'Ἠλίας'.

95 All of the synoptics contain the reports of the opinion of certain people that Jesus was Elijah (Mt. 16.14; Mk 6.15; 8.28; Lk. 9.8, 19). All report Elijah's presence at the Transfiguration (Mt. 17.3; Mk 9.4; Lk. 9.30, 33).

Matthew 17.10-12 and Mk 9.11-13 report the conversation between Jesus and the three witnesses of the Transfiguration. The heart of that conversation is Jesus' explanation of Elijah's eschatological appearance: Elijah restores all things when he has first come; he has come, and men have done to him whatever they wish (Mk 9.11-13). Luke has no parallel here. Matthew 27.47-49 and Mk 15.35, 36 record the confusion over Jesus' cry from the cross and the people took it to mean that Jesus cried for Elijah. Luke does not have a parallel to this.

Only Matthew has the specific statement concerning John, 'and if you will receive, he himself is Elijah who is to come' (11.14).

Except for the parallel passage noted above, Luke is unique in his references to Elijah. John is to go before 'the Lord their God' in the spirit and power of Elijah (1.17; cf. Mal. 4.5, 6).

explanation 'the disciples understood that he spoke to them concerning John the Baptist'[96] (v. 13). Apparently, Matthew knew of interpretations that confused this conversation as an explanation of Elijah's appearance in the Transfiguration.

Luke avoids this conversation entirely. To him there is no sense in which the function of John's preaching may be confused with Elijah's presence in the Transfiguration.

Luke is the only synoptic writer to use events out of the life of Elijah for illustration (4.25, 26; 9.54), and he seems to use an Elijah typology to describe the ministry of Jesus.[97] Lampe has suggested the following evidence of this typology in Luke: the Nazareth sermon, the choosing of disciples as Elijah chose Elisha, the raising of the widow's son, and the disciples' expectation that Jesus would call fire down on the Samaritan villagers. Luke is unique in his association of the word 'exodus' with Moses and Elijah. Lampe suggests that this may appeal to Elijah's 'exodus' when he and his disciple passed through the waters to the place of his translation. He suggests that there are parallels between the ascension of Jesus and the ascension of Elijah.[98]

As we asked concerning Moses we must ask concerning the Elijah traditions: Why did such a tradition arise around the figure of Elijah? The most significant circumstance of his life that gave rise to this expectation is that he was translated. Elijah's zeal for the law thrust him into an eschatological role. With this there developed a tradition of the sinlessness of Elijah.[99] he is given the role of the returning forerunner as reward for his zeal and sinlessness. The fact that Elijah is named in Mal. 4.5 as the forerunner is, of course, the scriptural ground of the growth of this tradition. In what capacity does he appear in the Transfiguration? What is his distinction from Moses? What is his complementary function with Moses?[100]

---

96 Marshall, *Luke: Historian and Theologian*, p. 147.

97 Marshall, *Luke: Historian and Theologian*, p. 147.

98 Lampe, 'The Holy Spirit in the Writings of St. Luke', in D.E. Nineham (ed.), *Studies in Luke–Acts* (Oxford: Basil Blackwell, 1955), pp. 176-82.

99 Carruth, 'The Jesus-as-Prophet Motif in Luke–Acts', p. 38.

100 It seems an oversimplification to answer the questions with the statement that Moses and Elijah represent the law and the prophets respectively. Certainly, this kind of symbolism of the two is not developed in any of the Luke–Acts literature. This bifurcation of the Scriptures is not what is intended by the NT phrase 'the law and the prophets'. This phrase is intended to express the solidarity of the OT. It would seem that the translation of Elijah is not critical to this question,

The traditions defined Elijah most commonly as forerunner of the Messiah.[101] The fact common to all the traditions (including Mal. 4.4-6) is the eschatological nature of Elijah's return. He was not a 'writing prophet' and the words which are recorded of him in the historical books are messianic. So, we must judge his appearance here as a fulfillment of his ministry not as a fulfillment of his predictions.[102]

The fulfillment of Elijah's ministry serves two purposes. First, it distinguishes his function from Moses' function. Secondly, it complements Moses' function.

On the first, Moses is the symbol of all the law and the prophets. Divine mandate and divine promise are represented in him. So those portions of the OT that represent the commandments of God – the demand of holiness – are seen in Moses. We may also see in him the promises which involve the prediction of Messiah. We do not see the prediction of Messiah in Elijah. Elijah does have a function here, however. It is precisely that eschatological function that is attributed to him in Mal. 4.4-6 and 3.1 – the one who prepares the way of God by proclaiming the demands of the law.[103] Why should he appear in

---

because it is not common to both Moses and Elijah. The tradition of the translation of Moses has too little acceptance in the tradition to be strongly considered here.

101 Jeremias, 'Ἡλίας'.

102 Conzelmann depicts Elijah's (and Moses') presence here as the symbol of the withdrawal of his ministry (*The Theology of St. Luke*, pp. 12-27); cf. Caird, *The Gospel According to St. Luke*, p. 133: 'What Peter did not realize was that Moses and Elijah belonged, with John the Baptist, to the old order that was passing away …'; Caird, 'The Transfiguration', p. 293: 'Now, however the law of Moses and the spirit of Elijah were both being rendered obsolete by the determination of Jesus to follow the way of the cross and by his redemptive suffering to suffer God's way of dealing with sin'.

The presence of Moses and Elijah for the purpose of symbolizing their removal does not take into account the continued use of the law in the rest of the Luke–Acts record. Not even in the controversy of Gentile freedom is the law replaced by apostolic decree. In Luke the law is not simply an 'epoch'. 'If Luke had championed the idea the law as provisionally valid, an epoch, he would have proved that the Jewish accusations were valid. But that is precisely what he tries to disprove.' Jacob Jervell, *Luke and the People of God: A New Look at Luke–Acts* (Minneapolis: Augsburg Press, 1972), p. 145.

103 Kee, 'The Transfiguration in Mark', p. 146:

> The evidence thus points to the conclusion that Elijah was considered in first-century Judaism as an almost exclusively eschatological figure. There is no hint of his being numbered among the prophets, but his roles in relation to the establishment of God's Rule are manifold and all of them crucial. It is in this

this setting? Because the one who defines the holiness of the kingdom and predicts its redeemer (Moses) and the one who prepares the way of the kingdom (Elijah) are also participants in it.

We must examine briefly the Moses-Elijah-Messiah typology in order to show Elijah's complementary role to Moses. Moses stands as a predecessor of Christ and Elijah a precursor.[104] The introduction of the 'exodus' suggests the complementary role of these two men. Moses was the leader of the first exodus; Elijah led a symbolic exodus and ascended.[105]

There is a Moses-Messiah typology in rabbinic literature that would seem to show the complementary nature of the Moses-Messiah typology and the Elijah-Messiah typology. Though the Moses-Messiah typology is preserved in rabbinic literature it did not arise in that period. 'There are references to show that it goes back to a period prior to the NT ... it finds attestation in the Damascus document, Joseph(us) and the NT'.[106]

The NT stands out from the OT and other Jewish tradition by picturing two eschatological witnesses of the Messiah and his kingdom (the Transfiguration account and Revelation 11). The appearance of Elijah with Moses in the Transfiguration sets the NT apart from the traditions reflected in the older Rabbinic literature.[107] There is, however, the motif of the suffering servant which brings these two together and, in the Transfiguration, brings them to Jesus (especially Luke's account). The concept of suffering is present even in Mark and Matthew who do not mention Jesus' 'exodus'. 'From the

---

history-of-religions background that we must look for light on the meaning of Elijah as one of the companions of Jesus on the mount of Transfiguration.

104 Ziesler, 'The Transfiguration Story and the Markan Soteriology', p. 266. Helmut Gollwitzer, *La Joie de Dieu* (Neuchatel and Paris: Editions Delachauxet Nestlé S.A., 1966), p. 101: 'La personne de Moïse etait considérée comme le parfait modele du Messie ... Elie, de son coté, se presente comme precurseur des derniers temps'.

105 Lampe, 'The Holy Spirit in the writings of St. Luke', pp. 176-77; Evans, 'The Central Section of Luke's Gospel', pp. 37-53: Based on Lk. 9.51, 52 the key word for Luke is ἀναλήμψεως which is governed by συμπληροῦσθαι and ἔξοδον is governed by πληροῦν in 9.31. Evans develops the travel narrative according to the pattern of the exodus of Moses and uses as his pattern the Testament of Moses. Though this author uses the Moses typology, he does show the cogency of the exodus and ascension pattern. It seems also that Ziesler has shown the relation between Moses and Elijah in this connection.

106 Jeremias, 'Μωυσῆς'.

107 Jeremias, ''Ηλίας'.

standpoint of biblical theology, the establishment of the date of the apocalyptic tradition of the martyrdom of the returning Elijah is of great importance. For it enables us to see that Mk 9.12f. is right when it assumes that the idea of a suffering forerunner is not strange to the contemporaries of Jesus.'[108] That there is a suffering-servant motif associated with Moses seems evident in Acts 7.17-44.[109]

Luke's description of the appearance of Moses and Elijah and their conversation with Jesus is more explicit than Mark's account. The first detail that Luke gives is that Moses and Elijah appeared 'in glory' with Jesus. This glory symbolizes the same for all. It is chiefly representative of the nature of the kingdom of God yet to come. This manifestation of the kingdom is to have as its chief characteristic the presence of the glory of God. By this glory Moses and Elijah are identified as participants in this kingdom glory with Jesus, exactly as they are later enveloped in the cloud (v. 34).[110]

That this is the symbolism intended by representing Moses and Elijah as appearing in glory is shown by the use of this word in Scripture. Everything in heaven is represented by the radiance associated with glory. Those who appear before God appear in glory. It is applied to believers in the life to come (1 Cor. 15.43; Col. 3.4); it is applied to the glorious body of Jesus at the Parousia (Phil. 3.21). 'The state of being in the next life is thus described as participation in the radiance or glory…'[111]

Moses and Elijah together occupy the role of heavenly messengers in the Transfiguration. This is even implied in Mark when the content of the conversation is not reported.[112] Luke does report the content of the conversation. Moses and Elijah were talking with Jesus concerning τὴν ἔξοδον αὐτοῦ ἣν ἤμελλεν πληροῦν Ἰερουσαλήμ.

---

108 Jeremias, 'Ἠλίας'.

109 Jeremias, 'Μωυσῆς'.

110 Johnson, 'The Transfiguration of Christ', pp. 141-42: Johnson probably makes too much of the contrast between Moses' death and Elijah's translation, but his assessment of these participants in the kingdom seems to be correct:

> An illustration of the inhabitants of the kingdom to come. On the Mount were Jesus, who is the Messiah; Peter, James and John, the representatives of the theocratic nation. With him were Moses, a saint who died, and Elijah, a saint who was raptured without dying, the two together representing the two types of believers in the church of Jesus Christ (cf. 1 Thess. 4.13-18).

111 BAG, pp. 202, 203; Kittel and von Rad, 'Δόξα'.

112 Walter Grundmann, *Das Evangelium nach Lukas* (Berlin: Evangelische Verlagsanstalt, 1934), p. 192.

In this clause there are three particular elements of interpretation: (1) ἔξοδον, (2) ἣν ἤμελλεν πληροῦν, and (3) Ἰερουσαλήμ.

The word ἔξοδος has broad application: the dissolution of a marriage, banishment, marching out, coming to an end, and rarely of death.[113]

The definitions and imagery of this word suggest the application which it has here in Luke. The basic meaning is departure, but it is related also to deliverance. It suggests here, then, all of the redemptive events recorded by Luke in the closing of his gospel and in the beginning of Acts: namely Jesus' death, resurrection, and ascension. These three components represent salvation in Luke–Acts. The symbolism is threefold: suffering, glory, and redemption. For Luke, salvation does not rest in the cross alone, but the cross as it is unified with glory, issuing in redemption.[114]

The second element of particular interest in this verse is the clause ἣν ἤμελλεν πληροῦν. The clause is expressive of necessity, particularly of divine appointment. Πληροῦν, in particular, enforces this connotation. It carries the sense of fulfilling a norm, a promise, a demand; and in the NT, when it is so used, it is always used of the divine will and never of the human will. It also carries an eschatological meaning.[115]

From this point on in Luke the necessity of fulfillment becomes a theme for Luke. It dominates the 'travel narrative', the passion section of Luke, the resurrection appearance of Jesus, and the ascension passages in Luke and Acts. All of these passages are thematically unified around necessity, fulfillment, suffering, and ascension.

The third emphasis of this verse is the city of Jerusalem. This city is to be the site of all that is embraced in the word ἔξοδος, and it is so designated by divine will. It is, by divine appointment, the place of suffering and exaltation.

Jerusalem is also the place where all redemptive activity takes place: the crucifixion, resurrection, ascension, and Pentecost.[116]

There is a specific tension in the introduction of 'exodus' in the scene of glory. The 'exodus', though carrying a connotation of

---

113 W. Michaelis, ''Εξόδος', *TDNT*.

114 Reumann (ed.), *Understanding the Sacred Text*, p. 368.

115 Gerhard Delling, 'Πληρόω', *TDNT*; Reiling and Swellengrebel, *A Translator's Handbook on the Gospel of Luke*, p. 381; BAG, p. 677.

116 Pilgrim, 'The Death of Christ in Lukan Soteriology', p. 122.

deliverance, is a word of suffering, even death. Yet this message is spoken by messengers who appear in glory to Jesus who has just been translated into glory. Luke's account, then, brings the suffering of Jesus into a relationship of necessity to his glory. At the same time the glory is not lessened by the suffering. Thus, suffering and glory are in Luke harmonious.

This culmination of suffering, glory and deliverance in Jerusalem is the reason that the Transfiguration stands at the head of and is the actual beginning of the trek toward Jerusalem.[117] We have earlier seen how Luke shows Jerusalem as a common goal in several of his pericopes.

In summary, Moses and Elijah appear in this scene as eschatological figures. Moses represents the fulfillment of all of Scripture in this presentation of the kingdom of God and in testimony of its King. He also represents here the culmination and fulfillment of the Moses-Messiah typology. Elijah is here as the precursor of the kingdom. There are thus two eschatological witnesses to the kingdom.

These two are represented as being seen in glory with Jesus. In this symbol they are participants with him in the heavenly glory and kingdom.

The message of Moses and Elijah is the 'exodus' which Jesus must fulfill in Jerusalem. The word 'exodus' includes (by Luke's later redaction) all the redemptive activity that would take place in Jerusalem in Jesus' last days. By joining exodus and glory in a common scene, Luke harmonizes the glory of the kingdom of God with the suffering of Jesus.

Peter's proposal (vv. 32, 33).

Luke alone gives information that implies that the Transfiguration was a night experience (vv. 32, 37). The sleepiness of the three disciples is described as extreme: βεβαρημένοι ὕπνῳ. The next clause stands in contrast to this condition: διαγρηγορήσαντες δὲ εἶδον.[118]

---

[117] Conzelmann, *The Theology of St. Luke*, p. 59; Pilgrim, 'The Death of Christ in Lukan Soteriology', p. 184; Ramsey, *The Glory of God and the Transfiguration*, p. 39.

[118] John Reumann, *Jesus in the Church's Gospels* (Philadelphia: Fortress, 1968), p. 129: 'Luke adds that the disciples, who had been drowsy, now saw the glory of the scene and Jesus' special glory (9.32).' Contra: Reiling and Swellengrebel, *A Translator's Handbook on the Gospel of Luke*, pp. 381-82; B. Weiss, *A Commentary on the New Testament* (trans. G.H. Schodde and E. Wilson; New York: Funk & Wagnalls, 1906), p. 78: 'Luke explains by stating that the disciples, while Jesus was praying had been

It seems that the preferred translation in this light is 'And Peter and the men who were with him were burdened down with sleep; but when they had remained awake, they saw his glory...'. Though this is not critical to our interpretation, this descriptive detail shows that these three disciples were dissociated from both the prayer of Jesus and the Transfiguration of Jesus until the point of their seeing his glory and the glory of Moses and Elijah. This circumstance suggests a parallel between Gethsemane and the Transfiguration.[119] The suggestion of a 'typology' between the two scenes is probably exaggerated but there is basic comparison. 'Tout d'abord la scene n'est pas sans analogie avec celle ju jardin des Óliviers.'[120]

By the designation 'His glory' Luke implies that the glory in which Jesus was seen originated in his person. This is the first distinction that Luke has specifically made between Jesus and Moses and Elijah (except by the predominance of attention and description). The distinction which now appears prepares for the declaration of sonship to follow. The phrase 'his glory' appears three times in reference to Christ (9.26; 9.32; 24.26) 'and significantly shows that the evangelist thinks of the divine glory in the mission of Christ as being "the glory of Christ"'.[121] With this statement Luke's reference to Jesus' presence

---

overpowered by sleep, and now suddenly awakening, see the brilliant vision.' Browning, *The Gospel According to St. Luke*, p. 102: 'The Disciples slept then were awakened'.

119 Caird, 'The Transfiguration', p. 291; Conzelmann, *The Theology of St. Luke*, p. 59: he suggests a typological connection; 'We find all together the suffering, the sleeping of the disciples and the fact that on "awakening" they see his glory. The Mount of Transfiguration foreshadows the Mount of Olives, in both its aspects, for it is the place of prayer and arrest as well as the scene of the Ascension.' Helmut Flender, *St. Luke, Theologian of Redemptive History* (trans. R.H. and I. Fuller; Philadelphia: Fortress, 1967), p. 74: 'The transfiguration story points ahead to the coming events in Jerusalem. The allusion to Jesus' agony on the Mount of Olives is obvious.'

120 A. Feuillet, 'Les perspectives proposés á chaque évangéliste', *Biblica* 39 (1958), p. 290. Both scenes depict Jesus as praying; his disciples are asleep or almost asleep. Both scenes are oriented toward the events about to take place in Jerusalem.

121 Ramsey, *The Glory of God and the Transfiguration*, pp. 39, 40; contra, Kee, 'The Transfiguration in Mark', p. 144: '... the radiance (of Jesus) is connected with "borrowed glory" ... just as Moses shone when he stood in the presence of God'. This fails to take into account Luke's desire to show a distinction between Jesus and Moses and Elijah. It also fails to take into account the order of the two parallel events. Moses' face shined in 'borrowed glory' because his glorious appearance followed his entering the cloud. Jesus appeared in glory before the cloud appeared. Kee also fails to take seriously the word μεταμορφόω in Mark, which is the basis of his article.

begins to take on the formal characteristics of references to divine presence: i.e. that his presence is recognized by his glory. This, in itself, distinguishes Jesus from the two who were seen standing with him.[122] This attachment of glory to the person of Jesus also interprets his work as saviour; with this element, Luke also introduces an interpretation of the 'exodus'. As the 'exodus' carries with it the concept of deliverance, Jesus' 'glory' carries with it the concept of deliverer: 'the New Testament like the LXX, does not use δόξα merely to convey the idea of brightness of God's presence but as a kind of token word for a larger whole of which the major element is that of the salvation of men'.[123]

Luke with this designation seems to establish another tie-in with 9.27. In 9.26 there is a description of the Son of man coming 'in his glory'; 9.27 predicts the coming of the kingdom of God. The Transfiguration scene portrays Jesus in glory and in 9.32 speaks of this glory as 'his glory'. The intention of Luke seems to be to show that the glory of the Son of man is identifiable with the kingdom of God and 'that the Transfiguration is a proleptic manifestation of the glory of the Son of Man ... For him (Luke) the Transfiguration is a manifestation of the glory of Jesus (the Son of Man)'.[124] These are also the essential elements of the kingdom of God. This verse thus by identifying Jesus' glory with his presence also identifies Jesus' glory with the presence of his kingdom: 'When the three saw Jesus' glory they saw the kingdom of God'.[125]

It is difficult on the basis of Luke's explanation of Peter's remark to determine if Luke is kinder to Peter than Mark is. Commentators

---

122 Browning, *The Gospel According to St. Luke*, pp. 101-102: 'At the transfiguration the glory is no mere reflection, but Messiah's own glory, such as will be forever his after the ascension ...'

123 L.H. Brockington, 'The Septuagintal Background to the New Testament Use of Δόξα', in D.E. Nineham (ed.), *Studies in Luke–Acts* (Oxford: Basil Blackwell, 1955), p. 4; Marshall, *Luke: Historian and Theologian*, p. 169: 'Thus salvation is closely bound up with the person of Jesus ... Consequently, the exaltation of Jesus is the supreme saving event in Luke's eyes ...'

124 Farrell, 'The Eschatological Perspective of Luke–Acts', p. 42.

125 Farrell, 'The Eschatological Perspective of Luke–Acts', p. 43; Evans, 'The Transfiguration of Jesus', p. 103: 'Here was his Kingdom-glory. The Son of Man had entered into the state in which he was to reign, in the presence of Peter, James and John. They beheld the Son of Man coming into his Kingdom (Matt. xvi. 28); they saw the kingdom of God come with power (Mark ix. 1); they saw the kingdom itself (Luke ix. 27).'

differ here,[126] but it is not difficult to see the prominence that Luke gives Peter in Luke–Acts.[127]

The proposal of Peter begins with 'Ἐπιστάτα which is peculiar to Luke, who does not use the title 'Ραββί. Instead, he uses this title where Mark and Matthew use 'Ραββί, διδάσκαλε κύριε. It is equivalent of the Aramaic רבי.

Peter asserts as his reason for the proposal: 'It is good for us to be here'. The proposal suggests that it is good that we are here and that we remain here. Very clearly this observation ignores the conversation of Jesus with Moses and Elijah; and in ignoring it, it also sets aside the goals of that conversation: the 'exodus' and Jerusalem. It is thus another example of the disciples' attempt to avoid Jesus' message of his passion.[128] This observation and proposal have the additional burden of opposing what the language of the conversation in Luke had indicated as the will of God.[129]

The most obvious error in Peter's proposal to build the tabernacles (σκηνὰς) is the delay.[130] Jesus and his two heavenly visitors will be detained in the mountain in order to occupy the tents. The disciples will be detained in order to build the tents.[131]

---

126 The language of this verse does not convey whether Luke seeks to be more severe than Mark. The conclusion which one makes will not seriously affect his interpretation of the Transfiguration. Among those who see a conciliatory handling of Peter are the following: Boobyer, *St. Mark and the Transfiguration Story*, p. 78; Martin, 'The Transfiguration', p. 189. Among those who see a severe treatment of Peter by Luke are the following: Rollins and Rollins, *Jesus and his Ministry*, pp. 193-94; Johnson, 'The Transfiguration of Christ', p. 138; Harrison, 'The Transfiguration" p. 321.

127 Talbert, *Luke and the Gnostics*, pp. 85-88. Peter often appears as spokesman for the apostles in the gospel. In Acts he is the leader prior to Pentecost (Acts 1), the preacher on the Day of Pentecost (Acts 2), and is the most prominent leader in Jerusalem in the first eleven chapters of Acts. So, if Luke is harsh with Peter here, it is not characteristic of Luke.

128 Kee, 'The Transfiguration in Mark', pp. 147-48.

129 Johnson, 'The Transfiguration of Christ', p. 138: 'But his (Peter's) words are not only senseless, they are positively sinful. In effect, they would turn him from his destined earthly goal, the cross.'

130 Harrison, 'The Transfiguration', p. 321. The suggestion that Peter's proposal was offensive because it placed Jesus on the same level with Moses and Elijah seems not to fit with Luke's development of the story. He has already shown that with Jesus 'His glory' is not a 'borrowed glory'. The context of the pericope has prepared the disciples to see in Jesus the glory of the Son of man, which supersedes the glory of Moses and Elijah.

131 Groves, 'The Significance of the Transfiguration of Our Lord', p. 91.

In order to examine this proposal further, it is necessary first to examine the word σκηνὰς.[132]

Whether the Transfiguration was understood to have occurred at the season of the feast of tabernacles is of no consequence in the interpretation. If Peter's proposal is a proposal to institute an eschatological form of the feast of tabernacles, he is put in the position not only of being unware of what he said, but of being unaware of the ritual of the feast.[133]

It is possible that the concept of dwelling in 'tents' had become a part of eschatological tradition by the time of this writing. In this case, it could have had its origin in the Sinai-feast of tabernacles tradition, and by time developed in ways that were independent of the origin of the tradition. This, apparently, is the case. 'One possibility is that dwelling in σκηναί as in the wilderness, is an attribute of the eschatological consummation'.[134] It is difficult to find preparation for

---

132 W. Michaelis, 'Σκηνή', *TDNT*. The etymology of the word indicates primarily a temporary field or desert dwelling, as the tent of a nomad or soldier. It is this meaning that serves as the basis for its other applications. Its predominant application in Scripture relates either to the dwelling place of God (or a god) or a meeting place with God (or a god). In the Hebrew heritage it is used to commemorate meeting with God in the feast of tabernacles.

This connection has led quite a number of students of Scripture to conclude that the Transfiguration took place at the time of the feast of tabernacles, and that this was the provocation of Peter's suggestion (Ellis, *The Gospel of Luke*, pp. 142-43; Ramsay, 'The Time of the Transfiguration', pp. 557-62; Walter Roehrs, 'God's Tabernacles Among Men: A Study of the Transfiguration', *Concordia Theological Monthly* 35 (1965), pp. 256-80). Most commentators recognize a feast of tabernacles' symbolism here even if they do not attach a historical or literal connection. It must be observed, however, that whatever Peter proposed is rejected by Luke as being an incorrect response to the Transfiguration. It is not simply an error of timing as Boobyer indicates. Basing his study primarily on Mark, he avoids the difficulty of Peter's suggestion by raising the question of Peter's timing: 'If the evangelist (Mark) thinks of this scene as a prediction of the second coming of Jesus, then Peter's words are out of place, because their offer is made too soon' (Roehrs, 'God's Tabernacles Among Men', p. 78). Peter's response is entirely wrong; therefore, whatever interpretation we place on it is an interpretation of what Peter is represented as thinking and not an interpretation of what Luke intended as the meaning of the Transfiguration.

133 In the feast it was the congregation that dwelt in the tents and they dwelt in them only temporarily. True, Yahweh was understood to dwell in the tabernacle which housed the altars and mercy seat; but here Peter proposes only to build tents for the three seen in glory. Boobyer attempts to meet this problem by citing Rev. 7.15-17 'which associates the Lamb with God in this eschatological tabernacling of the people of God' (Boobyer, St. *Mark and the Transfiguration Story*, p. 78).

134 Michaelis, 'Σκηνή'.

eschatological interpretation of σκηνή in the OT. There are NT texts that seem to bear this out and also indicate that the symbolism of σκηνή had taken on the sense of permanent dwelling.[135] Luke 16.9 is of particular interest because of its combination of words: εἰς τὰς αἰωνίους σκηνάς. Here the concept of eternity and the age to come seem to be carried by this symbolism.[136] Revelation 7.15-17 does give evidence of an eschatological dwelling of God among the redeemed. The New Jerusalem is called ἡ σκηνὴ τοῦ θεοῦ and God σκηνώσει μετὰ αὐτῶν (men) (Rev. 21.1-4). There is also a σκηνή symbolism in the incarnation theology of John, reflected especially in Jn 1.14 which may reflect a reference to the Transfiguration.[137]

Even though Luke rejects as a complete misunderstanding Peter's suggestion, it does offer us valuable information. It reflects the similarities between Sinai and the Transfiguration. It reveals a milieu in which the tabernacle had become an eschatological symbol – a symbol of the age to come, of God's tabernacling among the redeemed, and of the permanence of these tabernacles.

Riesenfeld is correct to see the eschatological motif in the reference to the tabernacles. His attempt to turn this into evidence for a cultic enthronement festival *Sitz im Leben* lacks evidence.[138]

Peter's proposal that they build a tabernacle for each of the persons seen in glory still reveals his confusion over the meaning of the experience; hence, Luke's evaluation that he did not know what he was saying. What he is saying is correctly assessed by Ramsey: 'Here and now let the tabernacling begin, with Messiah and Moses and Elijah dwelling in glory'.[139]

Summary: By physical description and by spiritual issues Luke establishes basic analogies between the Transfiguration and Gethsemane: the night scene, the prayer, the sleepiness of the disciples and the relationship to Jerusalem.

---

135 Michaelis, 'Σκηνή': 'One should rather remember that already the LXX σκηνή being used for משכן ... had taken on something of the continuous and lasting'.

136 Geldenhuys, *Commentary on the Gospel of St. Luke*, p. 416; Michaelis, 'Σκηνή': 'Luke 16.9 speaks of eschatological σκηναί in the plural ...'

137 Roehrs, 'God's Tabernacles Among Men', p. 22; Brown, *The Gospel According to St. John I-XII*, p. 33.

138 Harald Riesenfeld, *Jésus Transfiguré* (Copenhagen: Ejwar Munksgaard, 1947), pp. 258-61, 264-80; there does seem to be some evidence for this in Hebrews 1; contra: Ziesler, 'The Transfiguration Story and the Markan Soteriology', p. 264.

139 Ramsey, *The Glory of God and the Transfiguration*, p. 115.

As the scene progresses Luke begins to show the distinction between the glory of Jesus and the glory seen on Moses and Elijah. The glory of Jesus is presented in the pattern of divine glory, which Luke ties to the presence of the kingdom of God.

Peter's proposal is confused, but it does shed some light on the concept of σκηνὴ. It had taken on eschatological significance and this had given some eschatological meaning to the feast of tabernacles. Thus, the tabernacles reflect both a Sinai tradition and an eschatological interpretation of that significance.

The voice of witness (vv. 34, 35).[140]

The first prominent feature of this verse is the cloud: νεφέλη. Its appearance, in effect, closed off and answered Peter's proposal. It did so because of the significance of the cloud itself and because of the voice of witness that came from the cloud.

The symbolism of the cloud has become fixed in the Old and NTs and related literature. It is established first by the special cloud that is a representation of the presence of Yahweh to lead Israel (Exodus 13.21).[141]

---

140 A brief look at the grammar and wording of v. 34 will be helpful in order to prepare for the applications that follow. The opening of this verse shows the real answer to Peter's proposal: 'While Peter was still saying these things, a cloud came …' The next grammatical emphasis of the verse is that the cloud descended on Jesus and the three disciples and enveloped them all within it; 'and they were afraid as they entered into the cloud' (Reiling and Swellengrebel, *A Translator's Handbook on the Gospel of Luke*, p. 384). The effect of this translation is to show that the three observers of the Transfiguration are now enveloped into its glory not by personal transformation, but by inclusion in the cloud (Babcock, 'The Transfiguration', p. 325; Lindsay, *The Gospel According to St. Luke*, p. 141; Rollins and Rollins, *Jesus and his Ministry*, p. 196); contra: Creed, *The Gospel According to St. Luke*, p. 135; he cites with disapproval Nordern (*Die Geburt des Kindes*, pp. 96-97), who supposes that perhaps only upon Jesus did the cloud descend; Reiling and Swellengrebel seem to take issue with their own suggested translation above (*A Translator's Handbook on the Gospel of Luke*, p. 384).

141 The presence of Yahweh continues to be so represented in the experience of Israel as recorded in the OT. It is represented at Sinai (Exod. 19.16); it settled on the completed tabernacle and remained there, throughout the wilderness wanderings (Exod. 40.34-38). This same symbolism appears in the dedication of Solomon's temple (1 Kgs 8.10; 2 Chron. 5.13). The cloud appears in prophetic vision experiences of the prophets and represents the divine presence. In Isa. 6.4 it appears under the symbolism of smoke (Hebrew ענן). Ezekiel 1.4-2, 8 and 10.1-22 both describe the presence of God under the symbolism of the cloud (Riesenfeld, *Jésus Transfiguré*, pp. pp. 130-31; Boobyer, *St. Mark and the Transfiguration Story*, pp. 78, 79). 'The cloud is a common Old Testament symbol for the presence of God …' (Reumann [ed.], *Understanding the Sacred Text*, p. 129).

The designation for this cloud is the 'shekinah', which was developed in the Targums 'as 'buffer' to enable the divine intervention to be described without the language of direct description'.[142] Its special function is to describe God as present in order to lead and protect his people and to provide communion with them (Exod. 25.8; Lev. 26.12; Isa. 57.17).[143] It is a 'frequent symbol for the presence of the activity of God (Lev. 16.2; 2 Chron. 5.13, 14, etc.)'.[144] More specifically the Shekinah is the representation of the Person of God, combining both the concepts of the word of God and of the glory of God.[145]

The Shekinah took on a specific eschatological character, and also continued to represent the presence of God. It combined the two meanings in order to express the idea of God's dwelling among his people in the last day.

The eschatological meaning of the Shekinah, represented in the Greek word νεφέλη, is virtually its exclusive use in the NT.[146] It has become a special Parousia symbol.[147]

---

142 Reumann (ed.), *Understanding the Sacred Text*, p. 18; Brown, *The Gospel According to St. John I-XII*, p. 33: 'In rabbinic theology *shekinah* was a technical term for God's presence dwelling among the people'.

143 Ramsay, 'The Time of the Transfiguration', p. 19.

144 Browning, *The Gospel According to St. Luke*, p. 102.

145 'Of the three periphrases employed by the Rabbis to avoid pronouncing the name of Yahweh, three were preeminent – the 'Word', the 'Glory', and the 'Presence' ('Shekinah'). Of these the 'Word' was used by the Targums for the invisible presence, as the 'Glory' for the visible presence of God. Both, however, were superseded in popularity by the term 'Shekinah', and it is in connexion with 'Shekinah' that the vision is most commonly mentioned. But 'Shekinah' stood for both the visible and the invisible presence' (Kenneth E. Kirk, *The Vision of God* (New York: Harper and Row, 1966), pp. 21, 22).

146 In only three places in the NT is the word νεφελή used in a sense other than eschatological. Luke 12.54, Jude 12 (both of which are eschatological passages, though νεφέλη is not used as an eschatological symbol) and 1 Cor. 10.1f (where Paul uses it of the cloud in the wilderness [Exod. 13.21]).

147 The Son of man comes on the clouds of heaven with power and great glory (Mt. 24.30; Mk 13.26; Lk. 21.27); the Son of man is seated at 'the right hand of power and coming on the clouds of heaven' (Mt. 26.64; Mk 14.62); the cloud that separated Jesus from the disciples at the ascension became a symbol of the return (Acts 1.9); the returning Jesus is announced as coming on the cloud (Rev. 1.7); the Son of man is seated on a white cloud (Rev. 14.14); the translated and resurrected saints will be caught away in the clouds (1 Thess. 4.17), and in Rev. 11.12 the two witnesses are taken into heaven in a cloud. The angel of judgement descends wrapped in a cloud (Rev. 10.1).

I have not mentioned here Mt. 17.5; Mk 9.7 and Lk. 9.34, 35; I will deal with them in the body of the material.

The cloud in this passage (and its parallels, Mk 7.9 and Mt. 17.5) is the Shekinah and as such is an eschatological symbol.

The Shekinah symbolism recalls the Sinai motif that is evident in the language of this verse; the cloud came and it 'tabernacled' over and about them, and its pattern is Sinai.[148] The concept 'tabernacling' or dwelling is already in evidence at Sinai, but it is further developed by the recurrence of the cloud over the tabernacle in the wilderness and the temple of Solomon in Jerusalem. It is a symbol of Yahweh's presence among his people.[149]

The disciples correctly understood this cloud to be the descent of the presence of God among them.[150] This recognition is the reason for the fear of the disciples as they entered the cloud. This is the usual reaction of people in Scripture who come into the divine presence.[151]

This event is more intimate than the OT manifestations on which it is patterned. The three disciples, who until this time have been observers only, are enveloped in the cloud and thus drawn into the event as participants.[152] On the face of the matter, those on whom the Shekinah descends and to whom it appears are God's people and kingdom (Exodus 19.3-9).

The cloud symbol here, though eschatological, is not an instrument of the coming of Jesus (Parousia), but of the witness to him. In this function, it is still in the Sinai tradition, and it is an eschatological witness. It is the witness that is appropriate to Jesus'

---

148 Hans-Peter Müller, 'Die Verklärung Jesus, Eine motivgeschichtliche Studie', *ZNW* 51 (1960), p. 56, 'To the appearance belongs the motif of the ascent on the mountain'.

149 Lampe, 'The Holy Spirit in the writings of St. Luke', p. 167; Albrecht Oepke, 'Νεφέλη', *TDNT*: 'In the OT the dark cloud is a sign of the intrinsically inaccessible God who graciously offers himself in fellowship'.

150 Babcock, 'The Transfiguration', p. 325:

> They enter into the cloud, or the glory (2 Peter 1.17). It is the cloud into which Moses entered (Exod. 24.18; cp. 24.9); it is the cloud of smoke of Isaiah's vision (6.4) when he saw the glory of Christ (12.41); it is the cloud of which Joel prophesied (2.30; cp. Acts 2.19;); it is possibly referred to by St. John 'we beheld his glory … John beareth witness to him… the law as given by Moses'. (Jn 1:14, 15, 17) …'

151 Ellis, *The Gospel of Luke*, p. 143: 'The overshadowing 'cloud' of God's Shekinah confirms Peter's apprehension of the divine presence'.

152 This is a grammatically defensible conclusion. The infinitive εἰσελθεῖν interprets ἐπεσκίαζεν. They (αὐτούς – subject of the infinitive) entered into the cloud which was overshadowing them.

appearance in the last day and after he has entered into his glory: namely, the declaration that he is God's 'elected Son'.

We have seen the divergencies of Luke from Mark. The significant difference here is Luke's ἐκλελεγμένος instead of Mark's ἀγαπητός. We need to attempt to discover the background of this witness by comparisons with similar pronouncements in Scripture.

The most obvious comparisons to be made (other than the synoptic parallels) are: (1) the baptismal witness (Lk. 3.22; Mk 1.11; Mt. 3.17), (2) Ps.2.7 and (3) Isa. 42.1.[153]

The similarities between the baptismal scene and the Transfiguration are clear. For Luke, both mark the beginning of specific stages in Jesus' ministry.[154] The witness in each case is a voice from heaven – the symbolism for the voice of God. Luke, in each case, mentions the prayer. The most important parallel for our concern is the word of witness itself. In Luke and in Mark the baptismal witness is in the third person: σὺ εἶ. The designation at the baptism in each case ὁ υἱός μου ὁ ἀγαπητός (Luke, Mark, and Matthew), Mark and Matthew have this formula in the Transfiguration witness. Luke differs in the Transfiguration by his designation ὁ εκλελεγμένος. It would appear that both these forms of witness have a common origin: Isa. 42.1. The differences in wording do not bar that conclusion. The heart of the matter is that the witness in each case presupposes 'a relationship to God that evidently obtains prior to and independently of the Lord's mission in the world ...'[155] The belovedness and/or election of the Son did not rest on what the Son had done, but what he was: namely, the 'elected of God'.

Of the OT passages that are cited in this connection, the most frequently mentioned are Ps. 2.7 and Isa. 42.1. Genesis 22.2 is sometimes suggested. Deuteronomy 18.15 is, of course, mentioned in the command, 'Hear him...'

Bretscher has analyzed Ps. 2.7 in this light and has pointed out the lack of similarity between the psalm and this passage. There is clear agreement only in the words 'my son'. The psalm does not refer to

---

153 I will not deal with 2 Pet. 1.17, 18 because it reflects an interpretation of the Transfiguration and not an influence on the formation of the tradition of the Transfiguration.

154 Conzelmann, *The Theology of St. Luke*, p. 180.

155 Stonehouse, *The Witness of St. Luke to Christ*, p. 166.

the Son as 'beloved'. It does not mention Yahweh's pleasure in him, nor is the son designated as 'begotten'.[156]

Isaiah 42.1 is connected with this witness as a messianic 'servant of Yahweh' passage. Bretscher denies that this word of witness is derived from Isa. 42.1.[157] he fails to take into account the distinctive features of Luke's redaction.

Luke's divergence from Mark offers several alternatives: (1) he went his own way with his own interpretative presuppositions, or (2) he used a source that was totally independent of Mark, or (3) he adopted a reading that is compatible with two streams of tradition, one of which is reflected in Mark and the other in Luke.[158] If the last of these alternatives can be shown to have strong support, inquiry concerning the first two is unnecessary on this passage.

Jeremias has presented a very convincing argument in support of the conclusion that Luke's wording represents one of two streams of tradition both originating with Isa. 42.1.[159] This verse brings together

---

156 Bretscher, 'Exodus 4.22-23', p. 302: It should be observed that Luke does cite this passage, but in connection with the declaration of Jesus' sonship at the resurrection (Acts 13.33). Paul makes the same application of the resurrection in Rom. 1.4. It would appear that the NT writers apply Ps. 2.7 in a way different from the declaration of the voice from heaven.

157 Bretscher, 'Exodus 4.22-23', pp. 303-304: he bases this conclusion largely on the incongruities between Mark's record and the Septuagint translation of Isa. 42.1 and on his, conclusion that Mt. 12.18 represents 'a later theological development' (p. 304). Bretscher misses the point of studying Luke's account as an individual author's account which, though dependent on Mark, must be judged under its own redactional and tradition criteria. One cannot solve Luke's redactional question by concluding the inquiry with Mark.

158 On 1 and 2 above: Certainly, unique Lukan presuppositions and interpretations may be shown; however, it is hardly acceptable to conclude that Luke wrote independently if it can be reasonably shown that his record has a common origin with Mark.

159 J. Jeremias, 'παῖς θεοῦ', *TDNT*: a summary of Jeremias' study and conclusions will be helpful.

In Isaiah the suffering servant is עבד יהוה, which is understood corporately of Israel; but its predominant application is to an individual either of the royal messianic line or the prophetic line. In Isa. 49.7; 50.4-9 and 52.13-53.12 the suffering servant is comforted in his sufferings and recognizes that they are ordained of God.

In the later books of the OT the concepts of 'servant' and 'child' tend to come together. Isaiah and Daniel follow a course that allows עבד to be rendered by παῖς. The translation of עבד with παῖς has a parallel in Wisdom. There is also a suffering servant of Yahweh who has become the child of God. Jeremias concludes 'that in verses where παῖς θεοῦ means 'servant of God' the OT use of עבד יהוה lives on with its various ramifications' (V, p. 679).

several themes of the suffering servant and in combination with Lk. 9.35b applies them to Jesus as the suffering servant.

Hellenistic Judaism and Palestinian Judaism treated Isa. 42.1-4 differently. In Hellenistic Judaism, the passage was taken to refer to Israel. Palestinian Judaism 'takes it to be wholly Messianic'.[160]

The similarities between Isa. 42.1 and Lk. 9.35b are impressive. The concept עבד יהוה is expressed by עבדי this, in turn, is translated in the Septuagint as παῖς μου (παῖς θεοῦ). So these two phrases are equivalents.

The παῖς μου of Isa. 42.1 is also a chosen one בחירי. In Lk. 9.35 Jesus declared to be ὁ υἱός μου ὁ ἐκλελεγμένος.[161]

The reasoning of Jeremias cited in note 148 seems to be supported by the text before us. The OT reference which Luke has in mind here may have reflected the influence of a Hebrew text preserved in Palestinian Judaism in its worship formulae. These worship formulae may have been taken over in Palestinian Christianity.

The term 'servant of God' is a messianic term; in evidence Jeremias cites both canonical and non-canonical Jewish sources. In the Septuagint the translation of עבד with παῖς in Isaiah is clear. There is a tendency to treat Isa. 42.1-4 and 53 as applying to Israel. Corporately, Palestinian Judaism treats them as applying to an individual messianic figure. This is seen in the interpretation of Isa. 49.6 in Sirach 48.10 and in Ethiopic Enoch 37.71. The traits of the Messiah are drawn from Isaiah and he is designated as the 'Elect'.

Jeremias claims that Lk. 23.35 reflects a tradition from late Judaism. The words of mockery (ὁ χριστὸς τοῦ θεοῦ, ὁ ἐκλεκτός) reflect a Jewish interpretation of Isa. 42.1 which understands the Messiah as 'the elect one' (V, p. 689).

This position is somewhat hindered by the infrequent use of παῖς θεοῦ of Jesus in the NT. However, Mt. 12.18-21 lifts the Septuagint translation of Isa. 42.1-4 exactly and applies it to Jesus. This application is strengthened by the occurrence of this expression in Acts: 'In the 4 ref. from Ac ... the par. use of παῖς σου in 4.24-30 for David (v. 25) and for Jesus (27-30) shows that Luke is using archaic expressions which he had borrowed from the language of liturgical prayer' (V: p. 701). Jeremias also cites Lk. 9.35 as evidence of this tradition. He also cites what appears to be the oldest reading of Jn 1.34 (οὗτός ἐστιν ὁ ἐκλεκτὸς τοῦ θεοῦ) as a messianic title, drawn from Isa. 42.1.

The evidence which Jeremias presents leads him to the conclusion that the designation עבד יהוה as παῖς θεοῦ is a pre-synoptic tradition and is a formula drawn from the Hebrew text. This influence is more significant than the Septuagint, even though Luke depends heavily on the Septuagint. The passages cited by Jeremias show that the 'christological interpretation of the servant of the Lord of Dt. Is. belongs to the most primitive age of the Christian community, and very soon came to be a fixed form' (V, p. 709).

[160] Jeremias, 'παῖς θεοῦ', p. 684.

[161] Jeremias, 'παῖς θεοῦ', pp. 701, 702.

This conclusion is further supported by the recurrence of the suffering servant themes of Isaiah in Luke's account of the Transfiguration: namely, the suffering, the divine ordination of the suffering and the implication of exaltation in the word ἔξοδος.

The use of the word ἐκλελεγμένος appears to bring together the themes of election and sonship בהירי עבד. Here Jesus' sonship corresponds to the election of עבד יהוה (παῖς θεοῦ) and the reading in Luke represents an alternate reading of Isa. 42.1.[162]

Other suggestions for the scriptural origin of the word of witness here are Gen. 22.2 (the Septuagint) and Exod. 4.22.

The Genesis passage reports the command of God to Abraham: 'Take your son, your only son Isaac, whom you love and go to the land of Moriah'. This interpretation depends too heavily on a typological application of the Genesis story.[163] It should be further observed that the particular typology that sees in Isaac's proposed sacrifice a type of Jesus' sacrificial death could have arisen only in the Christian community. Hence, no Jewish background for its use can be offered.

The suggestion that Exod. 4.22 is the scriptural basis of Lk. 9.35 chiefly depends on the following arguments: (1) the desire to link the theme of Israel's sonship to the sonship of Jesus; (2) the exact literal translation of Exod. 4.22 from Hebrew to Greek; (3) the peculiarity of 2 Pet. 1.17; and (4) the amplification of the designation 'first born' to mean 'beloved' and 'elected'.[164] The suggestion is novel, but not

---

162 Jeremias, 'παῖς θεοῦ', pp. 701, 702.

163 Bretscher, 'Exodus 4.22-23', p. 304.

164 Bretscher, 'Exodus 4.22-23', pp. 305-10: This conclusion does not seem to offer an adequate explanation of the origin of this word of witness. The first argument is adequately met in Isa. 42.1. The bifurcation represented by the corporate application of this passage and the individual messianic application may represent two sides of the same thought. The Messiah may be conceived as embodying all Israel; so, Isa. 42.1 may in fact join the themes of Israel's sonship and Messiah's sonship. Luke 9.35 gives it a unique Christian application. The second argument represents a translation method that is not here in evidence in the synoptic gospels – certainly not in Luke who patterns his writing, very carefully after the Septuagint. The third argument depends too heavily on a reading that (1) lacks conformity to Gen. 22.2 (ἀγαπητός instead of πρωτότοκος – Bretscher's suggestion) and (2) lacks evidence of being pre-synoptic in its origin. Bretscher does present sufficient evidence for his fourth point. There is evidence that the designation 'first born' was expanded to such meanings as 'only child' (Esdras 6.58; Psalms of Solomon 13.9; 18.4; 2 Baruch 5.1; 21.21), 'election' (Dead Sea Scrolls fragments – 'The Words of the Heavenly Lights' [G. Vermes]), Yahweh's servant (Bretscher here

convincing. Bretscher himself finally has to argue from Isa. 42.1. He also depends on Luke's use of both ἀγαπητός and ἐκλελεγμένος as a single word of witness. It would seem that he should be able to show a Lukan use of the concept πρωτότοκος (which word does not appear in the NT) or at least a concept of μονογενής.

It seems that the most likely OT passage to account for this word of witness is Isa. 42.1. It brings together the several themes of the suffering servant, and applies them to Jesus as the messianic figure. Jeremias has shown that the concept of the servant of Yahweh was the equivalent of Son of God in at least some segments of the early Christian background. He has also shown that there is some parallel for this in the rest of Luke–Acts.

The significance of this statement derives from two sources: (1) the setting in which it occurs and (2) the meaning of this witness. The first of these lays the groundwork for the second.

The obvious descriptive characteristics of the setting are these. The scene is Jesus' appearance in glory, the appearance of Moses and Elijah with him and their discussion of Jesus' 'exodus'. This scene is further enhanced by the appearance of the cloud and the issuance of the voice of witness from the cloud.

This is a kingdom setting, identified by the glory of the King and the glory of those who appear with him in the kingdom. This is the glory in which Jesus is always presented in Luke–Acts after the ascension. Riesenfeld is correct in seeing an enthronement motif here.[165] This conclusion is further strengthened by the similarity of this scene with the appearance of the Son of man in Dan. 7.13, 14. 'Two elements make up the primary motif of the transfiguration story, the revelation of the Son of man (Dan. 7.13) and the vision of God at Mount Sinai.'[166] The former of these motifs is shown by the changed appearance of Jesus and his appearance in glory, and the

---

argues that Hosea 11.1; Jer. 31.9; 38.9; Isa. 42.1 are paraphrases of Exod. 4.22.), and 'beloved child' (which is implied in Gen. 22.2 itself). The weakness of this evidence, however, is that it does not show that the term πρωτότοκος is the provenance of all the amplifications. The amplifications are related, but not necessarily dependent.

165 Riesenfeld, *Jésus Transfiguré*, pp. 265-80.

166 Ellis, *The Gospel of Luke*, p. 142; Farrell, 'The Eschatological Perspective of Luke–Acts', p. 42: 'For him (Luke) the Transfiguration is a manifestation of the glory of Jesus (the son of Man)'.

night vision. The glory that is seen in this scene is also depicted by Luke in the vision of the Son of man in Acts 7.56.

The witness to Jesus here is designed to show God's approval of him, to affirm his sonship and with this affirmation to announce his messianic kingship.

As a statement of approval,[167] this witness is comparable to the witness at the baptism. The first comes to Jesus at the initiation of his ministry showing that 'Jesus had accepted God's commission to be both Messiah and Servant of the Lord, and the voice from heaven had come to him to confirm him in the course he had chosen'.[168] The second witness comes to Jesus at the announcement of his kingship and the preview of his kingdom.

The Transfiguration presents a complex picture of the kingdom; it combines the passion with a proleptic view of the form of the apocalyptic kingdom. 'The transfiguration is a prophetic preview of both the future glory and the true nature of Jesus' messiahship.'[169] God's seal of approval is here placed on Jesus in this kingdom situation.[170]

The voice in affirming Jesus' sonship is the word of his enthronement. The sonship affirmed is that unique sonship which we have seen in the study of Isa. 42.1ff. It is here designated by the 'quasi-technical' use of the word ἐκλελεγμένος.[171]

The designation of Jesus as ὁ υἱός μου ὁ ἐκλελεγμένος is designation peculiar to Luke. The design of the word ἐκλελεγμένος is to express a particular relationship between God and Jesus.[172] This

---

167 Browning, *The Gospel According to St. Luke*, p. 103: 'The divine voice, coming at the end of the scene, sets the seal of divine approval on Jesus ...'

168 Caird, *The Gospel According to St. Luke*, pp. 131, 132; Conzelmann, *The Theology of St. Luke*, p. 58.

169 Ellis, *The Gospel of Luke*, pp. 141, 142: We have here more than an awareness of suffering, but an awareness of inauguration; contra: Conzelmann, *The Theology of St. Luke*, p. 58.

170 Kee, 'The Transfiguration in Mark', p. 149.

171 Creed, *The Gospel According to St. Luke*, p. 135; Reiling and Swellengrebel, *A Translator's Handbook on the Gospel of Luke*, p. 384: 'ἐκλελεγμένος = "chosen," equivalent to *eklektos* (cp. 23.35), and both a messianic title'.

172 The word ἐκλέγω (ἐκλέγομαι) expresses separation (as to choose one or more persons or things from a larger group), a special relationship between the one who chooses and the chosen (as to choose a person or thing for one's own) and a particular purpose (as to be chosen for a designated aim) (BAG, pp. 241, 242). This is not a word unique to Luke in the NT, but he does use the word more frequently than any other NT writer. He uses it in the following circumstances. In Lk. 10.42

relationship is seen in terms of the election itself (the electing God and the elected Son), and the purpose of the election. Nothing is said here of the ground of the election; hence, we judge that the word here (as it does in other places) carries the connotation of sovereign election.

The word designates a peculiar relationship between the 'electing' Father and the 'elected' Son. At the baptism (Lk. 3.22) and in other synoptic accounts of the Transfiguration (Mk 9.7; Mt. 17.5) Jesus is the 'beloved' Son. The two designations have converged from a common OT origin and become interpretative each of the other.

This uniqueness is carried into the function for which the subject is elected. In this case the two terms 'beloved' and 'elected' had become messianic designations. The electedness of the Messiah includes both the glory into which he is here translated and the sufferings of which he is told by Moses and Elijah. The election embraces all aspects of the revelation of the Messiah in the Transfiguration. This messianic designation points out the Messiah both in his sufferings and his glory.

The servant passages of Isaiah, other OT witnesses, and the subsequent interpretation in Jewish tradition began to bring together the titles 'Son', 'Messiah', and 'King'.[173]

This divine witness also brings together the various OT references that allude to the messianic kingship.[174] The term 'Son of God' is a

---

and 14.7 the word is used of human choices. It is used of human choices under special circumstances of divine providences in the following instances: Acts 6.5 (of the choosing of Stephen, Philip, and Prochorus by the congregation) and Acts 15.22, 25 (of the sending of certain ἐκλεξαμένους ἄνδρας to accompany Barnabas and Paul). All other occurrences of this word in Luke–Acts are related to divine election: Lk. 6.13 and Acts 1.2 (of Jesus' choosing the apostles), Acts 1.24 (in the prayer that the Lord would show whom he had chosen to fill Judas' apostleship), Acts 13.17 (of God's choice of the patriarchs) and Acts 15.7 (of God's choice of Peter that through his mouth the gentiles should hear the word of the gospel). The word generally in its middle form preserves the middle connotation; hence, in divine election, it carries the notion to choose for oneself (BDF, §316.1).

173 George Wesley Buchanan, *Hebrews* (The Anchor Bible; Garden City: Doubleday, 1972), pp. 13, 14; Zimmerli and Jeremias, 'παῖς θεοῦ' Riesenfeld, *Jésus Transfiguré*, pp. 269-70.

174 Johnson, 'The Transfiguration of Christ', pp. 138-39: 'The voice from the cloud unites the Psalms (2.7), the prophets (Isa. 42.1) and the law (Deut. 18.15) in an authoritative testimony of his Sonship and Messiahship'. Müller, 'Die Verlärung Jesu', p. 56: The second motif which Muller identifies is the appearance of the cloud and the heavenly voice which proclaims Jesus' eschatological majesty'. Lindsay, *The Gospel According to St. Luke*, p. 142.

title for a Jewish messianic king, and the announcement of enthronement.

The union of the messianic title ὁ υἱός μου ὁ ἐκλελεγμένος with the prophetic allusion αὐτοῦ ἀκούετε brings together in this one witness the kingly office and the prophetical office.[175] This allusion to Deut. 18.15 brings 'the authority of the eschatological prophet into a single statement with the announcement of the messianic King'.[176]

It may be objected that the OT does not make a direct application of Deut. 18.15 to the eschatological prophet, but rather to a succession of prophets descending from Moses.[177] There is evidence of the prophet-king motif in Judaism.[178] Samaritan tradition interpreted Deut. 18.15 of an eschatological figure after the type of Moses.[179] There are clear references to this text in Qumran literature in which it was 'used in association with the conception of the eschatological prophet'.[180]

The fundamental answer to these objections is that the NT presents a tradition that specifically takes Deut. 18.15, 18 as the prediction of the appearance of an eschatological prophet.[181] More

---

175 The union of these two offices in the interpretation of Moses (Deut. 18.15) predate the Christian era; Meeks cites 'The Exodus', a drama written by a certain Ezekiel (c. second century BCE): 'It is apparent that Moses' kingship – one might even say divine kingship – and the closely related office of prophecy were taken for granted by Ezekiel and his audience …' (*The Prophet-King*, p. 149). The 'triple office' of John Hyrcanus (ruler, priest, and prophet) probably belongs 'to a "firm tradition" that Josephus took over' (Meeks, *The Prophet-King*, pp. 144-45, citing *Bellum Judaicum*, 1.65).

176 Lindsay, *The Gospel According to St. Luke*, p. 142: 'In the words themselves of the majestic installation there is a remarkable honouring of the Old Testament and all its parts … (Ps. ii.7) … (Isa. xlii.1) … (Deut. xviii.15)'. Johnson, 'The Transfiguration of Christ', pp. 138-39; Ellis, *The Gospel of Luke*, p. 143: '… probably a reference to the eschatological prophet of Deut. 18.15 LXX (cf. Acts 3.22; 7.37; Jn 6.14). If so, Jesus is here identified with the royal "Son" (Ps. 2.7), the chosen Servant (Isa. 42.1) and the prophet like Moses.'

177 Ferdinand Hahn, *The Titles of Jesus in Christology* (trans. Harold Knight and George Ogg; London: Lutterworth, 1969), p. 356; Meeks, *The Prophet-King*, pp. 180, 199, 200, 215: Rabbinic literature generally followed the same interpretation.

178 See note 164.

179 Jeremias, 'Μωυσῆς'; Carruth, 'The Jesus-as-Prophet Motif in Luke–Acts', p. 58; Hahn, *The Titles of Jesus in Christology*, p. 359.

180 Hahn, *The Titles of Jesus in Christology*, p. 357; Carruth, 'The Jesus-as-Prophet Motif in Luke–Acts'.

181 This is not to claim that NT writers (or the early Christian community generally) spoke in isolation from their own milieu: 'a popular expectation of an eschatological prophet distinct from Elijah was lively in the first century A.D.'. (Carruth, 'The Jesus-as-Prophet Motif in Luke–Acts'); this is also evident from

specifically, Luke in his presentation of Jesus presents a 'prophetic christology' which may draw on traditions already present; but it certainly represents a specific redaction of materials by Luke.[182]

In the light of Luke's redaction, it should be observed that Luke's order αὐτοῦ ἀκούεσθε is an exact reproduction of the Septuagint order in Deut. 18.15 (contrary to Mark and Matthew).[183] Luke uses the full statement of Deut. in Acts 3.22 and applies it to Jesus in Peter's defense before the Sanhedrin. If we may connect this with the Transfiguration witness, it means 'This is the Moses-prophet, and more than a prophet – one who is a Son. But even so, it is uttered not by a man but by the divine voice.'[184]

Quite clearly this announcement intends to show that Jesus' authority supersedes the authority of Moses and Elijah. This is evident throughout Luke's account of the Transfiguration. It is a superseding of fulfillment and not a repudiation of Moses and Elijah. In this scene, then, Luke preserves the unity of the time of preparation with the time of fulfillment. By command the disciples are to move from hearing Moses and Elijah to hearing him who fulfills their ministries.[185]

The close of the Transfiguration (v. 36a).

Luke is the briefest of the synoptics in his closing formula for the Transfiguration. This may be attributed to his personal style, which tends toward abbreviation. For Luke, the message of the divine voice is the signal for the end of the Transfiguration account. The meaning of such a closing is that the revelation intended in this experience has come to an end. Hereafter, the authority of Jesus is to be observed; the command, 'Hear him' prepares readers for the emphasis on teaching that follows.[186]

---

prophet-king tradition of Jn 4.14, 15 (Meeks, *The Prophet-King*, p. 99); Hahn, notes that an eschatological prophet (Deut. 18.15) 'can … be assumed for late Judaism' (Hahn, *The Titles of Jesus in Christology*, pp. 364-65).

182 Meeks, *The Prophet-King*, pp. 27, 28; see n. 1, p. 28.

183 Lampe, 'The Holy Spirit in the Writings of St. Luke', p. 174.

184 Moule, *The Gospel According to Mark*, pp. 162, 163.

185 Lampe, 'The Holy Spirit in the Writings of St. Luke', p. 174.

186 The attempt of some commentators to force onto this statement a theological implication of the removal of the law (or the old covenant), or of a disavowal of Moses and Elijah fails to take into account that the revelation was over. If we are to get this meaning from this statement, it would seem that it would necessarily be a part of the structure of the vision itself. It must be recognized that the

The next statement of Luke εὑρέθη Ἰησοῦς μόνος means nothing more than that the appearance of Jesus had returned to its natural appearance and the heavenly visitors had disappeared with the cloud.

The three disciples had experienced a view of the apocalyptic kingdom which they must preserve and cherish, but which could not continue as a way of life. It could not continue because the 'exodus' at Jerusalem had not taken place. This is one of the revelations of the Transfiguration.

The silence of the disciples (v. 36b).

In this half verse, Luke departs from Mark by simply observing that the disciples kept silent about the things that they had seen. The statement is very emphatic. The double negatives imply an imposed silence. This is as close as Luke comes to reflecting the command of silence that is recorded in Mk 9.9. This phrase 'in those days' may be taken as Luke's parallel for Mark's 'until the Son of man should have risen from the dead' (9.9). The 'days' of Luke probably refer to the time from the Transfiguration until the resurrection. The statement probably reflects Luke's knowledge of the conversation recorded in Mk 9.9, 10. Luke omits any reference to Elijah's mission in the ministry or person of John the Baptist; hence, he also omits the conversation in which this subject arose. He covers the essential point of the silence of the disciples by his own observation.

Shekinah and the glory were also gone. Contra: '... because he (Jesus) is the fulfiller of the O.T., Moses and Elijah can now disappear' (Browning, *The Gospel According to St. Luke*, p. 103). 'As though to enforce the command, he (God) withdrew Moses and Elijah from sight, so that the disciples beheld no man save Jesus only' (Harrison, 'The Transfiguration', p. 321).

4

THE TRANSFIGURATION IN LUKAN THEOLOGY

Three canons govern the selection of the material for the following segment of study: uniqueness, peculiarity of expression and peculiarity of emphasis. The thematic studies that follow represent the application of these canons individually and in combination. In the introduction of these themes Luke has made interpretative adjustments appropriate to his editorial aims and theology.

This chapter seeks to bring together elements from the exegesis in support of the thesis. The elements of special importance are the following: the kingdom of God, prayer, glory, and ἔξοδος.

One of the theses of this study is that the Transfiguration account in Luke is a proleptic presentation of the kingdom of God in the experience of Jesus and his three intimate disciples, and that this account is used in a similar manner in worship in the Christian community.

The Theology of Luke Presented in the Special Themes of his Transfiguration Account

1. The kingdom of God

In Lk. 9.27, Luke does not speak of the arrival of the kingdom. Instead he speaks of seeing the kingdom: hence, what is anticipated in that statement is not the event of Parousia. He is not envisioning the process of the kingdom's coming or of the Son of man's coming, but the end product – the kingdom established.

Within this context, our identification of the kingdom of God need not deal with all aspects of its coming. We need to identify the kingdom sufficiently to show the fulfillment of this promise in the context, specifically the Transfiguration.

Luke uses a number of expressions for the kingdom of God. He represents it by the Judaic expressions of 'throne of David' (Lk. 1.32, 33), the 'twelve tribes of Israel' (Lk. 1.32, 33; 22.29, 30), and the 'kingdom restored to Israel' (Acts 1.6). In addition to the formal term 'kingdom of God',[1] Luke represents the kingdom as Jesus' kingdom (Lk. 23.42, 43) and (in the words of Jesus) as 'our Father's kingdom' (Lk. 11.2) originating from the presupposition of 'my Father's kingdom'.[2]

We may divide the references to the kingdom in Luke into two categories: those that describe the present form of the kingdom and those that describe the future form of the kingdom. These are held in tension throughout Luke–Acts.

The present nature of the kingdom is presented in specific Lukan themes which are intended to identify the kingdom in the present age. The kingdom is present where the divine presence is manifested either by the visible presence of Jesus among men (Lk. 17.20)[3] or by

---

[1] Hans Conzelmann, *An Outline of the Theology of the New Testament* (trans. John Bowden; New York and Evanston: Harper and Row, 1968), p. 108: This is Luke's equivalent of Matthew's 'kingdom of heaven' (Compare Lk. 13.18 and Mt. 13.31-33).

[2] Joachim Jeremias, *The Prayers of Jesus* (trans. John Bowden *et al.*; London: SCM Press, 1967), pp. 56-57:

> … the juxtaposition of πάτερ and ὁ πατήρ when they follow each other in the same prayer (Mt. 11.25, par. Lk. 10.21 beginning, end) shows that an Aramaic אבא also underlies πάτερ in Jesus' prayers. The position is very clearly illustrated by the tradition of the prayer in Gethsemane: the ἀββά used by Jesus according to Mk 14.36 is rendered ὁ πατήρ by Mark (14.36), πάτερ μου by Matthew (26.39), and πάτερ by Luke (22.42) … The important thing is that we have discovered that all five strata of the Gospel tradition report unanimously and without any hesitation *that Jesus constantly addressed God as 'my Father'* with the exception of Mk 15.34 (par, Matt. 27.46), *and show that in so doing he used the Aramaic form* אבא (emphasis original).

[3] In contrast to the Pharisee's expectation of an immediate but yet unseen and unrealized in breaking of the kingdom (the age to come), Jesus answered here that the kingdom of God is 'among you' (ἐντὸς ὑμῶν, 17.20, 21). More specifically the statement means that the kingdom of God is 'in your midst by virtue of the fact that Jesus is present and active in your midst' (Bo Reicke, *The Gospel of Luke* [trans. R. MacKenzie; Richmond: John Knox Press, 1964], p. 85; Norman Perrin, *The Kingdom of God in the Teachings of Jesus* [Philadelphia: Westminster, 1963], p. 175). Jesus'

the manifestation of the Holy Spirit. After the ascension it is the Holy Spirit that 'constitutes a continuing presence of the kingdom of God … Luke regards the Holy Spirit as the mediator of the reign of God, "the anticipator of the end in the present"'.[4] The kingdom is brought into being by its proclamation. Prior to the ascension this proclamation is primarily in Jesus, but it is also carried out by his disciples.[5] After the ascension this proclamation is by the action of the Holy Spirit in the church.[6] Under any of the circumstances the kingdom is constituted by the word of proclamation.

To preach the kingdom means that 'the kingdom itself is being manifested (see (Luke) 10.9, 17ff.; 11.31f.; 16.16; 17.20f.; 23.32-49)'.[7] The kingdom is present through the preaching of Jesus and/or the performance of his mighty works. This is so because the proclamation is the divine Word; as such the divine Word has in itself the power of its own fulfillment. So, when the kingdom is preached, the kingdom is formed.

In this same light, the content and power of the proclamation brings into being the hallmarks of the kingdom, or its essential characteristics: the preaching of the gospel to the poor, the announcement of deliverance to the captives, the universal offer of salvation (the vision of the inclusion of the gentiles in the kingdom and the salvation of the lost), the giving of sight to the blind, the sending out of the shattered free, participation in the benefits of the kingdom (as

---

correction of the Pharisees' misconception declares that the kingdom does not come with observation; therefore, it cannot be identified by such physical and temporal observations as 'Behold here or Behold there'. Instead, Jesus declares that it is among you, and the implication is that Jesus' audience did not know it; 'The logion (vss 20-21) has as its basic point that the Kingdom of God is in the midst of the Pharisees in the ministry of Jesus, though they did not see it since there were no unambiguous evidences of it' (Charles H. Talbert, 'The Redaction Critical Quest for Luke the Theologian', *Perspective* 11 [1970], pp. 178-79).

[4] Ellis, *Luke*, p. 13; Lampe, 'The Holy Spirit in the Writings of St. Luke', pp. 171-72:

> The same power of the Spirit works miracles after Pentecost at the hands of Peter and John, Stephen and Philip, and it characterizes the apostolic preaching just as it did that of Jesus himself. This power is … therefore, that St. Luke brings the ideas of the power of the kingdom and the working of the Spirit of God into very close relationship with each other; they are virtually identical.

[5] Ellis, *Luke*, p. 13: 'The unique and revolutionary aspect of Jesus' message was his assertion that in his ministry the new creation already was breaking in upon the present age'.

[6] Marshall, *Luke: Historian and Theologian*, pp. 134-36.

[7] Ellis, *Luke*, p. 13.

in prayer, especially the Lord's Prayer [Lk. 11.1-13], and the announcement of the acceptable year of the Lord [Lk. 4.17-19, 42-44]).[8] This is an effectuating proclamation; so, the kingdom exists, and its benefits are realized by proclamation.

These are the elements of the identification of the kingdom in the present age. It is in this sense that the kingdom is imminent[9] without implying that the Parousia is imminent.[10] This aspect of the kingdom's being (in breaking) does not depend on a prior Parousia.

Throughout Luke–Acts the concept of the future manifestation of the kingdom of God (the day of the Son of man – Lk. 17.24)[11] stands in tension with this concept of the present existence of the kingdom.

Luke identifies the future aspect of the kingdom of God by the fulfillment of various eschatological symbols and expectations. The initiating mark of this future manifestation of the kingdom is the Parousia in which the Son of man appears publicly[12] in the manner of a lightning flash (Lk. 17.22-24). Other symbols and expectations are: the reestablishing of the throne of David and the rulership over the twelve tribes of Israel by the Messiah on the throne of his father David (Lk. 1.32, 33; 22.29, 30), the gathering of the redeemed at the 'feast of salvation' (the eschatological meal fulfilled – Lk. 13.28, 29; 22.16-18; 22.29, 30), the gift of eternal life (Lk. 18.29, 30), the final judgement (Lk. 13.28, 29) and the Father's appointment of the kingdom to Jesus (Lk. 22.29, 30, 69, 70).

If the kingdom in its present form is constituted by its proclamation, those who make this proclamation (Jesus and his disciples) must have a special authority. The claim at Nazareth was that Isa. 61.1, 2a

---

8 Marshall, *Luke: Historian and Theologian*, p. 136.

9 Marshall, *Luke: Historian and Theologian*, p. 136.

10 Talbert, 'The Redaction Critical Quest', pp. 185, 186: cf. Lk. 21.8 and 17.20-18.8, 'Both passages set up stages which must elapse before the parousia occurs'.

11 ἐν τῇ ἡμέρᾳ αὐτοῦ is doubtless the correct reading here; it is supported by א, A, K, L, W, X, Δ, Θ, Π, Ψ, 063, Family 1, Family 13, a host of minuscules, Byzantine lectionaries, and most of the ancient versions. There is impressive evidence for a shorter reading. However, the number and the quality of witnesses for the longer ending would seem to prevail here. However, note Metzger, *A Textual Commentary on the Greek New Testament*, p. 167 (Lk. 17.24): 'Although copyists may have inadvertently omitted the phrase ἐν τῇ ἡμέρᾳ αὐτοῦ because of homoeoteleuton (-που ...-του), the Committee was impressed by the combination of the Alexandrian and the Western types of text (𝔓[75], B, D, it.[a, b, d, e, 1])'.

12 Talbert, 'The Redaction Critical Quest', p. 186.

was fulfilled in Jesus (Lk. 4.21). The anointing of the Spirit that had come upon him at his baptism had equipped him for this proclamation[13] and the voice of witness from the opened heavens had given him his authority (Lk. 3.21, 22). Jesus was anointed for this proclamation (Lk. 4.18). He was commissioned for this purpose and it was necessary for him to preach the kingdom of God (Lk. 4.43). During his ministry the disciples (i.e. 'the twelve') accompanied Jesus as the preacher (Lk. 8.1) and went before him preaching under authority of his commission (Lk. 9.1-6). When the crowd followed Jesus and the returning apostles into the desert, Jesus spoke to them of the kingdom of God (Lk. 9.10, 11). Luke, in this context, places three characteristic elements of the kingdom in proximity to each other: the proclamation (9.11), a communal meal (9.12-17) and the confession of Peter (9.18-20).[14]

The same pattern of preaching is carried by Luke into Acts to designate the announcement of the kingdom. The resurrected Jesus spoke of the things of the kingdom of God (Acts 1.3); he ate with the apostles (Acts 1.4 – συναλιζόμενος), and promised the eschatological gift of the Holy Spirit (Acts 1.4-8).

Philip preached at Samaria the things concerning the kingdom of God (Acts 8.12), Paul's and Barnabas' activity is designated as 'preaching the gospel' (εὐαγγελιζόμαι, Acts 14.7). Paul's activity is represented by 'proclaiming' (κηρύσσων) the kingdom of God (28.31) and 'witnessing' (μαρτυρέω) of the kingdom of God (Acts 28.23).[15]

The key word in the preaching of the kingdom of God is εὐαγγελιζόμαι, which has become a technical term for the proclamation of the Christian message.[16]

---

13 Charles H. Talbert, *Literary Patterns, Theological Themes and the Genre of Luke–Acts* (SBL Monograph Series, 20; Missoula, MT: Scholars Press, 1974), p. 117.

14 Talbert, *Literary Patterns*, p. 27.

15 Lampe, 'The Holy Spirit in the Writings of St. Luke', pp. 171, 172, 192: 'In Acts ... the phrase "kingdom of God" appears but seldom, and when it is mentioned it is identified with the content of the apostolic gospel'.

16 The promise to Zacharias of the birth of John (Lk. 1.19) and the doxology announcing the birth of Jesus (Lk. 2.10) employ this word. It is also used to describe the preaching of John the Baptist (Lk. 3.18). It appears that John is to be given a place among those who preached the gospel (cf. Lk. 16.16; cf. 13.28, 29). He occupies 'a place in the era of fulfillment, yet one which partakes of the nature of preparation' (Marshall, *Luke: Historian and Theologian*, p. 146).

Luke has fused the two concepts of 'preaching the gospel' and of 'preaching the kingdom of God' into one. This is evidenced in the synoptic tradition by the fact that they have used the word εὐαγγελιζόμαι by itself to mean 'to preach the gospel', and Luke has attached the word to the kingdom in the clause εὐαγγελιζόμαι τὴν βασιλείαν.

The Lukan identification of the constituents of the kingdom is applicable both to the kingdom as present and as future. A special emphasis of Luke is the inclusion of the poor in the kingdom of God (Lk. 6.20; 18.24). The patriarchs and all the prophets are in the kingdom and are so manifested in the day of judgement (Lk. 13.28, 29),[17] and people are drawn from all of humankind to be manifested in the kingdom. The constituents of the kingdom in the eschatological sense have the distinction of having endured temptation with Jesus (Lk. 22.29, 30). The penitent thief is incorporated in the kingdom (Lk. 23.42, 43). The Samaritans were potentially included in the kingdom as a part of the mission of God to Israel.[18] It should also be noted that Luke records the Samaritan mission and conversions prior to the mission to the gentiles indicating that preaching to the Samaritans was considered a part of the Jewish mission.[19]

Excursus on the Present and Future Nature of the Kingdom in Luke

The present (or imminent) nature of the kingdom appears in Luke on the lips of Jesus in the following situations. In 9.27 Jesus promises that some of those before him would not taste of death until they saw the kingdom of God. Though there is a future emphasis here,[20]

---

[17] This apparently includes Moses and Elijah as well as John the Baptist, contrary to Conzelmann: 'It is true that this period (the period of the Law and the Prophets) comes to its close with John, greatest of the prophets, but his status does not carry him beyond it, for even he does not proclaim the Kingdom of God' (Conzelmann, *The Theology of St. Luke*, p. 101); 'As far as Elijah and Moses are concerned, Luke answers the undecided question in the story of the Transfiguration, ix, 28-36. With their appearances here the role of both of them is completed' (Conzelmann, *The Theology of St. Luke*, p. 25).

[18] Jervell, *Luke and the People of God*, p. 78: '…For Luke the Samaritans are not considered Gentiles, but "the lost sheep of the house of Israel." The Samaritans receive the Spirit, which Luke sees as Israel's "possession" (8.15ff.).'

[19] Jervell, *Luke and the People of God*, pp. 110, 121: 'Luke 9.51-56 shows that Jesus found himself in Samaritan territory, and that he wished to be accepted there'.

[20] Ellis, 'Present and Future Eschatology', pp. 34, 35:

it is not the predominant emphasis. The meaning is that some in Jesus' generation could expect to see the kingdom. So the predominant emphasis here is the manifestation of the kingdom in the present age. It is a restricted experience; hence, it is not the seeing of the kingdom by virtue of its proclamation.

Luke 10.9, 11 (Q) proclaims that the kingdom of God has come near (ἤγγικεν, v. 9) and 'proves' that it has come near (ἤγγικεν, v. 11) by a symbolic act of divine judgement (vv. 10, 11a). By the present proclamation and symbol and by the expectation of future divine judgement, Luke has maintained the tension of present-future eschatology in the form of a petition to God. The petition is eschatological[21] though not apocalyptic in its expectation. The petition expects an immediate answer which is to be fulfilled by the daily supply of bread, the remission of sins, and deliverance from temptation, which are all characteristics of the kingdom of God.

Luke 16.16, 17 is generally attributed to Q. Luke has considerably shortened the saying (cf. Mt. 11.12, 13); he has preserved the distinction between the two stages of salvation history. In Mt. 11.12 we have a statement of persecution. It seems best, however, to take Lk. 16.16 as a statement regarding entrance into the kingdom.[22]

In contrast to the Pharisees' expectation of an immediate but yet unseen and unrealized inbreaking of the kingdom (age to come) Jesus answers that the kingdom of God is 'among you' (ἐντὸς ὑμῶν, 17.20, 21).[23]

These verses are peculiar to Luke; they represent a special emphasis. Though vv. 20, 21 are joined to the narrative of the healing of the ten lepers (vv. 11-18),[24] it seems best to take them as Luke's

---

Luke ix.23-36 ... represents a deliberate juxtaposition of present and future eschatology. It is within this frame of reference that Luke ix. 27 should be understood. While Luke employed the scheme he did not create it. The structure of the present passage is the work of a pre-Markan editor, perhaps the one who stands behind both Mark and Q.

21 Jeremias, *Prayers*, pp. 98, 99.

22 BAG, p. 140.

23 Reicke, *The Gospel of Luke*, p. 85: 'Jesus' answer in 17.20b-21 that the kingdom has in fact already come (the much discussed *entos hymon* most likely means "among you") ...'; Norman Perrin, *The Kingdom of God in the Teachings of Jesus* (Philadelphia: Westminster, 1963), p 175.

24 From the L tradition: Talbert, *Literary Patterns*, p. 54.

introduction to vv. 22-37, which are from Q.[25] By joining this special material to the Q material Luke keeps his parallel emphasis of present and future eschatology. Verse 20 means that the kingdom is 'in your midst by virtue of the fact that Jesus is present and active in your midst'.[26]

There is an implication of the present character of the kingdom in Jesus' sorrow over the failure of the rich young ruler to enter the kingdom of God (18.24, 25).

In Lk. 23.42, 43 (L) the words of the penitent thief set the framework of the answer of Jesus. The thief anticipates that it lies in the power of Jesus to grant him admission to his kingdom. His request does not necessarily anticipate an immediate realization of the kingdom. Jesus' words (σήμερον μετ' ἐμοῦ ἔσῃ ἐν τῷ παραδείσῳ) promise the thief more than he anticipated. He promises an immediate realization of the kingdom.[27]

Luke expresses the inquiries of others concerning the immediate realization of the kingdom in three places. In each case, the expectation of the inquirer is for an immediate (though yet unrealized, unseen and therefore future) presentation of the kingdom in an apocalyptic sense. Luke treats this expectation as erroneous and represents Jesus as correcting the misunderstanding.

In Lk. 17.20 the Pharisees ask when the kingdom of God will come. Jesus responds with the correction that it does not come with observation; so it cannot be said with truth 'it is here or there'. Instead it is among you, and the implication is that you do not know it (vv. 20b, 21).

---

25 Matthew does not have a parallel for Lk. 17.22 concerning the day of the Son of man. He introduces the warning not to be deceived by those who cry 'Behold here is the Christ or there' (Mt. 24.15-22). Matthew's emphasis is entirely future.

26 Farrell, 'The Eschatological Perspective of Luke–Acts', p. 61; Haenchen, *The Acts of the Apostles* (trans. Basil Blackwell; Philadelphia: Westminster, 1971), p. 141 n. 2: '… as Luke understands it Jesus is not declaring that the kingdom is in unbelieving Pharisees, but that in his own person it is in the midst of them …'

27 LaGrange, *Evangile Selon Saint Luc*, p. 591:

> Après les mots ἀμήν σοι λέγω … Jésus accorde plus que le larron n'implor. C'est le jour meme, au moment de sa mot, qu'il retrouvera le Christ. Plutot que de chercher exprissément ce qu'est ce paradis … Le mot de παραδεῖσος 'jardin delicieux' euoquait pour le larron l'image d'un lieu de bonheur (IV Esdr. VII, 36; Hem LXI, 12, etc.).

According to Luke, Jesus gave the parable of the ten pounds in order to correct and warn (Lk. 19.11-27). Verse 11, as an introductory statement (Luke's peculiar transition), shows that Luke understood this parable to teach that the Parousia was not to be expected immediately.[28] This parable, then in this context is a corrective for those who expected the immediate manifestation of the kingdom in a visible event. They supposed that the kingdom's coming would be related to Jesus' arrival in Jerusalem.[29] Luke's use of this parable shows that there is to be a period marked by the fulfilling of a visible stewardship before the kingdom comes as a visible entity.[30]

In Acts 1 the disciples asked the resurrected Jesus if he would at that time restore the kingdom to Israel. Their expectation was the immediate inbreaking of an apocalyptic new age marked by the government of Israel (Acts 1.6). Jesus corrected this expectancy (without denying that the kingdom would be restored to Israel) by giving the promise of the Holy Spirit (Acts 1.8). From other passages in Luke–Acts, it is evident that this is an eschatological promise and expectation.[31] The Holy Spirit is Israel's expected eschatological possession.

Not all future and apocalyptic expectations voiced in Luke–Acts are considered erroneous by Luke. There is a future concept of the kingdom that is also apocalyptic, and it is portrayed by Luke as

---

28 Jeremias, *Parables*, p. 59:

> To provide a setting for the conflated parable an introductory saying (19.11) has been prefixed which exhibits a number of Luke's literary characteristics (although it need not have come from Luke himself); it states that the parable was related in order to refute false was to appear immediately. Hence we can see how Luke interpreted our parable: ...

Jeremias notes the possibility that this interpretation did not originate with Luke; see p. 99 n. 40.

29 Talbert, 'The Redaction Critical Quest', p. 173.

30 Jeremias, *Parables*, p. 59.

31 Lampe, 'The Holy Spirit in the Writings of St. Luke', p. 184:

> The connection between the Kingdom and the Spirit appears in the fact that the risen Lord's command to his disciples to await the promise of the Spirit-baptism seems to form part of a discussion about 'the things concerning the Kingdom of God', and the apostles' reception of the power of the Spirit constitutes the answer to their question concerning the restoration of the Kingdom to Israel.

p. 193: 'The last days have now dawned, and the ancient hope of the gift of the Spirit is to be fulfilled through the crucified and exalted Messiah ... At Pentecost they actually received the Power of the Spirit in which Jesus had preached, healed and exorcised'.

correct and as existing side by side with the motif of the present existence of the kingdom.[32]

The announcement of the conception of Jesus (Lk. 1.32,33) anticipates a future and endless reign of the child to be born. He is to reign on the throne of his father David and his is to be a rulership over the house of Jacob. This announcement reflects a Jewish apocalyptic hope.

Luke 1.20-30 contains three segments: Luke's introduction (vv. 22, 23a), Jesus' exhortation and parable (vv. 23b-27; Q) and the warning of judgement (which Luke actually begins in the words of the householder in the parable – v. 27) and description of the kingdom of God (vv. 28, 29; Q).[33] The parable is applied in two apocalyptic motifs: the future judgement and the 'Messianic banquet'.[34] In each of these the kingdom is represented in consummation . The judgement is a familiar apocalyptic characteristic of the kingdom of God. The patriarchs and all the prophets are seated in the kingdom, and they are joined by people from all the directions of the earth. For Luke this means that they are partakers of the fulfillment of the kingdom represented by the patriarchs and prophets 'seated at the feast of salvation'.[35] This is the kingdom of God in consummation as distinct from the kingdom of God in Parousia.

From Q, Luke reflects an apocalyptic symbol (14.15) joined to the parable of the Great Banquet (14.16-24 parallel Mt. 22.1-14). The particular difference between the manner in which Luke handles this material is in the introduction which has no Matthew parallel.[36] By

---

[32] Jervell, *Luke and the People of God*, p. 78.

[33] Talbert, *Literary Patterns*, p. 56: 'Luke 13.18-30 consists of two collections of Q traditions. 13.18-21 (=Mt. 13.31-33) and 13.22-30 (= Mt. 7.13-14, 22-23, 8.11-12) which are found in different order in Matthew'. The identification of Q in some parts of this passage seems strained. Verses 22, 23a have no Matthew parallel; v. 22 is a part of Luke's movement in the journey material. Verses 25-27 are parallel in thought with Mt. 7.22, 23 but the verbal and contextual identifications are remote at best.

[34] Talbert, *Literary Patterns*, p. 56.

[35] Jeremias, *Parables*, p. 96.

[36] Whether this introduction stood in Q is doubtful. It is not a saying of Jesus and is nowhere reflected in Matthew. It must be attributed either to Luke's redaction or to an L Tradition. Talbert notes the 'Lukan introduction', and attributes this to Luke's interest in literary parallelism with Lk. 13.22-30. Talbert and Vincent Taylor attribute the entire passage to Q (Talbert, *Literary Patterns*, p. 56; Vincent Taylor, *The Gospels* [London: The Epworth Press, 1938], 4th edn, p. 24). The parallelism

placing the parable here there is a union of the eschatological (v. 15) with the hortatory. The parable in this form, in fact, shifts the emphasis from the eschatological to the hortatory.[37] This structure does not deny the eschatological emphasis of the symbol,[38] but joins it to exhortation in view of the apocalyptic judgement.[39] Luke 17.22-37[40] is an esoteric discourse on the appearance of the Son of man. It is significant here because it has the position of elaborating privately to

---

seems remote; hence, it seems to offer little solution to the question of the source of this introduction.

[37] Jeremias, *Parables*, pp. 45, 97.

[38] Jeremias, *Parables*, p. 69.

[39] Jeremias, *Parables*, pp. 171-77: '... and by the words of μου τοῦ δείπνου, "my supper," he (Jesus) will have been referring to the Messianic banquet (cf. Luke 22.30), so Luke may have understood it, and may have seen in the parable an allegory of the Messianic banquet'.

[40] This is a complex passage. Verses 20, 21 are from an L tradition. The entirety of vv. 22-37 is generally represented as coming from Q. There are complexities within this passage, however. Verses 22, 23 and 31 could as well be attributed to the influence of Mark; v. 22 has no Matthew parallel; there is no Mark or Matthew parallel to vv. 28, 29. Verse 32 is peculiar to Luke and follows the suggestion made by the introduction of Lot in vv. 28, 29. It seems difficult to ascribe these to Q by the usual identification of Q. These complexities suggest that this passage was drawn together from a variety of sources and editorial structure.

Where Mark deals only with the days of tribulation, Luke contrasts these days with the days of the Son of man (v. 22). The days of the Son of man are regarded as days of blessedness in contrast to the intensive tribulation. Luke says nothing of the shortening of the days of tribulation for the sake of the chosen ones (Mk 13.20). Luke goes directly to warn against those who would claim that Christ is here or there. According to this arrangement of the text, they will make these claims of the secret presence of Jesus in the midst of the days of tribulation. According to Mk 13.22; 23 and Mt. 24.26 (for which there is no Luke parallel) this is the work of false Christs-and false prophets. In Mark and Matthew this explanation is the answer to these false claims. In Luke the answer is the dramatic presentation of the day of the Son of man – his appearance as a lightning flash across the sky (v. 24).

In v. 25, Luke introduces a further correction of this false apocalypticism; the Son of man must suffer before the day of the Son of man can come. Luke's point is that there can be no expectation of the Parousia until the days of the suffering have passed; the approach to Jerusalem must not raise false hopes in the disciples. By taking up the analogy with the days of Noah, Luke apparently intends to characterize the days following the suffering of the Son of man. After the suffering there will come days of normalcy and a presumptuous increase of evil (vv. 26-29). These days will continue until the revelation of the Son of man (v. 30). This day is marked by the judgement that is inherent in separation between those who await the day of the Son of man prepared for it and those who are not prepared (vv. 34, 35, 37) (Verse 36 is omitted by 𝔓[75], ℵ, A, B, K, L, W, X, Δ, Θ, Ψ and most other witnesses.). The gauge of preparation is in the giving of one's life or the attempt to preserve it (which Luke introduces by the example of Lot's wife [vv. 32, 33]).

the disciples on the answers that Jesus had given to the Pharisees in vv. 20, 21. The following apocalyptic symbols appear. The Son of man and his sudden appearance are likened to lightning (v. 24). The increase of evil culminating in sudden destruction is exemplified in Noah and his generation (vv. 26-28) and Lot and the people of Sodom (v. 29). The day of the Son of man has the same kind of prelude and culmination (vv. 30, 31). There is also a judgement motif here (vv. 33-37; compare 9.23-26). Jesus corrected the wrong apocalypticism of the Pharisees with which Luke introduces this section. The section itself goes on to correct the same type of error in the Christian community. He gave his disciples private instruction to correct the same kind of apocalypticism in the Christian community.

In Lk. 18.29, 30 'this age' and the 'age to come' are placed in contrast to each other, though each relates to an experience of the kingdom. We have noted earlier the present aspect of the kingdom in this passage. The age to come is distinct in character from this age, because in it the believer can receive eternal life. In this age, though in the kingdom, the believer receives those things that are related to temporal possessions and relations which have been given up for the sake of the kingdom of God.

The parable of the pounds (Lk. 19.11-27) has been commented on already as a correction of the thinking of some of the disciples who thought that the kingdom would appear immediately. The full application of this parable in Luke culminates in a judgement scene.[41] The judgement is a judgement of the stewardship of those in the kingdom (vv. 15-26) and of the enemies of the kingdom (v. 27).

While Jesus ate the passover meal with the disciples (Lk. 22.13-15) he anticipated the eating of the eschatological meal with them when the kingdom is fulfilled (22.16 πληρόω). The same eschatological meal is anticipated in the symbol of the wine cup; here Jesus says that he will not drink of it again until the kingdom has come (22.17, 18, ἔρχομαι). This passage combines the element of suffering with the eschatological element of the coming of the kingdom.

---

[41] Jeremias, *Parables*, p. 59: 'Luke, then would seem to have interpreted the nobleman who received a kingdom and demanded a reckoning from his servants on his return, as the Son of man departing to heaven and returning to judgement'. Jeremias argues that Luke's conclusion is wrong, but it remains that this is the form in which Luke passed on this material to his readers.

Luke 22.29, 30 combines the eschatological meal with the appointment of a kingdom to the disciples (based on the Father's appointment of a kingdom to Jesus) and their sitting on thrones judging the twelve tribes of Israel. Jesus' kingdom is thus identified with the twelve tribes of Israel, and as the kingdom of Jesus.[42]

Summary and conclusions

Luke has very carefully distinguished the following aspects of the kingdom of God: (1) the kingdom manifested in its present form (either by the presence of Jesus and his Word or by the presence and manifestation of the Holy Spirit), (2) the kingdom manifested at the Parousia, and (3) the kingdom manifested in consummation depicted in the blessedness of constituents gathered at the Messianic meal with Christ.

Concerning the first of these, we may note that Luke represents Jesus as expecting his disciples to discern the presence of the kingdom by his presence and proclamation and by the recognition of its essential characteristics. No special experiences are required, except the spiritual relationship to Jesus. This was a relationship common to discipleship. The Pharisees could not see it, but the disciples could. Hence, we judge that the restriction placed on those who see the kingdom in Lk. 9.27 excludes this concept of the kingdom from the fulfillment of this verse.

The manifestation of the kingdom by the Parousia is to be a public manifestation. This is Luke's consistent presentation of this event (Lk. 17.20 – 18.8; 21).[43] Hence, we may judge that all people will see the manifestation of the kingdom in the coming of the Son of man. This is not to be expected in Jesus' generation. There is to be a period of stewardship, political upheaval and tribulation that must transpire before the Parousia. 'This means … that Luke identified events of the second and third Christian generations as eschatological phenomena leading to the end'.[44] No special spiritual relationship was needed to be a witness of this manifestation of the kingdom. In fact, this teaching of the public nature of the Parousia is set over against the teaching of those who claimed private knowledge of Christ's presence.

---

[42] Haenchen, *Acts*, p. 723 n. 8.
[43] Talbert, 'Redaction Critical Quest', p. 186.
[44] Talbert, 'Redaction Critical Quest', p. 183.

The third form of the manifestation of the kingdom, which I have designated the kingdom in consummation, is also future and apocalyptic. We see this manifestation of the kingdom as observers of the judgement and of the gathering of the kingdom around the eschatological meal. Such a manifestation of the kingdom appears after and is the product of Parousia; and as the Parousia lies in the indefinite future, so does the consummate form of the kingdom.

The Transfiguration scene presents eschatological elements that are compatible with the presentation of the kingdom in this form. Some of the eschatological elements that appear here are the glorious appearance of Jesus, the glorious appearance of Moses and Elijah, and the appearance of the Shekinah. These are also apocalyptic; they relate to the kingdom of God in its fulfillment in the age to come. These are not elements of the Parousia.

Luke has bypassed the Parousia in this scene; he does not describe the coming of the Son of man or the process of the coming of the kingdom. Instead, Luke gives a picture of the kingdom already gathered around the glorified Messiah. It is a proleptical presentation of the kingdom to certain disciples who must yet await its eternal appearance at the end of the age. This presentation, however, shows the kingdom as it will be gathered around the exalted Messiah. These are conditions that are specifically of the age to come and are not a part of the temporal order.

Certain ones of the early Christian community expected to see these benefits within their age; according to Luke, however, they are supratemporal. Their manifestation awaits the age to come following the Parousia. Those who see such manifestations see them in their inheritance of eternal life. Luke 9.27 promises an exception to this expectation. Some will see this kingdom before the end of the age. So, in the Transfiguration, the kingdom has come and has been witnessed by three of Jesus' disciples.

We conclude, then, that the Transfiguration is a presentation that takes into account Luke's supratemporal concept of the kingdom and yet may be viewed by the three intimates of Jesus through special religious experience while they yet remained mortal.

2. Prayer

The emphasis which Luke places on prayer in the Transfiguration calls for more specific attention.[45]

It is common in devotional uses of this pericope to make the connection between Jesus' prayer and the Transfiguration paradigmatic for believers.[46] Within a certain context, this is certainly an admissible application; this has relevancy to Luke's emphasis on Jesus' piety. Another devotional emphasis is that the Transfiguration is the answer of the Father to the prayer of the Son.[47]

One of the reasons for the presentation of the Transfiguration account in the early Christian traditions was that it was a paradigm of worship in the early Christian community. Its use here, however, is more fundamental to Luke's eschatology than the usual devotional concept of personal and subjectively realized transformation. Luke has taken a cultic element and has integrated it to his story and his theology. The integration of cult and theology is demonstrated generally in the use of prayer in Luke–Acts. It is illustrated quite specifically in the pericope under study.

The most consistently recurring theme in Luke's presentation of the prayers of Jesus and Jesus' teaching about prayer is eschatology. Luke conveys this theme not only by the content of Jesus' prayers and teaching, but also by the circumstances and contexts in which they occur. Though the eschatological theme cannot be pressed in all occurrences of prayer in Luke, it appears consistently enough to justify this conclusion.

---

45 Harris, 'Prayer in Luke–Acts', pp. 64-72: 'A new step in *Heilsgeschichte* is initiated by divine revelation received in prayer. 9.28-29 is the second crucial place in Luke's Gospel where Jesus is pictured as praying' (p. 72).

46 Dillersberger, *The Gospel of St. Luke*, p. 255: 'During the prayer, then, the shape of his countenance was altered … Prayer nearly always alters the human countenance.' Caird, 'The Transfiguration', p. 291:

> But the evidence presented by Evelyn Underhill and others, that physical transfiguration has been known to accompany the intense devotional experiences of saints and mystics, has persuaded more recent writers that such desperate devices (i.e. the attempt to see the Transfiguration as a post-resurrection vision) are unnecessary.

J. Mathieson Forsom, 'The Transfiguration', *Expository Times* 17 (1905-1906), p. 140: The Transfiguration 'stands out as an instance of Christ's normal experiences when wrapped in prayer'.

47 Johnson, 'The Transfiguration of Christ', pp. 135-36.

This eschatological use of prayer in Luke–Acts is especially significant in those instances of prayer associated with eschatological events in the life of Jesus and the church. The first of these is the prayer of Jesus at the time of his baptism (Lk. 3.21, 22). The act of prayer is not specifically associated with the baptism, but with the things which followed. After Jesus had been baptized and while he was praying, events of eschatological significance occurred:[48] (1) the heaven opened; (2) the Holy Spirit descended on Jesus; and (3) the Voice came from heaven announcing Jesus' divine sonship.

The choosing of twelve apostles from among all the disciples was preceded by a night of prayer on Jesus' part (Lk. 6.12-16). Luke wanted to show that the praying of Jesus had a direct bearing on his choosing the twelve. 'The close relation between Jesus' nocturnal prayer and the choice of the twelve is made clear by Luke's temporal designations ...'[49] The apostleship was derived from Jesus' commission by God: hence, the emphasis on prayer prior to the choosing.[50] The choosing of twelve apostles relates the number of the apostles to the twelve tribes of Israel and Jesus' later promise that twelve would sit on thrones and would judge the twelve tribes of Israel (Lk. 22.29, 30). The connection emphasizes the divine origin of the commission and implies its eschatological nature.

Jesus was alone praying when he began the series of questions that provoked the confession of Peter (Lk. 9.18ff). This in turn provided the setting for the prediction of suffering (vv. 21, 22), the call to emulation of Jesus' cross (vv. 23-25), the description of the coming of the Son of man and the consequent judgement (v. 26), and the promise that some would see the kingdom of God (v. 27). Prayer, thus, stands at the head of this group of eschatological sayings.

---

48 Creed, *The Gospel According to St. Luke*, p. 57: 'The aorist participle βαπτισθέντος contrasted with the present participle προσευχομένοι makes the descent of the Spirit coincident with the prayer of Jesus, not with his baptism, which has already been completed'. Harris, 'Prayer in Luke–Acts', p. 38: 'The present tense is suggestive; it connects the heavenly revelation more closely with prayer than with baptism'.

49 Harrison, 'The Transfiguration', p. 53.

50 Walter Grundmann, *Das Evangelium nach Lukas* (Berlin: Evanglische Verlagsansalt, 1962), p. 137: 'Die Zwölf sind im nächtlichen Gebet ihm als die Apostel vom Vater bezeichnet worden; sie sind die, "die du mir gegeben hast" (John 17, 6 u.a.) – ein erneuter Zusammenklang zwischen lukanischer und johanneischer Uberlieferung'.

Luke 9.28, 29 places prayer at the heading of the events of Transfiguration. Prayer is intimately related to the change in Jesus' appearance and to the rest of the Transfiguration scene.

These three instances of prayer in Luke relate prayer to revelatory experiences. They also have in them eschatological symbols – the heavens opened, the Holy Spirit, the heavenly witness, the cross, the coming of the Son of man, the kingdom of God, and the manifestation of glory.[51]

Luke also introduces teaching about prayer that shows a connection with eschatology. The first such teaching that we will observe is the pericope of the 'Lord's Prayer' (11.1-4).[52] Jesus' praying is placed at the heading of this pericope. Provoked by the prayer of Jesus, one of his disciples asked him to teach them to pray 'just as John taught his disciples' (v. 1). The intention of the request is for Jesus to provide a prayer that is characteristic of his message.[53] The prayer which thus follows ties together Jesus' message of the kingdom of God and the disciples' expectation and experience of the kingdom. 'The Lord's prayer is in fact a brief summary of the fundamentals of Jesus' proclamation.'[54] This judgement of Jeremias is supported by the following aspects of the prayer: (1) the peculiar address to God (πάτερ), (2) the petition for the hallowedness of the Father's name, (3) the petition for the will of God to be done, and (4) the petitions which anticipate the blessings of the kingdom – the daily supply of bread, the remission of sins and deliverance from temptations. Jeremias judges this prayer to be 'the clearest and, in spite of its terseness, the richest summary of Jesus' proclamation which we possess'.[55] This union of the prayer with the proclamation of Jesus establishes the eschatological meaning and anticipation of the prayer.

There follows a parable of prayer in vv. 5-8 which probably comes from a pre-Lukan tradition.[56] Though the parable itself may not show

---

51 Harrison, 'The Transfiguration', p. 318: 'Luke informs us that Jesus' journey up into the high mountain had a definite purpose. He went to pray. This was so on all occasions when the voice from heaven testified of the Son. It was so at the river, on the mount, and in the Holy City.' Clearly, Harrison has appealed to data outside of Luke, but he has shown the pattern to be a NT pattern.

52 Verse 1 is introductory. Verses 2-4 are from Q.

53 Joachim Jeremias, *The Prayers of Jesus* (trans. John Bowden *et al.*; London: SCM Press, 1967), p. 77.

54 Jeremias, *The Prayers of Jesus*, p. 77.

55 Jeremias, *The Prayers of Jesus*, p. 77.

56 Jeremias, *Parables*, p. 87 n. 95; Talbert, *Literary Patterns*, p. 54.

specific eschatological symbols, the saying that applies the parable may have such symbolism (v. 8). This verse seems to be intended as a reinforcement of the petitions of the prayer. If this be true, it appears that Luke understood the parable to have the same eschatological symbolism as that seen in the prayer itself.

Luke draws a series of exhortations from Q (vv. 9-13) to apply this parable. They come to a climax in an eschatological promise (v. 13): namely, the promise of the Holy Spirit.[57] Jeremias notes that ''Ἀγαθά (Mt. 7.11) has the same eschatological significance as πνεῦμα ἅγιον (Lk. 11.13), since τὰ ἀγαθά ... frequently designates gifts of the Messianic Age ...'[58]

There is another prayer parable in Lk. 18.1-8. It is the application which appears at the end that especially shows the eschatological teaching (vv. 6-8). Beare and others have argued for a hellenistic origin of the parable.[59] Conversely, Jeremias argues for the antiquity of both the parable and the application. He argues that the assurance of God's unwavering faithfulness is 'an essential element in the preaching of Jesus'.[60] he also observes that the 'Aramaizing construction (v. 7b) is evidence of the antiquity of the tradition'.[61] The parable pictures the 'elect' as under duress and as crying out to God for their vindication. Jesus promises that God will vindicate them ἐν τάχει. The application also relates this vindication to the coming of the Son of man in the question, 'When the Son of man comes, will he find faith in the earth?' This question is the conclusion of the teaching begun in Lk. 17.20 concerning the coming of the kingdom. 'Thus the context of the parable, of the Unjust Judge in Luke's Gospel is a discussion of the eschatological question (cf. also 19.11)'.[62]

It appears from these three pericopes that Luke sees prayer as tied to eschatological expectation.

---

57 The reading πνεῦμα ἅγιον is supported directly by 𝔓75, ℵ, A, B, C. K, W, X, Δ, Π, Ψ, Family 1 and Family 13, and many minuscules, lectionaries and ancient versions. Some variation of 'good gifts' is supported by citations mostly from Patristic authors: Cyril, Origen and Ambrose. The reading πνεῦμα ἅγιον is to be preferred.

58 Jeremias, *Parables*, p. 145.

59 Francis W. Beare, *The Earliest Records of Jesus* (Oxford: Basil Blackwell, 1962), p. 188.

60 Jeremias, *Parables*, p. 153.

61 Jeremias, *Parables*, p. 155.

62 Harris, 'Prayer in Luke–Acts', p. 91.

The Lukan references that represent the content of Jesus' prayers are also significant for this study. The most significant of these for our purposes is Lk. 10.21-24: the prayer of Jesus on the return of the seventy (two). Of particular importance is the statement that 'He rejoiced in the Holy Spirit'.[63] This prayer has the special distinction of having the Holy Spirit as its Agent or Instrument of worship: 'prayer is, in fact, complementary to the Spirit's activity since it is the point at which the communication of divine influence becomes effective for its recipients'.[64] This connection of the Holy Spirit and prayer is characteristic of Luke–Acts (Lk. 24.51-53; Acts 2.1-15; 4.31).

Another special characteristic of prayer shown here is the aspect of rejoicing, and its anticipation of the rule of God. The rejoicing is verbalized in the confession (ἐξομολόγησις) which follows. The confession refers to specific aspects of the divine rule and eschatological acts. The Father is 'my Father'.[65] he is 'Lord of heaven and earth' (cf. Lk. 11.2). The things of the kingdom are revealed by the sovereign will of God. The Son acts under the authority of the Father and is the Agent for the revelation of the Father's nature and will. This is the fulfillment of what the prophets and kings had wished to see, to know and to hear. The context and content of this prayer are thus seen as the eschatological realization of the OT message and hope.

The prayer of Jesus in Gethsemane is in part recorded by Luke (22.42). The eschatological nature of this prayer must be primarily derived from the situation in which it is placed in the life of Jesus. It occurs in a special place: Gethsemane on the Mount of Olives.[66] It occurs in the night of Jesus' arrest and on the eve of his crucifixion (cf. Lk. 9.22, 31, 51). This prayer is placed between two exhortations to the disciples that they should pray in order that they not enter into temptation (vv. 40, 46; cf. 11.4).

Jesus' commitment of his spirit to the Father (Lk. 23.46) may properly be designated as a prayer. This prayer is a part of the total

---

[63] 'Ἐν τῷ πνεύματι τῷ ἁγίῳ is supported by ℵ, D, Ξ, 1241, and by 𝔓[75] and B with the omission of ἐν. There are other less prestigious witnesses to this reading. Variations of this formula all indicating that it is the 'Holy Spirit' in which Jesus prays are abundant: C, K, Π, Family 1, L, ℵ, 33, *et al.*

[64] Lampe, 'The Holy Spirit in the Writings of St. Luke', p. 169; Weiss, *A Commentary on the New Testament*, II, p. 90.

[65] Jeremias, *Prayers*, pp. 56, 57; Ernst Lohmeyer, '*Our Father*' (trans. John Bowden; New York: Harper and Row, 1952), pp. 34, 35.

[66] Conzelmann, *The Theology of St. Luke*, pp. 58, 59.

eschatological setting and teaching of the cross. It represents Jesus' special relationship to the Father (πάτερ). Jesus is conscious of his mission from the Father, and now he goes to the Father; lying in the background of this agony is the overriding consciousness of the Father's approval and witness earlier recorded by Luke (3.22; 9.34, 35). This is a part of Luke's total use of the cross to represent Jesus' route to glory and accomplishment of purpose. This prayer anticipates Jesus' going to the Father and thus echoes Luke's 'exodus' concept. Two instances of Jesus' prayers appear in Luke that do not appear to serve the eschatological theme: Lk. 22.32 and 23.34.[67]

The theme of prayer which is set up by Luke in the period of Jesus' presence among the disciples is continued in the book of Acts. What is characteristic of Jesus' life and of his disciples at that time becomes characteristic of the church.[68]

During the life of Jesus, prayer stands in direct relationship to revelatory experiences (Lk. 3.21, 22; 9.18-20; 9.28-36). Such a connection is seen in the book of Acts. Prayer precedes the casting of lots for the divine election of a replacement for Judas (Acts 1.24-46).[69] The church, according to Luke, conceived of this method as a route of revelation and it entered this expectancy through prayer. This is also a characteristic common to other eschatological communities.[70]

Prayer is integral to the vision of Ananias and Saul in which the identities and missions of each were revealed to the other (Acts 9.10-12). Luke presents a similar relationship between the visions of Peter and Cornelius (Acts 10.1-4, 30, 9-16). Peter describes this experience in Acts 11.5; here Luke uses the phrase ἐν ἐκστάσει ὅραμα to characterize his experience. Paul relates that he received a revelation while in ecstasy (ἐν ἐκστάσει) following prayer (Acts 22.17, 18). An observation which Harris makes of 22.17, 18 would seem to be appropriate

---

67 This reading is not firmly established, though it seems to have sufficient evidence to be accepted. It is supported by a significant number of uncial witnesses: ℵ (original hand), A, C, D (2nd corrector), K (with εἶπεν instead of ἔλεγεν), L, X, Δ, Π, Ψ. Those manuscripts that omit it are 𝔓[75], apparently ℵ's first corrector, the first corrector of D, W and Θ.

68 Harris, 'Prayer in Luke–Acts', p. 92.

69 William A. Beardslee, 'The Casting of Lots at Qumran and in the Book of Acts', *Novum Testamentum* 4 (1960), pp. 249, 250.

70 Beardslee, 'The Casting of Lots at Qumran and in the Book of Acts', pp. 249, 250.

to all of these experiences: 'Prayer serves as a means by which God directs *Heilsgeschichte* as Luke conceives it'.[71]

Prayer is related to the descent of the Holy Spirit at Jesus' baptism (Lk. 3.21, 22). The pattern apparently developed from this is in evidence in the disciples' receiving the Holy Spirit in Acts. Following Jesus' ascension and his promise of the Holy Spirit, the disciples were continually (ἦσαν) in the temple blessing God (Lk. 24.53).[72] Acts 1.14 picks up the same pattern of prayer. Each stands between the ascension (as the origin of the disciples' hope) and Pentecost (as the focus of their hope according to Luke). This motif (Acts 1.14) 'prepares for the Pentecost account (2.1ff), i.e. for the gift of the Holy Spirit in the community'.[73] The relation of prayer to the presence of the Holy Spirit and recurrences of the Spirit's baptism continue in the life of the early church according to Luke (Acts 4.31; 8.15). In addition to this function of prayer in the receiving of the Holy Spirit, the life of the early church under the immediate influence of Pentecost was characterized by prayer (Acts 2.41-43). In this summary prayer is represented as 'typical of the early community's life... he (Luke) is emphasizing prayer as one of its characteristic features'.[74]

The connection between prayer and the Holy Spirit is significant because of the eschatological nature of the gift of the Holy Spirit. There is apparently a parallel between the manner in which the Holy Spirit descended on the disciples after Jesus' ascension. The fact that Jesus rejoiced 'in the Holy Spirit' (Lk. 10.21) suggests another parallel; such a description is appropriate to the manner in which Luke describes the normative experience in worship in Acts. Specific attention may also be called to the ecstatic experiences related to prayer (Acts 1.14, cf. 2.1-4; 10.9-20, cf. 11.5; 22.17). Life in this eschatological community is a life characterized by prayer, the presence of the Holy Spirit and special ecstatic experiences used for special revelations.

---

[71] Harris, 'Prayer in Luke–Acts', p. 170.

[72] 'Εὐλογοῦντες seems to be the best reading here; it is supported by 𝔓[75], א, B, C (original hand), L and several of the versions. Ἀινοῦντες καὶ εὐλογοῦντες has impressive support (particularly numerical), A, C (second corrector), K, W, X, Δ, Θ, Π, Ψ, Family 1 and Family 13 and a host of minuscules. It is the longer reading and is suspect as a later expansion; the fundamentally stronger support of the shorter reading would lead one to adopt it.

[73] Harris, 'Prayer in Luke–Acts', p. 118.

[74] Harris, 'Prayer in Luke–Acts', pp. 136, 137.

There is a parallel between Jesus' prayer prior to the appointment of the twelve and the fasting of the church at Antioch prior to the appointment of Barnabas and Saul by the Holy Spirit (Acts 13.1, 2). The church subsequently fasted and prayed and sent the two forth by the laying on of hands (13.3).

There is a specific parallel between the prayer of Jesus from the cross (Lk. 23.34) and the prayer of Stephen (Acts 7.60); the same parallel is in evidence between Lk. 23.46 and Acts 7.59. 'As Luke emphasized the idea of suffering in Jesus' messiahship, so he emphasizes the element of suffering in the early church. He is showing how Stephen follows his Lord to death.'[75]

There are doubtlessly more general parallel emphases between prayer in the life of Jesus and the community surrounding him and the community in Acts gathered around the work of the Holy Spirit. The basic point of application, however, is that each community is an eschatological community and that one of the routes of identification with and participation in this community is prayer. This is also the instrument for receiving the benefits of the eschatological kingdom. This is especially shown by the relationship of prayer to the descent of the Holy Spirit, ecstatic experience and revelation.

The precise order of the Transfiguration is that Jesus went into the mountain in order to pray, not in order to be transfigured. As he was praying, he was transfigured. Luke intends a causal relationship between the prayer and the Transfiguration. The Transfiguration is a revelatory experience; its specific revelation is the kingdom of God and the glory of Jesus in the kingdom.

The preceding discussion of prayer has shown two patterns. The first is that prayer is the route into the realization of the kingdom in personal experience and the route by which kingdom benefits are received. The second is that prayer is the instrument of entrance into special experiences of revelation.

On the first of these patterns we may note by way of summary the following: the Lord's prayer (Lk. 11.1-4), the exhortations which follow the Lord's prayer (Lk. 11.9-13), the eschatological expectations associated with the parable of the Unjust Judge (Lk. 18.1-8), Jesus' rejoicing in the Holy Spirit (Lk. 10.21-24), Jesus prayer from the cross

---

[75] Harris, 'Prayer in Luke–Acts', p. 158.

committing his own spirit to the Father (Lk. 23.46) and the descent of the Holy Spirit in the book of Acts (Acts 1.14; 2.1-4; 4.31; 8.15).

On the second of these patterns we may note by way of summary the following: the opening of the heavens and the revelation which followed Jesus' baptism (Lk. 3.21, 22), the choosing of the twelve under the Father's commission (Lk. 6.12-16), the confession of Peter and the announcement of the suffering of the Son of man (Lk. 9.18-22), the revelations that are alluded to after Jesus rejoiced in the Holy Spirit (Lk. 10.21-24), the revelation expected in the choosing of Judas' replacement (Acts 1.24-26), the revelation to Ananias and Saul (Paul) concerning each other (Acts 9.10-12) and the revelation concerning Peter and Cornelius (Acts 10.1-4, 30, 9-16).

Prayer, as it is introduced in Luke's account of the Transfiguration, follows the same pattern revealed throughout Luke–Acts. Prayer is the threshold of the Transfiguration. Prayer is here instrumental in revelation represented by the Transfiguration. It is also instrumental in proleptical translation into the glory of the kingdom of God.

3. Glory

The significance of the word 'glory'[76] for our inquiry is represented by the fact that this is the chief symbol of Jesus' changed appearance

[76] The background for Luke's use of this word is the OT in the Septuagint. In the OT there are three prominent periphrases for God: the Word, the Glory and the Shekinah (Kirk, *The Vision of God*, pp. 21, 22). Of these terms, Glory became representative of the visible presence of God (Kirk, *The Vision of God*, pp. 21, 22) and hence the form of divine revelation. The Hebrew word that most often stands behind the Greek word δόξα is כבוד. The NT follows this Septuagint use in representing the presence of God (1) by brightness, (2) by power and miracle working, (3) by saving power, and (4) by God-likeness (Brockington, 'The Septuagintal Background to the NT Use of Δόξα', p. 1). Isaiah 6; 60.1-3, and Ezekiel combine the glory of God with the manifestation of his holiness and righteousness. Ezekiel consistently represents divine glory as a 'fiery appearance' (Ramsey, *The Glory of God and the Transfiguration*, pp. 12-16). This glory is also the, 'standing accompaniment of all direct revelation from heaven' (Brockington, 'The Septuagintal Background to the NT Use of Δόξα', p. 3). It is this brightness that represents the whole character of God – his sovereignty, holiness, righteousness and power (Ramsey, *The Glory of God and the Transfiguration*, pp. 13, 14; Brockington, 'The Septuagintal Background to the New Testament Use of Δόξα', p. 4). The aim of revelation of God in his glory is the presentation of the power of God for redemption (Brockington, 'The Septuagintal Background to the New Testament Use of Δόξα', p. 4). It can be said on the basis of the Septuagint use of δόξα 'that the glory of God is the salvation of men, particularly the salvation of Israel' (Brockington, 'The Septuagintal Background to the New Testament Use of Δόξα', pp. 6, 7). The cognate verb δόξαζω is used to represent the acts of praise or worship in which God is

in the Lukan Transfiguration account. Luke strengthens this emphasis by describing Moses and Elijah as appearing in glory with Jesus. The concept of glory is finally climaxed by the appearance of the cloud at the end of the Transfiguration scene.

Building on the OT (Septuagint) use of δόξα, Luke employs this word to express the visible manifestation of God. It is the manifestation of divine revelation.

Salvation and light are equated with glory in Luke under the following circumstances. Luke 2.9 describes the glory of God shining around the shepherds at the announcement of Jesus' birth; the words of the angels include the words of exultation: Δόξα ἐν ὑψίστοις θεῷ (2.14). This same theme of exultation is picked up in the praise of the multitude to Jesus in the triumphal entry (Lk. 19.38).[77] Messiah, in Simeon's address to God, is described as 'your salvation'; this term is in turn equated with 'a light of revelation to the nations' and the 'glory of your people Israel' (Lk. 2.29-32). The sum of these references is that the manifestation of divine glory is a symbol of God's saving self-revelation.

There are two references in Luke that use the word δόξα of the appearance of the Son of man: 9.26 and 21.27. They are both Parousia sayings and they use the word δόξα to describe the coming of the Son of man. In the latter the manner of the Parousia is described: 'And then they shall see the Son of man coming in a cloud with power and great glory'. Luke 21.28, independently of the other synoptics,

---

'glorified' and of the works of divine power that 'glorify' the name of God (Brockington, 'The Septuagintal Background to the New Testament Use of Δόξα', p. 5).

These themes are picked up throughout the NT; our interest must be narrowed to Luke's use of the concept of glory. We may present these in summary here and develop those that are pertinent to the Transfiguration inquiry in the body of this study. The verb δοξάζω is used of an act of worship in all cases except one (Acts 3.13 in which Peter says 'God ... has glorified his son'.); note Lk. 2.20; 4.15; 5.25; 7.16; 13.13; 18.43; 23.47; Acts 4.21; 11.18; 13.48; 21.20. Luke usually reserves this word for sacred use. The use of the verb has bearing on the use of the noun. The noun is used as an exultation in worship or as a term descriptive of worship in the following places (Lk. 2.14; 17.18; 19.38; Acts 12.23 [where it is used of Herod's irreverence]). The noun is used to describe Messiah (Lk. 2.29-32; 24.26). It is used to describe the Son of man in his heavenly estate (Lk. 9.31, 32; 9.26; 21.27; Acts 22.11). Stephen describes God in his appearance to Abraham as the 'God of Glory' (Acts7.2) and later he is said to see the 'glory of God' (Acts 7.55). There are three references in which the term is used in the secular sense (Lk. 4.6; 12.27; 14.10)

[77] Brockington, 'The Septuagintal Background to the New Testament Use of Δόξα', p. 5.

makes this appearance of the Son of man a redemptive appearance. 'Glory', a symbol of divine revelation, is used to describe the appearance of the Son of man; it is also associated with redemption.

While he was in Mesopotamia, Abraham saw ὁ θεὸς τῆς δόξης (Acts 7.2). The appearance of glory is the manifestation in which God revealed himself to Abraham and separated him from his homeland to the land of promise. Luke draws from this reference a union of divine revelation and salvation under the symbol of glory. In the same context, Luke describes Stephen as seeing 'the glory of God and Jesus standing at the right hand of God' (v. 55). In v. 56, Stephen confesses 'I see ... the Son of man standing at the right hand of God'. This position of the Son of man is designed to show that he shares God's throne[78] and consequently his glory. Luke's intention is to attribute this glory to Jesus as the Son of man. Again, glory is depicted as the visible manifestation of God and it is also tied to deliverance (cf. vv. 59, 60).

Acts 22.11 represents one of Paul's descriptions of his conversion (Acts 9.3-9). He describes the revelation of the resurrected and ascended Lord in these terms: τῆς δόξης τοῦ φωτὸς ἐκείνου. This glory was the visible instrument of revelation to Paul (Saul). It was manifested for the purpose of his salvation. In this way revelation and redemption join in the common symbol of glory.

In these references two themes appear rather consistently in the manifestations of glory: revelation and redemption. Glory is the appearance of God when he makes himself known in special acts of revelation. The aim of that revelation is redemption.

Luke adds another dimension to his use of glory – the eschatological. It is evident in some of the passages just cited. Christ enters glory through sufferings (Lk. 24.26). Luke preserves this image of the glory of Jesus in the intermediate state between the ascension and the Parousia (Acts 7.55, 56; 9.3-7; 22.6-11; 26.12-17). In the conversion of Paul (Saul), Luke describes Jesus as manifesting himself from heaven in blinding and glorious light. This description is comparable to the description of the glory in which the Son of man comes (Lk. 9.26; 21.27).

---

[78] Haenchen, *Acts*, p. 183.

These uses of glory in Luke–Acts prepare us for an interpretation of glory as a motif in the Transfiguration.[79]

The glory that is ascribed to Jesus in this scene is the same glory that characterizes the appearance of the Son of man in his day (Lk. 17.24; 21.27, 28). It is the same glory that is ascribed to the ascended Lord who appears from heaven (Acts 7.55, 56; 9.3-9). It is the glory in which he shares the divine glory (Acts 7.55, 56). The symbolism intended here is the same as that intended in other places. The glory represents a special revelation of Jesus and one that is specifically a saving revelation.

The glory manifested here is the glory of the new age seen in the coming of the Son of man (Lk. 9.26; 21.27, 28).

In summary, the transfigured appearance of Jesus brings into a single scene most of the symbolism in Luke's use of δόξα: the instrument of divine saving self-revelation, the apocalyptic appearance of the Son of man which is also his intermediate heavenly appearance, and the visible instrument of revelation and salvation.

This is the glory of the reigning Messiah. The presentation of him in glory manifests Jesus as King. The glory is also reflected in the appearance of Moses and Elijah. It is the glorious reign of the Messiah which Peter, John, and James see, and which is represented by the story of the Transfiguration.

4. Ἔξοδος

We have seen in the exegesis the essential etymology and application of the word ἔξοδος. Our special interest here is to see how this word and the sentence in which it stands fit into the redactional scheme of Luke.

For Luke here, as in the rest of his writings, there is a strong Septuagint influence. His concept of 'exodus' relates to the deliverance of Israel from Egypt. This connects Jesus with Moses; 'like his namesake Joshua in the Old Testament he is Moses' successor, and as such accomplishes an exodus or deliverance'.[80] Though the connotation

---

[79] The glory manifested in the Transfiguration is not primarily a description of Jesus' preexistent glory breaking through the veil of the flesh. Luke's usual emphasis in the use of δόξα is future (Ramsey, *The Glory of God and the Transfiguration*, p. 29). Neither is this a manifestation of Jesus' glory to be seen after the resurrection and before the ascension (Thrall, 'Elijah and Moses', p. 310). There is no biblical account that can be cited to justify this conclusion.

[80] Leaney, *A Commentary on the Gospel of St. Luke*, p. 167.

of death is in this word and conversation, there is an overarching concept of deliverance: '... the Greek word for death (exodus) is one which carries overtones of Divine deliverance'.[81] In this word Luke is establishing a symbol of redemption.

With the Transfiguration account, we have the introduction of the travel narrative.[82] Transfiguration stands as a heading for that section and introduces the elements that are critical to the travel narrative: suffering, resurrection an ascension.[83] These events represent for Luke Jesus' departure from his disciples,[84] and they are epitomized in the word ἔξοδος.

The word suggests the pattern of a 'new exodus' to be defined by Luke in the travel narrative. The first exodus was a redemptive journey for Israel; hence, the application of this motif must have the 'new exodus' culminate in deliverance.[85]

The travel narrative seems to be cast in the typology of the exodus.[86] In the Transfiguration the words ἔξοδος and πληροῦν form a

---

[81] Caird, 'The Transfiguration', p. 291.

[82] Conzelmann, *The Theology of St. Luke*, p. 196. 'The complex of events formed by – the prophecy of the Passion – the Transfiguration marks the next main division ... In Luke it is the Transfiguration that forms the climax both as regards the order of events and their inner meaning.'

[83] Ellis, *The Gospel of Luke*, p. 142: 'It (ἔξοδος) probably includes the whole of Messiah's redemptive work: death, resurrection and ascension.'

[84] John Reumann, *Jesus in the Church's Gospels* (Philadelphia: Fortress Press, 1968), p. 368: 'It is surely significant that in presenting the transfiguration Luke speaks of the 'departure (ἔξοδος) which he (Jesus) was to accomplish at Jerusalem' (9.31) – i.e. He refers to the cross and resurrection'. Evans, 'The Transfiguration of Jesus', pp. 39, 40: Evans concludes that Luke (following the pattern of the 'Testament of Moses') places Jesus' death, resurrection, and ascension together with the entire travel section under the 'sign manual' of the word ἀνάλημψις.

[85] Caird, *The Gospel According to St. Luke*, p. 132: 'The Greek word which Luke uses for death is an unusual one – exodus; and it is clear that he used it because of its Old Testament associations with divine deliverance.'

[86] Evans, 'The Transfiguration of Jesus', pp. 37-53: In Lk. 9.51, 52 the keyword is ἀναλήμψεως, which is governed by the verb συμπληροῦσθαι. There is a parallel for this thought in the Transfiguration scene; the parallel words are ἔξοδος and πληροῦν respectively (Lk. 9.31). Both ἔξοδος and ἀναλήμψεως are to take place in Jerusalem under the motif of fulfillment.

The entire central section (the travel narrative) 'is placed under the sign of ἀνάλημψις' (p. 39). This corresponds to the Septuagint μετατιθέναι which is used to describe the translation of some of the saints of the OT; hence, it involves more than ascension.

In the 'Testament of Moses' the death of Moses is called ἀνάλημψις; this concept evolves to become the Assumption of Moses. The 'Testament of Moses' is a unit; the former expresses the thought of journey and goal, whereas the latter expresses (in combination with ἦν ἤμελλεν) necessity and fulfillment. Luke 9.51, 52 has a similar pair of words: ἀνάλήμψεως and συμπληροῦσθαι. These verses mark the point at which Jesus began his trek to Jerusalem.[87] The goal of this journey as represented throughout this section of Luke is Jerusalem with all that takes place there – death, resurrection, and the final step of ascension.

With this alignment of concepts, the word ἔξοδος takes on the meaning of deliverance in Luke. So the description of Jesus' death in Lk. 23.33-49 contains elements of redemption appropriate to these concepts. Jesus from the cross itself can promise the penitent thief, 'Verily I say to you, "Today, you will be with me in paradise"' (23.43). It is difficult to separate this promise from the context of Jesus' kingship, even though the words of kingship are on the lips of the thief. He asks a part in Jesus' kingdom and Jesus responds by promising him life in 'paradise'.[88] The image is that of a redeemer king in the pattern of the coming of the Son of man (Lk. 21.27, 28).

Luke connects the rending of the veil in the temple with the other extraordinary events that took place at the time of the crucifixion (Lk. 23.44, 45), though this event is common to the synoptics. This veil is the symbol of that by which all but the priests are barred from the most holy place – the place where redemption is accomplished. Luke introduces this without amplification (and so do the other synoptics). The symbolism of the veil represents the restrictive access to the Holy of Holies. The people were shut off from this place of most intimate worship and redemptive offering.

Hence, we judge Luke to be showing here that the death of Jesus is the opening of the way into redemption.[89] It is significant that this event immediately follows Jesus' promise to the thief. This is not specifically a doctrine of vicarious atonement; this question is not presented. It is, however, a doctrine of deliverance through Jesus' death.

Jewish supplement to Deuteronomy. In the same pattern, Luke places Jesus' death, resurrection and ascension into the entire travel section under the word ἀνάλημψις. The travel section is cast in the pattern of a 'Christian Deuteronomy'.

87 Evans, 'The Transfiguration of Jesus', pp. 39-50.

88 K. Schmidt, 'Βασιλεία', *TDNT*: 'The thief crucified with him asks the suffering and dying Messiah King to remember him when he comes εἰς τὴν βασιλείαν σου …' (Lk. 23.42).

89 Geldenhuys, *Commentary on the Gospel of St. Luke*, pp. 611, 616; that Luke is familiar with the temple services and symbolisms is evident in Lk. 1.5-11.

Luke does not include in his record of Jesus' death the agonizing cry ελωι ελωι λεμα σαβαχθανι (Mk 15.34: cf. Mt. 27.46). Luke alone of the gospel writers records the words of Jesus when he cried with a 'great voice: Father, into your hands I commit my spirit' (23.46).[90]

Luke intends to show that the death of Jesus was his own deliverance. He designates death as necessary in Jesus' path to glory in the words of Jesus to the Emmaus disciples (Lk. 24.26). The whole concept of 'exodus' embraces death as it does resurrection and ascension.

The necessity of the 'exodus' at Jerusalem is enforced by the clause ἣν ἤμελλεν πληροῦν. The clause expresses the necessity of divine appointment,[91] and it also carries an eschatological meaning.[92]

---

[90] As early as Lk. 2.22-32, Luke presented the idea of the redemption of Jesus. As the firstborn son, he must be presented to Yahweh (Exod. 13.1-15); this presentation was an act of redemption by sacrifice (Exod. 13.12, 13, 15). The prescribed redemption sacrifice is given in this same passage. The background of this ritual was the sentence of death upon the firstborn (in remembrance of the exodus from Egypt – Exod. 13.13). Every firstborn son had to be redeemed from this sentence. Luke presents Jesus' coming under these same conditions. Luke's citation of the OT basis for this ceremony indicates his familiarity with this aspect of the tradition. The fact that Luke does not develop the concept of vicarious atonement as a motif in his books may indicate that he did not understand the tradition which he cited or that this motif was not within his focus in presenting Jesus in his gospel.

It would seem to be significant, however, that the concept of redemption (λύτρωσις – ransom, redemption) is a significant motif in Luke 1 and 2. In the song of Zacharias God 'has overshadowed and made redemption for his people' (1.68). Anna spoke of Jesus 'to all who expected redemption in Jerusalem' (2.38).

This same condition and the necessity of Jesus' redemption under Jewish law is implied by his observing Passover (Lk. 2.41). The fact that Jesus was baptized places him in a condemned and restored relationship. John's baptism is the 'baptism of repentance for the remission (εἰς ἄφεσιν) of sins' (Lk. 3.3; Mk 1.4). In Luke (3.7-9) it is the multitude that is rebuked for presenting themselves for baptism without an acknowledgement of sin. Luke (3.10-14) follows with examples of penitence. The effect of this succession in Luke is to show that the approach to John's baptism demanded an acknowledgement of condemnation. Hence, baptism was symbolic of restoration. Jesus comes to be baptized within this consciousness of condemnation and consequent restoration. The concept of 'redeemed' as by substitutionary sacrifice is not here; however, the idea of 'redeemed' in the sense of restoration is here.

These references do not constitute a development of Luke's concept of ἔξοδος issuing into redemption. They do, I think, show a redemption motif early in the book of Luke.

[91] BAG, p. 677: 'Its (πληρόω) use here implies that Jesus' death is in some way a fulfillment of his mission'.

[92] Delling, 'Πληρόω': 'The characteristic feature of the NT concept of the fulfillment of God's Word is the eschatological content'.

It is frequently used for the fulfillment of Scripture, including the fulfillment of OT types.[93] In Peter's sermon on the day of Pentecost the necessity of Jesus' death is combined with Peter's accusation of the Jews for the murder of Jesus (Acts 2.23).

From the point of the Transfiguration this necessity of fulfillment in Jerusalem dominates Luke's gospel. ἔξοδος is a necessity of Jesus' mission. The noun is governed by the infinitive πληροῦν. When Luke formally begins the 'travel narrative', he uses the word ἀναλήμψις to represent Jesus' goal; in order to indicate divine appointment, he uses the infinitive συμπληροῦσθαι ἀνάλήμψεως to govern ἀναλήμψις.[94] This theme of necessity appears in Lk. 13.31-35. Jesus insists (against the warning of the Pharisees) πλὴν δεῖ με σήμερον καὶ αὔριον καὶ τῇ ἐχομένῃ πορεύεσθαι (v. 33a). The third day is representative of Jesus' fulfillment of purpose as v. 32 shows: καὶ τῇ τρίτῃ τελειοῦμαι. The necessary fulfillment was the death of Jesus in Jerusalem. The dependent clause ὅτι οὐκ ἐνδέχεται προφήτην ἀπολέσθαι ἔξω Ἰερουσαλήμ is governed grammatically by δεῖ; hence the necessity of Jesus' dying and of his dying in Jerusalem are affirmed here.[95]

Luke combines these themes in two accounts of the ascension. In Lk. 24.44-53 the words of the resurrected Jesus are placed just before the record of the ascension. It is necessary (δεῖ) that 'all things written concerning me in the law of Moses and in the prophets and in the psalms be fulfilled' (v. 44). This necessity included the Messiah's suffering and resurrection from the dead on the third day (v. 46). Another necessity announced here is that remission of sins be preached to all nations in his name (v. 47).[96] This is the necessity of divine appointment as it was revealed in the Scriptures: hence, the appeal to

---

93 BAG, p. 677.

94 Evans, 'The Central Section of Luke's Gospel', pp. 37, 38; Lampe, 'The Holy Spirit in the Writings of St. Luke', pp. 181-82.

95 Pilgrim, 'The Death of Christ in Lukan Soteriology', p. 121:

> The idea of a divine task or mission receives its clearest statement ... verse 33. A divine imperative necessitates his journey to Jerusalem and the fate which awaits him. The δεῖ does not originate out of the fact that Jerusalem was the geographical site of his death, but arises out of the pre-determined plan of God. Jesus must die in Jerusalem.

96 There is a series of initiatives of purpose here that justifies this conclusion grammatically: 'παθεῖν τὸν χριστὸν καὶ ἀναστῆναι ... καὶ κηρυχθῆναι ...' BDF, §390.

Moses, the prophets and Psalms. These are encapsulated in the clause οὕτως γέγραπται (v. 46).

The joining of the necessity of preaching remission of sins to the necessity of the Messiah's resurrection brings together the theme of deliverance and the 'exodus' of Jesus.

Following these words, Jesus gave the promise of the Father (enduement with power – the Holy Spirit [v. 49]), led the disciples to Bethany, blessed them and departed from them (vv. 50, 51).

Luke begins the book of Acts by a recapitulation of those things recorded in Lk. 24.44-52 (Acts 1.1-11). The 'first book' to Theophilus covered the work and teachings of Jesus until the day he was 'taken up' (ἀνελήμφθη) (vv. 1, 2). The authority which comes from God's confirmation of the Son and the commandment 'Hear him' (Lk. 9.35) seems to be presupposed by Luke's here relating that Jesus gave commandments to the apostles whom he had chosen (v. 2). The authority lies in the fact that Jesus had died, had been raised from the dead and is now about to be taken up into heaven. All of the components of the 'exodus' are here brought together.

Jesus, after the suffering, shows himself alive 'in many sure signs' (v. 3a). In this period, he spoke to them the things concerning the kingdom of God (v. 3b).

Verse 4 introduces two aspects of the kingdom that are specifically eschatological: the eating together[97] and the promise of the Holy Spirit (vv. 4, 5, 8). This order is significant: It is the crucified and resurrected Lord who now stands at the threshold of the ascension (the Messiah who enters his glory through sufferings [Lk. 24.26]) who gives the promise of the Holy Spirit. After the promise of the Holy Spirit, Jesus commanded the apostles to be witnesses (v. 8); then, he ascended, and a cloud received him from the eyes of the apostles. The two heavenly messengers (ἄνδρες δύο) described the ascension with these words: ὁ Ἰησοῦς ὁ ἀναλημφθεὶς (v. 11).

This comparison of the Transfiguration with the ascension brings together all of the components in Luke's meaning of the word 'exodus'. These components (death, resurrection and ascension) are not separate events. They are brought together and unified in the Transfiguration. The Transfiguration accomplishes this unification by

[97] Davies, 'The Prefigurement of the Ascension in the Third Gospel', p. 230: συναλιζόμενος. Cf. Haenchen, *Acts*, p. 141 n. 3.

bringing suffering and glory together in one scene and in the Person of Jesus. It is Jesus in his kingly glory who receives the message of his exodus (inclusive of its sufferings) and also the necessity of it. In the ascension accounts, it is the resurrected Jesus who brings these together in his instruction to the disciples at Emmaus (Lk. 24.26) and at Jerusalem (Lk. 24.46, 47; Acts 1.3-11). The Transfiguration, then, not only presents the kingdom of God; it also presents the route by which the kingdom of God is brought to its fulfillment.

5. The kingdom of God proleptically presented in the Transfiguration scene

It is here that all of the components of the kingdom are drawn together and presented in one scene. The Shekinah in its descent on Mt. Sinai constituted the people of Israel as the people of God; they are designated as the 'kingdom of priests' and 'a holy nation' (Exodus 19. 5, 6). In the Transfiguration's appeal to the Sinai tradition, the same sense of the kingdom of God is conveyed. By placing Peter, John, and James under a common 'tabernacle' with Moses and Elijah, the narrative of the Transfiguration incorporates them into the same kingdom with the transfigured Jesus.

The 'exodus' must take place and it must occur in Jerusalem. Luke cannot conceive of the kingdom or the exaltation of the King without 'exodus'. In this sense and in the sense of divine appointment the 'exodus' of Jesus is already accomplished.[98]

In the Transfiguration, Jesus has already been glorified. He has crossed the barrier between mortality and immortality and stands in the transfigured form of the eternal kingdom.[99] This is the form in which he appears in all of the post-ascension scenes in the book of Acts: in heaven itself (Acts 7.55-60) and from heaven (Acts 9.3-9). The glory in which Jesus appears here is the glory ascribed to the Son of man in his coming.

The representation of the kingdom by the symbol of glorification is carried further by the glory that is ascribed to Moses and Elijah. The fact that they appear with Jesus helps to distinguish this scene from a Parousia scene. The Parousia is always described as public (Lk. 17.24; 21.27). The Son of man always appears alone in the Parousia (Lk. 12.39, 40: 17.24; 21.27). Moses and Elijah do not accompany the

---

[98] Evans, 'The Transfiguration of Jesus', p. 103.
[99] Evans, 'The Transfiguration of Jesus', p. 103.

Son of man in his coming, but they are doubtless among the prophets of the OT who gather for the eschatological meal in the kingdom of God (Lk. 13.28). They are identified with Jesus in the kingdom. We have concluded earlier that the Transfiguration depicts the kingdom a step beyond the Parousia. This conclusion would seem to be enhanced by these observations.

In Jesus, the prophets, and the disciples, we have a representation of the kingdom of God: 'There is the splendor of the glorified Redeemer, whose redeeming death, not yet accomplished, is spoken of between him and the representatives of the past economies of the kingdom; and there are the three apostles as representing the subjects of the kingdom'.[100]

The inclusion of Peter, John, and James in the kingdom is represented dramatically by their being enveloped in the Shekinah. So, they not only see the kingdom; they enter it in this spiritual experience. This envelopment in the Shekinah is represented by the word ἐπισκιάζω (which is common to the synoptics). Luke, however, in Lk. 1.35 makes a special and connected use of the word in the angel's description of the descent of the Holy Spirit on Mary: καὶ δύναμις ὑφίστου ἐπισκιάσει σοι.[101] In 1.35 it is specifically the 'power from above' (the Holy Spirit) that tabernacles upon Mary and by this tabernacling produces the Redeemer. 'Επισκιάζω carries the meaning of the divine presence. In the Transfiguration the symbol for 'tabernacling' is the cloud (the Shekinah).

Luke combines the Sinai-Shekinah motif with an eschatological cloud motif. This is not uniquely Lukan. Luke does, however, reinforce and interpret this motif by his other uses of νεφέλη in Luke–Acts. By his use of the singular noun, he seems to unify all references to the cloud.[102] Though Luke does not seek to conform precisely to Dan. 7.13 (which has the plural 'clouds'), he is appealing to the Jewish

100 Rowe, 'The Transfiguration', p. 33.

101 Lampe, 'The Holy Spirit in the Writings of St. Luke', pp. 167-68: 'It is highly significant that St. Luke here (1.35) employs the same word which is used in the Common Synoptic narrative to describe the overshadowing of Jesus and the disciples by the cloud at the Transfiguration'.

102 Luke 21.27 has the singular; its synoptic parallels have the plural. Acts 1.9 uses the singular in describing the ascension. All the Transfiguration accounts use the singular.

apocalyptic idea.[103] The cloud in Luke does not perform the same function that the clouds perform in Daniel. The cloud here does not present the Son of man to the Ancient of Days. The symbolism does fit into the same eschatological idea. The particular idea in Daniel is the presentation of the Son of man to the Ancient of Days, from whom the Son of man receives an everlasting dominion, glory and an indestructible kingdom (Dan. 7.13, 14).

Luke uses νεφέλη in two eschatological functions: as a Parousia symbol (Acts 1.9; Lk. 21.27), and as a symbol of divine witness to Jesus (Lk. 9.35).

The cloud and the voice of witness in the Transfiguration are to be distinguished from the Parousia.[104] We come to this conclusion for the following reasons. First, Moses and Elijah are not represented in the traditions as appearing concomitantly with the Messiah. The NT does not represent Moses as accompanying the Messiah. The role that is ascribed to Elijah is always that of forerunner and not that of an attendant.

Second, Jesus is not here represented as coming on the cloud (as may be implied by Acts 1.11). The cloud here is the representation of the presence of God in witness to Jesus as the 'elected Son'. This witness function is out of the Sinai tradition and is also eschatological.

Third, the voice of witness is appropriate to the consummation of all things by the declaration of Jesus' divine sonship.

Fourth, the command, 'Hear him', gives Jesus' words the authority of divine words.

The first two of these reasons have been discussed in the exegesis. The last two need additional study at this point. In order to do this, we observe the setting in which this witness occurs and the meaning of the witness. The first of these lays the groundwork for the second.

The characteristics of this scene already noted identify it as a kingdom setting. It presents the glory of the King and the constituents of his kingdom. This is the glory in which Jesus is always presented in Luke–Acts after the Ascension. Additionally, the Voice from

---

103 Ramsey, *The Glory of God and the Transfiguration*, p. 109; Lohmeyer, 'Die Verklärung Jesu', pp. 185-215.

104 Contra: Caird, *The Gospel According to St. Luke*, pp. 291-92; Davies, 'The Prefigurement of the Ascension in the Third Gospel', p. 232; Boobyer, *St. Mark and the Transfiguration Story*; Ramsey, *The Glory of God and the Transfiguration.*

heaven is Jesus' acclamation as King. We have already observed a converging of the titles 'Son', 'Messiah', and 'King' in the consciousness of Judaism in the pre-Christian era. This was reflected in subsequent literature.[105] There is a similar union of sonship and messianic kingship in the Qumran literature. J.M. Allegro offers the following translation of 4Q Florilegium:

> (And) the Lord (tel)ls you that he will build a house for you, and I will set up your seed after you, and I will establish his royal throne (Foreve)r I (will be) to him as a Father, and he will to me as a son. He is the shoot of David, who will arise with the Interpreter of the Law, who ...[106]

The term 'son of God' is a title for a Jewish messianic king. The announcement of that title is in some sense an announcement of enthronement. This is true in Jesus' baptism when he begins his ministry and begins by the authority of the divine witness to gather his kingdom. It is true in the Transfiguration when Jesus is seen in the culmination of the kingdom, which is his enthronement in glory. 'Jesus' enthronement, which was announced to him at baptism, is now seen proleptically in the apocalyptic vision granted to the inner circle of his followers.'[107]

This is consistent with the manner in which Luke pictures Jesus in the post-ascension scene in Acts. The giving of the Holy Spirit is Peter's supreme proof of the Father's exaltation of Jesus to his own right hand (Acts 2.33). This position is an enthronement position: 'Jesus, sitting at God's right hand shares his throne'.[108] It is this act that is explained in v. 36; the exaltation designated Jesus both Lord and Christ.

---

105 Buchanan, *Hebrews*, pp. 13, 14; *TDNT*, 'παῖς θεοῦ', by Jeremias, v: 654-717; Riesenfeld, *Jésus Transfiguré*, pp. 269-70.

106 J.M. Allegro, 'Further Messianic References In Qumran Literatue', *JBL* 75 (1956), p. 176.

107 Kee, 'The Transfiguration in Mark', p. 149.

108 Haenchen, *Acts*, p. 183. Hahn, *The Titles of Jesus in Christology*, p. 106: 'In this way (i.e. by the use of the LXX text in Ps. 110.1) the kyrios title became embedded in the context of the idea of exaltation'. 'Accordingly, it is thought, Jesus did not first enter on his kingly office at the end of the age, after a period of temporary reception into heaven, but was enthroned before the heavenly powers immediately after his ascension into heaven, and therewith took over his royal functions' (p. 169).

The vision of Stephen depicts Jesus in glory (Acts 7.54-56). Stephen saw the glory of God and Jesus standing at the right hand of God (v. 55). In consequence of this vision, Stephen designates Jesus as the Son of man (v. 56). The witness of Jesus' glory in Saul's conversion (Acts 9.3-9; 22.6-11; 26.12-17) warrants the designation of Jesus as Lord (9.5; 22.8; 26.15).

The command ('Hear him'; cf. Deut. 18.15, 18) underlines 'the eschatological aspects of Jesus' kingship'[109] with the concept of the messianic King.[110]

In this section we have attempted to show that the Transfiguration was described in Luke as a presentation of the kingdom of God. This is the fashion in which the kingdom will appear at the end of the age, but this presentation does not close out this age. It was a presentation of the kingdom to Peter, John, and James and an envelopment of them in it that did not remove them from this world order – the time and space restrictions of mortality. In the moments of the Transfiguration scene and particularly in the moment of the Shekinah they were in the kingdom.

The physical presence of Jesus in the Transfiguration is of central importance to Peter, John, and James. They had accompanied him to the mountain and had seen his natural appearance transcended by the glorious, but they still identified the glorious appearance with the physical presence of Jesus. This is also confirmed by Jesus' return to natural appearance after the Transfiguration.

It is this personal presence of Jesus that made the Transfiguration experience possible for the disciples. It was the recollection of the promise of Lk. 9.27 that gave interpretation to the Transfiguration.

The Relation of the Transfiguration Account to the Ascension Accounts

This study has attempted to show that Lk. 9.27 and the Transfiguration represent the kingdom of God established (consummated) rather than the kingdom of God coming (Parousia). The Parousia is the appearance of the Son of man initiating the apocalyptic events that close out this world order (Lk. 21.27, 28).

---

109 Kee, 'The Transfiguration in Mark', p. 149.

110 See Chapter 3, p. 127, esp. note 165.

The kingdom consummated follows the Parousia. This consummation is dependent on the gathering of its constituents at the Parousia (Lk. 21.28) and the final judgement (Lk. 13.26-29). This consummated kingdom is gathered around the Messiah in the messianic meal (Lk. 13.28, 29). The Transfiguration depicts the kingdom of God gathered around the exalted Messiah – a view of the kingdom a step beyond the Parousia.

The literary and content parallels between the Transfiguration account (Lk. 9.28-36) and the Ascension accounts (Lk. 24.50-53; Acts 1.1-11) suggest that these are companion pericopes. This is quite generally accepted along with the conclusion that both anticipated the Parousia.[111]

The latter part of this conclusion is open to question. In order to show the basis of my reservation here, it will be helpful to show the similarities and contrasts between Luke's Transfiguration account and his ascension accounts.

In the exegesis, we have shown the similarities between Lk. 24.46-53 and Acts 1.4-14. These may be seen graphically in the following chart from Davies:[112]

PARALLELS BETWEEN LUKE 24 AND ACTS 1

Luke 24.46-53	Acts 1.4-14
46 εἶπεν αὐτοῖς	7 εἶπεν πρὸς αὐτούς
48 ὑμεῖς μάρτυρες	8 ἔσεσθέ μου μάρτυρες
47 καὶ κηρυχθῆναι... εἰς πάντα τὰ ἔθνη, –	
ἀρξάμενοι ἀπὸ Ἰερουσαλήμ	ἔν τε Ἰερουσαλὴμ καὶ ἐν πάσῃ τῇ Ἰουδαίᾳ καὶ Σαμαρίᾳ καὶ ἕως ἐσχάτου τῆς γῆς
49 καὶ ἰδοὺ ἐγὼ ἐξαποστέλλω τὴν ἐπαγγελίαν τοῦ πατρός	4 περιμένειν τὴν ἐπαγγελίαν τοῦ πατρὸς

[111] Davies, 'The Prefigurement of the Ascension in the Third Gospel', p. 230, p. 232; J.G. Davies, he *Ascended into Heaven* (London: Lutterworth Press, 1958), p. 41: '... but St. Luke also affirms that the latter (Parousia) is foreshadowed by the Ascension; if therefore the Transfiguration was a pre-figurement of the Parousia, it must logically be a prefigurement of the Ascension too, and as such it is presented in the third gospel'. Boobyer, *St. Mark and the Transfiguration Story*; Ramsey, *The Glory of God and the Transfiguration.*

[112] Davies, he *Ascended into Heaven*, p. 187.

ὑμεῖς δὲ καθίσατε ἐν τῇ πόλει ἕως οὗ ἐνδύσησθε ἐξ ὕψους δύναμιν	παρήγγειλεν αὐτοῖς ἀπὸ Ἱεροσολύμων μὴ χωρίζεσθαι 8 λήμψεσθε δύναμιν ἐπελθόντος τοῦ ἁγίου πνεύματος ἐφ' ὑμᾶς
50 Ἐξήγαγεν δὲ αὐτοὺς ἕως πρὸς Βηθανίαν	12 ἀπὸ ὄρους τοῦ καλουμένου Ἐλαιῶνος, ὅ ἐστιν ἐγγὺς Ἰερουσαλὴμ σαββάτου ἔχον ὁδόν
51 διέστη ἀπ' αὐτῶν καὶ ἀνεφέρετο εἰς τὸν οὐρανόν	9 βλεπόντων αὐτῶν ἐπήρθη, καὶ νεφέλη ὑπέλαβεν αὐτὸν 10 ... εἰς τὸν οὐρανὸν
52 καὶ αὐτοὶ... ὑπέστρεψαν εἰς Ἰερουσαλὴμ	12 Τότε ὑπέστρεψαν εἰς Ἰερουσαλὴμ
53 καὶ ἦσαν διὰ παντὸς ἐν τῷ ἱερῷ εὐλογοῦντες τὸν θεόν	14 οὗτοι πάντες ἦσαν προσκαρτεροῦντες ὁμοθυμαδὸν τῇ προσευχῇ

The two pericopes have a common core of material and reveal common traditions. What is recorded in Lk. 24.46-53 is recapitulated and expanded in Acts 1.1-11. These two pericopes form the transitional material from the gospel to Acts.

The more important comparison is the comparison of Lk. 9.27-36 and Acts 1.1-12.[113] Davies has broadened the comparison to include Lk. 9.1-34 and Acts 1.1-12. He has interpreted this comparison more fully in the article cited earlier.[114]

An exegesis in resumé of Acts 1.1-12 will be helpful.

Two textual problems present themselves: in v. 9 (εἰπὼν βλεπόντων αὐτῶν ἐπήρθη καὶ νεφέλη ὑπέλαβεν αὐτὸν) and in v. 11

113 I have chosen the verses above for specific reasons. Luke 9.27-36 is chosen in conformity with our earlier exegesis of the Transfiguration. Acts 1.1-12 is chosen because all of this material is necessary to the comparison.

114 Davies, 'The Prefigurement of the Ascension in the Third Gospel'.

(εἰς τὸν οὐρανόν following ἀφ' ὑμῶνa). The text as accepted in *The Greek New Testament* is the preferable text both in v. 9[115] and in v. 11.[116]

The question of συναλιζόμενος (v. 4) is more a lexical problem than a textual one.[117] The question concerns the choice between καὶ συναλιζόμενος, παρήγγειλεν, and συναυλιζόμενος.

Συναλιζόμενος seems the better choice for two reasons: the textual evidence and meanings of the two words in question. The adoption of συναλιζόμενος is supported by 'all known uncial manuscripts, with the possible exception of D, and the overwhelming majority of the minuscule manuscripts'.[118] Συναυλιζόμενος is supported by 'about thirty-five minuscule manuscripts ... as well as many patristic witnesses'.[119] It is also supported by many of the ancient versions. Συναυλιζόμενος means 'lit(erally) spend the night with, then also gener(ally) be with, stay with'.[120] This idea is incongruent with the Luke–Acts record of the resurrection appearances of Jesus.[121]

---

115 The text in v. 9 is supported by ℵ[1], A, B. (εἰπὼν αὐτῶν βλεπόντων), C, E, Ψ, 049, 056, 0142, a host of minuscules, the Byzantine lectionaries and many of the ancient versions. ℵ[C] supports this reading except for the form εἰπόντων instead of εἰπὼν. The evidence for the text as presented has the overwhelming manuscript support. This choice is further enhanced by the fact that it is the more difficult of the two readings.

116 The text as presented here is supported by: ℵ, A, B, C, E, Ψ, 049, 056, 0142, 33, 81, 88, 104, 181, 326 (margin), 330, 436, 451, 614, 629, 630, 945, 1241, 1505, 1739, 1877, 2127, 2412, and 2492, the Byzantine lectionaries, most of the Old Latin, the Vulgate, a number of the versions and of the Church Fathers.

The number and value of witnesses for this reading are almost overwhelming for its adoption. It is burdened, however, by appearing to be an accidental inclusion by copyists because of the frequency of this ending in the context.

All things considered, it seems best to adopt the reading of the text as presented: cf. Metzger, *A Textual Commentary on the Greek New Testament*, p. 283.

117 Metzger, *A Textual Commentary on the Greek New Testament*, pp. 278-79.

118 Metzger, *A Textual Commentary on the Greek New Testament*, pp. 278-79: 'The Committee agreed that the manuscript evidence requires the adoption of the reading συναλιζόμενος'.

119 Metzger, *A Textual Commentary on the Greek New Testament*, pp. 278-79: This reading is also adopted by the following modern scholars: H.J. Cadbury and Kirsopp Lake, and as the text of RSV; cf. BAG, p. 791: 'So HJ Cadbury, *JBL* 45, '26, 310-17; K Lake; RSV text – On the whole question cf. also CC Torrey, *The Composition and Date of Acts*, '16, 23f.'

120 BAG, p. 791.

121 These appearances are in the nature of appearances at specific places and times to witnesses appointed beforehand by God (Acts 10.40, 41). The resurrected Jesus did not dwell in a given place to become the subject of merely human witnesses chosen by human initiations and curiosity.

Συναλίζομαι cannot be narrowed to one meaning. Bauer, Arndt and Gingrich give the following distinctions: συναλίζω eat (salt) with ... συνᾶλίζω bring together, assemble, pass(ive) come together ...'[122] The first of these two meanings is preferred by a number of modern scholars: E. Haenchen,[123] O. Cullmann,[124] and J.G. Davies.[125] This meaning is congruent with other instances of meetings of the risen Jesus with witnesses[126] to his resurrection (Lk. 24.43; Acts 10.41). The Lukan motif of the sacral meal adds weight to this choice of meanings.

The passage before us suggests the following outline: Luke's introduction of his book (vv. 1, 2); the appearance of the resurrected Jesus (vv. 3-5); the apostles' apocalyptic expectations and Jesus' answer (vv. 6-8); the ascension of Jesus (vv. 9-11); and the return of the apostles to Jerusalem (v. 12).

The progression and the content show affinity with the Transfiguration (Lk. 9.27-36) and its context. The specific ideas that may be seen in these vv. (without spreading into the entirety of Luke 9) are: the esoteric revelation at a meeting between Jesus and the apostles whom he had chosen (τοῖς ἀποστόλοις ... οὓς ἐξελέξατο); the revelation concerning the kingdom of God (τὰ περὶ τῆς βασιλείας τοῦ θεοῦ); the orientation toward Jerusalem (vv. 4, 8, 12); the apocalyptic expectation of the disciples and the provocation of Jesus' corrective answer (vv. 6, 7); the lifting up of Jesus (cf. ἔξοδος and ἀναλαμβάνω: vv. 2, 11); the cloud (v. 9); and two men (καὶ ἰδοὺ ἄνδρες δύο ... ἐν ἐσθήσεσι λευκαῖς: v. 10).

The prologue of Acts is a genuine Lukan composition and a continuation of Luke's purposes of narrative in the gospel. These verses recapitulate and serve a transitional purpose. 'In a few words (v. 1) he summarizes the contents of his former volume.'[127]

---

122 BAG, p. 791; Metzger, *A Textual Commentary on the Greek New Testament*, p. 278.

123 Metzger, *A Textual Commentary on the Greek New Testament*, p. 278 n. 3.

124 Oscar Cullmann, *Early Christian Worship* (trans. A.S Todd and J.B. Torrance; Chicago: Henry Regnery, 1953), p. 16.

125 Davies, he *Ascended into Heaven*, p. 187.

126 Haenchen, *Acts*, p. 141 n. 3.

127 W.C. van Unnik, 'The "Book of Acts" The confirmation of the Gospel', *Novum Testamentum* 4 (1960), p. 29; this assumption is basic to J.G. Davies' position (*He Ascended into Heaven*, pp. 42, 187, and 'The Prefigurement of the Ascension', pp. 229-33); contra the following authors cited by van Unnik, p. 30 nn. 1, 2, 3: Ph.

Verses 1 and 2 are designed to show that Luke intended his first book (πρῶτον λόγον) to embrace the record of Jesus up through the point of the ascension (ἀνελήμφθη). The introduction of this word connects specifically with Luke's scheme of the 'travel narrative' (Lk. 9.51).[128] This word signals the consummation of those things that must take place in Jerusalem which also equal Jesus' 'exodus'.

In v. 2, Luke recognizes the apostleship as the men elected of Jesus through the Holy Spirit[129] and as the special recipients of Jesus' commandments ἐντειλάμενος τοῖς ἀποστόλοις. Luke's frame of reference here is established on two parameters: (1) the esoteric nature of the commandments and (2) the eschatological nature of the company to which the commandments are delivered.

Verses 3-5 relate the purposes of the appearance of the resurrected Lord: (1) the demonstration of the resurrection (v. 3a '... to whom (i.e. the Apostles) he presented himself living after his suffering'), and (2) the speaking of 'the things concerning the kingdom of God' (v. 3b).

The first of these purposes is thematic with Luke; he establishes continuity between the suffering state and the resurrected state. He also establishes identity of person; the one who suffers is the one who is risen. According to Luke, Jesus established this by many decisive proofs.[130] The witnessing of these appearances is an essential credential of apostleship (Acts 1.22). According to this account these

---

Menoud, 'Remarques sur lies textes de l'ascension dans Luc-Actes' in: Bultmann-Festschrift, pp. 148ff; E. Norden, *Agnostos Theos* (Leipzig 1913, s. 312; K. Lake, in *Beginnings of Christianity*, V, pp. 1ff. For a summary of the literature on this question see Jacques Dupont, *The Sources of the Acts* (trans. Kathleen Pond; New York: Herder & Herder, 1964), pp. 24, 25 n. 22.

128 Evans, 'The Central Section of Luke's Gospel', pp. 39-42; Francis W. Beare, *The Earliest Records of Jesus* (New York-Nashville: Abingdon, 1962), p. 246.

129 Haenchen, *Acts*, pp. 138, 139: 'διὰ πνεύματος ἁγίου relates to the succeeding phrase, the choice of the apostles'. Cf. F.J. Foakes Jackson and Kirsopp Lake, *The Beginnings of Christianity: The Acts of the Apostles* (London: Macmillan and Co., 1932; Grand Rapids: Baker Bk; reprint edn, 1965), IV, p. 3, 'The Greek makes it obscure whether the writer means that Jesus was inspired in his choice of the apostles ..., or in the commands which he gave them ...'

130 BAG, p. 815: 'Sylloge Inscriptionum Graecarum, ed. Dittenberger, 867, 37 ... with reference to Artemis 685, 84 ...; Acts 1.3 (cf Jos. Ant. 5, 39 ... Ant. 17, 128)'. Jackson and Lake, *The Beginnings of Christianity*, p. 17: 'According to Luke and John the risen Lord had the same body as was buried and it still consisted of flesh and blood (Luke XXIV. 39; John XX. 27ff.)'.

appearances covered a period of forty days in which the risen Jesus was seen[131] intermittently[132] by the apostles.

The second of these purposes strengthens the bond between the gospel and Acts. 'This (περὶ πάντων ... ὧν ἤρξατο ὁ 'Ιησοῦς ποιεῖν τε καὶ διδάσκειν, v. 1b) is intended to call to the reader's mind the many references to the kingdom in the Gospel'.[133] This phrase is forward-looking as well; it covers not only what Luke had written under that banner in the gospel, but also what was to be written in Acts under the same banner (Acts 1.3, 6; 8.12; 14.22; 19.8; 20.25; 28.23, 31). The present-future tension is also continued from the gospel into Acts.

Central to the things of the kingdom of God is the promise of the Holy Spirit[134] which is here designated as the 'promise of the

---

131 BAG, p. 580, 'ὀπτάνομαι a new present formed fr. the aor. pass. ὤφθην 'I let myself be seen'. 'I appeared".'; BDF §101: ὁρᾶν; Jackson and Lake, *The Beginnings of Christianity*, p. 4: This word 'merely means 'was visible', and ... the etymological connexion with ὀπτασία cannot be pressed (cf. Zahn ad loc.)'.

132 BDF §223.1: 'A 1.3 ... during 40 days (not continuously, but now and then)'.

133 Farrell, 'The Eschatological Perspective of Luke–Acts', pp. 175, 176.

134 In Lk. 11.13 the juxtaposition of δόματα ἀγαθα with πνεῦμα ἅγιον identifies these with each other. Τὰ ἄγαθα is a semitism designating the gifts of the messianic age (Jeremias, *Parables*, p. 145); here the Holy Spirit is designated as the gift of the Father: This concept of the gift of the Father is taken up in Acts 1.4 and 2.33. This gift (the Holy Spirit) performs in the church the functions of the earthly Jesus among the apostles. This may be shown by the manner in which Luke describes the sending out of Barnabas and Paul (Saul) in Acts 13, 14. He describes this mission in the pattern of the sending out of the 70 (72) in Lk. 10.1-21. The comparison is shown below. The basis of this comparison is not parallels in vocabulary or literary form but a comparison of the inception, progress, and conclusion of the missions described.

Luke 10	Acts 13
v. 1 The Lord sent out the 70 (72) two by two.	v. 2 The Holy Spirit separated 2 men for this mission.
v. 2 The lord exhorted the disciples to pray that the Lord of the harvest would send workers.	v. 3 When the church had fasted and prayed they sent Barnabas and Paul (Saul) out.
v. 3 The 70 (72) were sent out by the commission of Jesus	v. 4 Barnabas and Paul (Saul) were sent forth by the Holy Spirit.
vv. 3-16 In his commission of the 70 (72) Jesus gave them authority to: pronounce peace on those who received them (vv. 5-7), heal the sick (v. 9a),	13.4 – 14.26 The Mission of Barnabas and Paul (Saul) followed many of these patterns: They healed the sick (14.8-10). They exhorted their hearers

Father'. This promise here is placed in the context of 'the things of the kingdom' and it is given in a meal setting (v. 4). The meal and the Holy Spirit both have for Luke eschatological significance. The meal is placed in an eschatological setting in the gospel in the following places: 12.37 and 13.28-30. It is placed with a resurrection appearance in 24.30, 31, 35, 41-43, which are eschatological scenes as well. This pattern continues in Acts 1.4,[135] 2.42, 46[136] and 10.40, 41.[137]

We have earlier noted the eschatological nature of the gift of the Holy Spirit. This significance of the Holy Spirit is in evidence here

---

preach that the kingdom is near (v. 9b), pronounce judgement on those who reject them – shake the dust of their shoes (vv. 10, 11). Jesus himself gave the imprecation against the cities (vv. 14, 15) and identified the commission with their Commissioner (v. 16). The 70 (72) rejoiced that the devils were subject to them (v. 17).	to enter the kingdom of God (14.22). They delivered imprecation against Jerusalem (13.27-29). They pronounced judgement against Elymas, who was addressed as υἱὲ διαβόλου (13.8-11).
v. 11 Jesus gave the 70 (72) authority to wipe off the dust from their feet in judgement against those cities that rejected them	13.51 Barnabas and Paul shook off the dust from their feet against Pisidian Antioch
v. 17 The 70 (72) regathered and recounted their mission and rejoiced that the devils were subject to them.	14.27 Upon their return to Antioch (in Syria), they rehearsed what God had done.
v. 21 Jesus rejoiced in the Holy Spirit	13.52 The disciples were filled with joy and the Holy Spirit.

This parallel study is significant to show that the Holy Spirit governed this preaching mission as Jesus had the preaching mission of the 70 (72). The Holy Spirit in the church acted as Jesus did among the disciples; the Holy Spirit was the source of the authority of the church's mission as Jesus had been of the mission of the 70 (72).

> The same power of the Spirit works miracles after Pentecost at the hand of Peter and John, Stephen and Philip, and it characterizes the apostolic, preaching just as it did that of Jesus himself. This power is, of course, the power of the kingdom of God, already operative in Jesus. It is clear therefore, that Luke brings the ideas of the power of the kingdom and the working of the Spirit of God into very close relationship with each other; they are virtually identical (Lampe, 'The Holy Spirit in the Writings of St. Luke', pp. 171, 172).

135 See nn. 119, 120, 121, 189.

136 Cullmann, *Early Christian Worship*, p. 15.

137 Haenchen, *Acts*, p. 141 n. 3: 'Assuming that συναλιζόμαι means "to eat (salt) together with someone"'. Luke speaks of the risen Jesus eating in Lk. 24.43 and Acts 10.41, also in the latter sense of communal meal with the disciples.

by the fact 'that the risen Lord's command to his disciples to await the promise of the Spirit-baptism seems to form part of a discourse about "the things concerning the Kingdom of God"'.[138]

Verse 5 is an explanatory verse of the promise of the Holy Spirit distinguishing John's baptism in water and Jesus' baptism in the Holy Spirit. It is not necessary for our purposes to develop the exegesis of this verse.[139]

Verses 6-8 deal with the apostles' apocalyptic expectations and Jesus' answer to them. The promise and command stated in v. 4 doubtless provoked the question recorded in v. 6. This promise of the Holy Spirit raised the hopes expressed in the question, 'Lord, in this time, will you restore the kingdom to Israel?' The word 're-store' ἀποκαθιστάνεις 'is a technical term in eschatology: the establishment of the right order by God (here Jesus) at the end of time …'[140] The apostles apparently still held the Jewish apocalyptic expectation that identified the kingdom of God as the establishment of the kingdom under an earthly Davidic throne and king, with the nation of Israel central to that world order.[141] They apparently also understood that one of the gifts of that restoration was the gift of the Holy Spirit. So, the promise of the Holy Spirit seemed to them to be the promise of the restoration of the kingdom to Israel.

Jesus' answer is twofold. First, he rebukes this presumption (v. 7). Second, he reiterates the promise of the Holy Spirit (v. 8).

The rebuke is in agreement with Mk 13.32 (parallel Mt. 24.36), which Luke does not record in his gospel, even though all of the synoptics are parallel in the contexts here. It should be recognized that all that is really said here is that the kind of expectation expressed by the apostles is in error. 'What is rejected in ch. i 6ff is not the idea of the Kingdom, but the idea of Jewish nationalism and apocalyptic computation of the day.'[142] 'Delay of the Parousia' must be read into this verse from other considerations. This is not to say Luke expected an immediate Parousia. He did not encourage his readers to expect the Parousia immediately; instead, he included all of the events from

138 Lampe, 'The Holy Spirit in the Writings of St. Luke', p. 184.

139 For a discussion of ὅτι Ἰωάννης see Jackson and Lake, *The Beginnings of Christianity*, pp. 6, 7.

140 Haenchen, *Acts*, p. 143 n. 2.

141 Jackson and Lake, *The Beginnings of Christianity*, p. 8.

142 van Unnik, 'The "Book of Acts"', p. 45.

the preaching of John in the category of eschatology.[143] From this time on, eschatological events are to be expected until the Parousia. 'In the tradition the ministry of Jesus is eschatological because in it God has begun his final action in the world …'[144] Luke has not pushed the Parousia into the distant and meaningless future. He has filled the present with the sense of the kingdom of God by the presence of Jesus, subsequently by the presence of the Spirit and Word of God and by the works of the kingdom in the church.

The Spirit is to endue the apostles with power; as a result of this receiving of power, the apostles are to be Jesus' witnesses. The concept of witness in Acts (represented by the words μαρτυρέω, ματύριον, μαρτύρομαι, and μάρτυς refers to a specific witness; it is a witness of the revelation that is in Jesus.[145] This answer is offered instead of the apocalyptic restoration of the kingdom to Israel. This is the kingdom offered in Jesus' physical absence as it had been offered by his presence (Lk. 17.20), but now offered through the agency of the Holy Spirit and manifested by the witness of Jesus.[146] 'Through the Spirit, the power and presence of Christ are known in the church.'[147]

This eschatological fulfillment in the church age is represented by the commission that is given the apostles. The commission covers the areas of witness under the terms Jerusalem, Judaea, Samaria, and ἕως ἐσχάτου τῆς γῆς. The totality of this mission is eschatological. The phrase ἕως ἐσχάτου τῆς γῆς is an eschatological expression

---

143 Marshall, *Luke: Historian and Theologian*, pp. 79, 109, 119.

144 Marshall, *Luke: Historian and Theologian*, p. 109; cf. W.C. van Unnik, 'Luke–Acts, A Storm Center in Contemporary Scholarship', in L. Keck and J. Martyn (eds.), *Studies in Luke–Acts* (Nashville: Abingdon Press, 1966), p. 28:

> Let me conclude by mentioning a few items … that merit exploration. (1) Has the delay of the *parousia* really wrought the havoc that it is sometimes supposed to have done, or did early Christians react differently from the way modern scholars would have done? In the light of the history of early Christianity this effect of the *Parousie-verzögerung* is highly overrated. The faith of the early Christians did not rest on a date but on the work of Christ.

145 van Unnik, 'The "Book of Acts"', p. 56: 'Except in these cases where it is used for somebody who is a man of good repute (vi 3, x 22, xv 12, xxii 12) it is always connected with the revelation in Jesus Christ'.

146 Lampe, 'The Holy Spirit in the Writings of St. Luke', p. 192: 'What the nature of the kingdom was to be they began to discover after the Resurrection. It turned out to be, not a restoration of the kingdom to Israel, but a mission to the world.'

147 Marshall: *Luke: Historian and Theologian*, p. 182.

'derived from the prophets'.[148] This commission, then, is to be the business of the church in the last days.[149]

Verses 9-11 describe the ascension itself. The language of v. 9 is designed to emphasize that the ascension of Jesus was a physical translation of Jesus into heaven; the bodily character of Jesus in the translation is identical to his bodily character in all instances since the resurrection. By such specific language Luke addresses himself to two problems: Jesus' physical absence from the church and gnostic spiritualization of Jesus' resurrection.[150]

The order which Luke emphasizes here is as follows: Jesus gave his commission (actually blessing; cf. Lk. 24.50); he was taken up while the disciples watched; then a cloud received him from their eyes.

This order of events establishes that the fulfilling of the commission was to be the activity of the church during the physical absence of Jesus. The manner in which Luke emphasizes the watchfulness of the disciples shows that the testimony of the ascension was to be part of the disciples' witnessing. This also establishes that the testimony concerning the witness was adequately confirmed.

The use of the cloud to receive Jesus is another eschatological symbol in the ascension scene. This interpretation of the cloud is in evidence in the Western text of Acts; the variant shows the consciousness of eschatological symbolism and affinity with the Transfiguration account.[151]

At this point all that can be said of the function of the cloud is that it was the instrument of receiving Jesus into heaven. It is his

---

148 van Unnik, 'The 'Book of Acts', p. 39; Jackson and Lake, *The Beginnings of Christianity*, p. 9: 'In the LXX a common phrase for distant lands., especially in the prophets (cf. Is. xlix.6, and many other passages), without any conscious reference to anyone place',

149 Lampe, 'The Holy Spirit in the Writings of St. Luke', p. 193: 'The last days have now dawned, and the ancient hope of the gift of the Spirit is to be fulfilled through the crucified and exalted Messiah … At Pentecost they actually receive the power of the Spirit in which Jesus had preached, healed and exorcised.'

150 Talbert, *Luke and the Gnostics*, p. 14: 'Also it has been proposed that the physical ascension of Jesus in Acts 1.9-11 should be viewed as an answer to such people as Gnostics who had a spiritual conception of Christ's immortality'.

151 Metzger, *A Textual Commentary on the Greek New Testament*, p. 282: 'According to one form of the Western text, preserved in Augustine and the Sahidic version, a cloud enveloped Jesus on earth before his ascension, and then he was lifted up (nothing is said of the disciples' watching the ascension)'. Haenchen, *Acts*, p. 149 n. 2.

vehicle into glory as is shown by the glorious appearance of Jesus that follows in the book of Acts. It is not said here, however, that Jesus took on a glorious appearance at the time of his ascension. This would have been contrary to Luke's aim to show that Jesus ascended in the same form in which he appeared in all of the prior resurrection appearances.[152]

The connection with glorification is adequately made by Luke. All subsequent appearances of Jesus in Acts depict him in glory, as Davies also notes.[153] In this sense the ascension is the final step in Jesus' 'exodus' (cf. ἔξοδος – ἀνάλημψις). It is Jesus' entrance into glory, and this had been foreseen in the Transfiguration.[154] It is also on the basis of the ascension that Jesus is designated Lord and the One who gives the Holy Spirit (Acts 2.30-36).

Verse 10 describes the appearance of the two messengers. The disciples were completely engrossed in the departure of Jesus: καὶ ὡς ἀτενίζοντες ἦσαν εἰς τὸν οὐρανὸν ... Luke introduces the two messengers with a phrase identical to his introduction of Moses and Elijah in the Transfiguration: καὶ ἰδοὺ ἄνδρες δύο ... (Lk. 19.30; Acts 1.10b), but more particularly from the Septuagint.[155] The attire of these men in white clothing suggests that they are understood by Luke as angels.[156] In the light of the immediate identification of this event with the Parousia (v. 11) the function of angels in Parousia is suggested (Lk. 9.26). Their primary purpose in this scene is to be messengers of the risen and ascended Jesus. This message follows in v. 11.

The first aspect of their message is a rebuke of the disciples for remaining in this place gazing (ἀτενίζοντες – v. 10) into heaven. The implication of the rebuke is that the apostles were now to be going

---

152 Contra: Davies, he *Ascended into Heaven*, p. 54: 'To St. Luke the Ascension was the occasion of the glorification of Jesus; he then assumed a radiant shining form ...'

153 Davies, he *Ascended into Heaven*, p. 54.

154 Davies, he *Ascended into Heaven*, p. 41; Lampe, 'The Holy Spirit in the Writings of St. Luke', p. 181; Haenchen, *Acts*, p. 149 n. 2.

155 Haenchen, *Acts*, p. 150 n. 1: 'Luke borrows καὶ ἰδοὺ from LXX, using it 24 times in his gospel, and eight times in Acts ... It lends an OT, Palestinian colour.'

156 Haenchen, *Acts*: 'The shining garments of heavenly beings are mentioned in II Macc. 11.8; Mk 9.3 par, 16.5 par; John 20.12 ...'; n. 4: 'Wellhausen's conjecture ... that they may be identified with Moses and Elijah is purely gratuitous.' Jackson and Lake, *The Beginnings of Christianity*, p. 9.

to Jerusalem in fulfillment of Jesus' commission (vv. 4, 8).[157] They must return to Jerusalem in order to receive the Holy Spirit because the Spirit is essential to their witness. Their witness is to be by the Holy Spirit, and this witness is to affirm both the ascension and the return of Jesus.

The second aspect of the message is the promise of Jesus' return. It is the clear intention of this promise to emphasize the exact identification of the returning Jesus with the ascending Jesus.[158]

The angels further promise that the manner of the departure is to be the manner of the return. This is emphasized by the redundancy of the verse: οὕτως ... πρόπον ...; this careful construction of the account of the ascension is designed to show the manner of the return of Jesus – the Parousia. The Parousia symbols in this passage are to be taken seriously; the eschatological signs identified here are the accompaniments of the Parousia: specifically, the cloud and the angels. In the light of Luke's other uses of the Mt. of Olives, it would seem that the site of the ascension (v. 12) also predicts the point of Jesus' return. Luke has been careful to show that Jesus' ascension was in the same body in which he suffered and in which he had been seen after the resurrection. This promise gives assurance that his return will be in the body of the resurrection. Though Luke does not ascribe glory to the visible appearance of Jesus, the fact that Jesus ascends into his glorious state implies that he will return in glory. Luke describes this kind of Parousia in Lk. 9.26 and 17.24.[159]

Verse 12 notes the site of the ascension as the Mt. of Olives. Its proximity to Jerusalem places it within the framework of the significance of Jerusalem. Yet this mountain also has its own significance as the place of Jesus' agonizing prayer before his arrest (Lk. 22.39) and now the place of his ascension.

We have previously noted the similarities between the Transfiguration and the ascension pericopes. The similarities identify both of these as descriptions of eschatological scenes. More specifically, they are apocalyptic in their anticipation. The central question is whether

---

157 Jackson and Lake, *The Beginnings of Christianity*, p. 6: Verse 4, μὴ χωρίζεσθαι: 'If the tense be pressed it means "give up leaving Jerusalem," and implies that to stay away was the apostles' intention.'

158 οὗτος ὁ Ἰησοῦς ὁ ἀναλήμφθεις; is emphatic and conveys the meaning 'this Jesus the one who has been taken up ...'

159 Note, however. the textual problem on the phrase 'in his day'. It is not supported by 𝔓75, B, D and some of the early versions.

they both anticipate the same apocalyptic event. It is our contention that they do not. Therefore, our interest at this point is to show the contrasts between the two scenes and to determine two things: (1) Do the contrasts justify our conclusion that the Transfiguration and ascension anticipate separate events? (2) If so, what are these events anticipated?[160]

We may list now the contrasts between these two accounts.

From the literary standpoint, both accounts are classified as legends; however, an important literary formal difference lies at the base of this consideration. The Transfiguration account has some of the formal characteristics of the theophany: a numinous appearance, the descending and overshadowing (tabernacling) cloud, the fear of the disciples in the presence of the cloud, and the voice from the cloud. From a literary standpoint the ascension account seems to be rather far removed from this genre.

We are not prepared to offer interpretative significance for each of the contrasts that may be drawn between the narratives. However, we are prepared to offer individual interpretation for a significant number of them so that the cumulative effect leads to the conclusion that Luke intended to foreshadow two different phases of the realization of the kingdom of God. The procedure following will be to state and interpret the contrasts that seem to be significant in this regard.

The witnesses of the Transfiguration were especially chosen from among the apostles, and they were shown a scene which they did not forthwith disclose to the other apostles. The Transfiguration was in the strictest sense an esoteric revelation. This is comparable to those descriptions of the kingdom of God which depend on an esoteric perception of it. The several representations of the messianic meal imply an esoteric identification of the kingdom (Lk. 13.28, 29; 22.15-20, 29, 30; 24.35). In contrast to these conditions, all of the apostles were witnesses to the ascension. The expectation of the ascension

---

160 An alternate pair of questions also arises here: (1) Are the contrasts overpowered by the similarities so that we must conclude that the Transfiguration and the ascension anticipate the same event? (2) If so, what is that event? We need not deal with these questions until we have fully examined the two questions above. If our thesis cannot be established, then we must examine the two pericopes under these two inquiries.

account and of the subsequent record in Acts is that the witnesses of this event were open in telling what they had seen and heard.

One of the most extreme contrasts between these two scenes is the appearance of Jesus. In the Transfiguration, Jesus appears in glorious light. This is the glory in which Jesus appears after the ascension, but never before the ascension other than the one case of the Transfiguration. It is the glory which he possesses in his position at God's right hand (Lk. 22.69; Acts 7.55, 56), in which he reveals himself to Paul (Saul) (Acts 9.3-7; cf. Acts 22.11) and in which he is to return from heaven (Lk. 21.27). The ascension is the threshold into glory, but that glory is not ascribed to Jesus on 'this side of the cloud'.

The two men who appear with Jesus in the Transfiguration stand in contrast to the two men who appear at the ascension. In the Transfiguration, the two men are named (Moses and Elijah); in the ascension, they are not. In the Transfiguration their names identify their relationship to Jesus. Their function is also identified by what they do in the Transfiguration: i.e. converse with Jesus. In the ascension the two men do not speak with Jesus at all, but speak only to the apostles, and they appear after Jesus has disappeared. Moses and Elijah are in the position of those who participate in glory with Jesus, and who are thus identified with him in that glory into which he enters in the kingdom of God. The two men at the ascension are in the position of messengers of Jesus after he had departed.

The clouds in each of these pericopes served to distinguish the two experiences reported. The most obvious contrast is in the distinctive functions in the scene. In the Transfiguration the cloud descends and envelops the mountain-top scene. It is the source of the heavenly voice. In the ascension the cloud serves only to separate Jesus from the eyes of the apostles. There are more subtle differences. The cloud in the Transfiguration is closely related to the function of the cloud in theophanies. In the ascension this is not a clear function of the cloud, if at all. In the Transfiguration the cloud is associated with the voice from heaven; hence, it relates to the theophanic symbol of the opening of the heavens. In the Transfiguration the cloud overshadows the mountain scene and conveys the eschatological concept of God's tabernacling among men, which Luke represents by the special word ἐπισκιάζω. In the ascension scene, Luke does not introduce the cloud by way of either of these symbols (theophany and tabernacling).

The response of the three apostles is in distinct contrast with the response of the apostles at the ascension. At the Transfiguration the response is one of fear, which is characteristic of theophanies. The ascension account does not ascribe such fear to the witnesses of that event; hence, there is absent this formal characteristic of the theophany.

The voice from the cloud reaffirms that Jesus is God's Son; this voice of exaltation is commensurate with the exaltation already seen in the glory of Jesus. It is the glory of enthronement (Lk. 22.69; Acts 7.55, 56) and the identification of kingship. In the ascension there is no heavenly voice.

The ascension pericope concludes with an interpretative sentence, (Acts 1.11) and the Transfiguration pericope offers no such concluding interpretative 'caption'. Luke clearly understands the ascension as a prefiguring of the Parousia. If Davies is correct in his conclusion that Luke intended the Transfiguration as a prefiguring of the ascension, Acts 1.11 is also the interpretation of the Transfiguration in Luke.

There are certainly parallels between the two pericopes; however, it seems better to account for these parallels on another basis. The parallels may be accounted for by the fact that both pericopes are eschatological and apocalyptic. This answer does not adequately explain the rather sharp contrasts noted above.

We have previously argued that there are two phases of Luke's concept of the future and apocalyptic manifestation of the kingdom of God: one public describing its coming (the Parousia) and the other esoteric describing it episodically in its consummation. On this thesis we can account for the differences between the two pericopes as well as the similarities. Davies and Boobyer both interpret the Transfiguration and the ascension as an anticipation of the Parousia; in order to do this, they must leave unexplained (or inadequately explained) the contrasts of the two pericopes. Their view implies that Luke did not have a coherent concept of Parousia since he described it with contrasting (if not contradictory) accounts. However, if the Transfiguration is taken as the prefigurement of the kingdom consummated (esoteric in nature and realization) and the ascension is taken as anticipating the Parousia (public in nature), the accounts are complimentary and not contradictory.

Transfiguration and Ascension as Cultic Narratives

In order to deal with this subject, it is essential to establish definitions. Two of these are common in biblical studies: ecstasy and cult. The third is not in common usage and hence must be established; it is the term 'experiencing the kingdom'.

Luke's use of the word ἔκστασις[161] in relation to worship does not describe a senseless (irrational) state, but a state of enrapturement in which the presence of God is supreme in the worshipper's consciousness.[162] For Luke the experience is usually connected with prayer.[163] It involves some special revelation. It supersedes the worshipper's normal mental and vocal capabilities and endues them with perception or speech that can be accounted for only by God's direct action.

---

161 BAG, p. 244: 1. 'distortion, confusion, astonishment, terror, lit. being beside oneself …' 2. 'trance, ecstasy, a state of being brought about by God, in which consciousness is wholly or partially suspended …'

The word appears in Luke–Acts under the following circumstances: (1) of astonishment in Lk. 5.26 and Acts 3.10 and (2) of a religious experience (trance) in Acts 10.10; 11.5; and 22.17. In both of the instances related to religious experience the ecstasy is preceded by prayer (Acts 10.10 and 11.5 refer to the same experience of Peter). Luke apparently does not associate this word with insensibility or being out of one's mind; it is not equated with 'madness' in Festus' chiding of Paul (Acts 26.24, 25).

The cognate verb ἐξίστημι follows the same pattern of use in Luke–Acts. It is used in the sense of amazement in the following places: Lk. 2.47; 8.56; 24.22; Acts 2.7, 12; 8.13; 9.21; 10.45 and 12.16. It is used in the sense of sorcery in Acts 8.9, 11.

In addition to these uses of the word ἔκστασις and ἔξίστημι there are experiences recorded by Luke that seem to answer to the concept of ecstasy, provided that we use the term to mean a yielding of one's consciousness to the presence of God. All of these occur under circumstances of divine worship: Acts 2.1-13; 4.24-31; 8.15-19; 10.44-48 (cf.11.15-17); 19.6. Acts 2.1-13; 10.44-48; 11.15-17; and 19.6 all speak of glossolalia; it is not my intention to imply that the word γλῶσσα by etymology conveys the sense of ecstatic. However, the experience here recorded indicates that those whose experiences are here; described are responsive to the Holy Spirit's presence and they are instruments for the manifestation of that presence.

162 Kirk, *The Vision of God*, pp. 196, 197.

163 Luke does not use the word ἔκστασις or its cognate verb ἐξίστημι of the Transfiguration. The setting, and description of the Transfiguration are similar to instances where he does use this word and the word of vision ὅραμα (BAG, p. 580: 'in our lit. of supernatural vision, whether the pers. who has the vision be asleep or awake'.). This word also is used in association with prayer (Haenchen, *Acts*, p. 347 n. 3: 'ὅραμα and prayer for him (i.e. Luke) belong together').

Luke's account of Pentecost (Acts 2.1-40) provides us with an example of this kind of experience. Luke takes great care to show that the believers were so enraptured that 'they began to speak with other tongues because[164] the Spirit was giving …'

He also is careful to point out that the speech, though in an enraptured state, was profound – speech as of the oracle of God (v. 4).[165] Luke carries this argument further by saying that Peter's speech was in the same vein of authority (v. 14), though it was not ἑτέραις γλώσσαις.[166] 'Here the believers were so carried out of themselves that they felt impelled to transcend human language and to commune in the language of angels or other mantic articulation.'[167]

This is a consistent description of ecstasy in Luke–Acts. Ecstasy understood in this way is an appropriate designation of the type of religious experience recorded of Peter, John, and James in the Transfiguration pericope.

Since the vocabulary of ecstasy is not used by Luke in the Transfiguration account, it is necessary here to argue from analogy.

In cases of special acts of divine revelation recorded in Luke–Acts, the witnesses of the revelation are 'beside themselves' in the sense of ecstasy; that is, they yield their self-consciousness to the wholly other-consciousness of the divine presence. They are more responsive to the divine presence than to their own mentality. We have noted these conditions already in the example of glossolalia in Acts. The conditions of ecstasy are also in evidence in Stephen's vision of the Son of man (Acts 7.55, 56). The conversion of Paul (Saul) is described in terms appropriate to the conditions of ecstasy (Acts

---

164 Καθῶς: BDF §453.2; Haenchen, *Acts*, p. 168: 'The Spirit causes the Christians it pervades to discourse in "other tongues".'

165 BAG, p. 101: 'ἀποφθέγγομαι speak out, declare boldly or loudly (of the speech of the wise man …; but also of the oracle-giver, diviner, prophet, exorcist and other inspired persons …)'.

166 F.F. Bruce, *The Acts of the Apostles* (London: Tyndale, 1951), p. 88: 'ἀποφθέγγεσθαι in ver. 4; probably here as there, the word implies inspired utterance'.

167 Amos N. Wilder, *Early Christian Rhetoric* (Cambridge, MA: Harvard University Press, 1971), p. 19. In this situation Luke takes care to show that this was not the senseless babbling of the drunk (v. 15); in Luke's report here, it was caricatured as the babblings of the drunk, but the glossolalia were understood to speak 'the great things of God' (v. 11). The speech reported here is not irrational babbling, but it does come from the Holy Spirit. It partakes of a sublimity and content beyond the unaided capabilities of the worshipper.

9.1-9), and it is referred to as the heavenly vision (Acts 26.19 οὐρανίῳ ὀπτασίᾳ). These instances demonstrate the conditions of ecstasy. They generally embrace the following: a revelation from heaven, the appearance of the Son of man in glory central to the revelation and the translation (in some degree of identity) of the witness into the scene.[168]

That the Transfiguration may be referred to as ecstatic would appear to be justified by the presence of these formal characteristics in Luke's Transfiguration account. The enrapturement of the three witnesses is represented by envelopment in the Shekinah, and witnessed to by the very existence of the account in synoptic and pre-synoptic tradition.

The word 'cult' is a modern imposition on biblical literature designed to designate the worship of the corporate body in either the OT or the NT. This is not inappropriate, but we must recognize that we are not dealing with specific biblical terminology. An appropriate definition is that given by S. Mowinckel; it is 'the visible socially arranged and ordered, efficacious forms through which the religious experience of communion between the deity and the 'community' is actualized and its effects expressed'.[169] This is not an entirely satisfactory definition for our purposes because it is general and not specifically Christian.

The instances of Christian worship that are recorded in Acts represent Luke's attempt to normalize the pattern of Christian worship. Luke describes Christian worship always in the perspective of the centrality of the exalted Lord.

The most important Christian characteristic is the obvious; Christian worship is the confession that Jesus is Lord. There are four specific agents of this worship experience which are also characteristic of the early Christian community: the Holy Spirit, the Word, the Sacraments, and prayer.[170]

---

168 David Edward Aune, *The Cultic Setting of Realized Eschatology* (Leiden: Brill, 1972), p. 93: Aune places another characteristic here: namely, 'pneumatic inspiration'; he also identifies the *Sitz im Leben* of this and other prophetic visions as 'in a cultic setting'.

169 Sigmund Mowinckel, 'Cultus', in *Religion in Geschichte und Gegenwart*, 3rd edn; Vol. IV, cols. 120-21, cited and translated by Aune, *The Cultic Setting of Realized Eschatology*, p. 9.

170 Cullmann, *Early Christian Worship*, p. 12: 'In the book of Acts (2.42 and 46; 20.7) instruction, preaching, prayer and breaking of bread are mentioned in such a

Another distinctive element of early Christian worship is its eschatological outlook. This outlook combines present eschatological realization and future eschatological expectation. Future expectation in Luke is divided even further. There is the Parousia, which is held to be future. In this event Jesus is expected to reappear. There is also the expectation of an apocalyptic kingdom in which the redeemed are gathered around the Messiah. This culmination of the kingdom is based on the prior occurrence of the Parousia and is described with such characteristics as the eschatological meal, inheritance of eternal life, the gathering of the patriarchs and all the prophets, and the final judgement.

In this relationship early Christian worship was backward looking and forward looking. Its backward look related to the time when Jesus was among men and the kingdom was known by his personal, visible presence among them. This backward look preserved the traditions of his words and actions as the divine Word.

Its forward look expected the Parousia and the subsequent fulfillment of the kingdom of God. There is a third distinction to be made here. In addition to its backward look and its forward look, there is in Christian worship an existential perception of the kingdom of God. The early church perceived the actuality of the kingdom by the telling and retelling of its narrative (and stories). This device brought together the past, the future, and the moment of experience into a true 'realized eschatology'. 'It (the story) presents the "way" of Christ, the way of life in two successive phases which are yet telescoped, the phase of incognito and abandonment and the phase of transfiguration.'[171]

The third term in need of definition is one coined in the process of this study: 'experiencing the kingdom'. This term is intended to cover a condition of worship in which the worshipper is translated by the Holy Spirit into an experience of the kingdom that is depicted or described in Sacrament or Word. An essential of this experience is the Holy Spirit; to use the term of mysticism, it is 'in the spirit'.[172]

---

way as to show that these elements were, from the beginning, the foundation of all worship life of the Christian community'.

171 Wilder, *Early Christian Rhetoric*, p. 29.

172 Rudolph Otto, *Mysticism East and West* (trans. Bertha L. Bracey and Richenda C. Payne; New York: Macmillan, 1932), pp. 132-33: '... the synoptic idea of the Kingdom, already present in early Christian teaching, is the germ of the fully developed idea of "life in the spirit"'.

This is the experience of being 'in the Spirit' as distinct from a forensic placement in the kingdom or in heaven.

The expression 'in the Spirit' is commonly associated with the theology of the Fourth Gospel; somewhat related terminology does appear in Lk. 10.21. This is not the precise analogy that we seek here. Luke describes experiences of human encounter with the Holy Spirit and with other manifestations of God (visions, etc.). These often represent for the believer or the community experiences of ecstasy. It is also evident from Luke that the early Christian community lived in an expectancy of such experiences. Peter thought he was seeing a vision when he was being delivered from prison (Acts 12.6-10). It is an experience which allows the individual and the corporate body to become present and proleptic participants in the kingdom of God.

The forward look of early Christian worship expects the coming events of the Parousia and the culminated kingdom. What is even more distinctive of early Christian worship is that it translates the worshipper into the apocalyptic fulfillment proleptically; that is, the worshipper experienced apocalyptic fulfillment while remaining 'within the framework of present time, history and worldly conditions'.[173] Cullmann ascribes this kind of experience to sacrament, especially the eucharist,[174] and seems not to lay strong emphasis on the Word. There is no need, however, to base this experience solely (or even primarily) on the eucharist. More fundamentally, the word is essential to the significance of sacrament. The word is an effectuating agent for spiritual experience. Christianity is a 'religion of the word'.[175] Peter used the citation of Joel 2.28-32 not only to defend the phenomena of Pentecost, but also to show the relationship of the promise of 'divine Word to prophetic visions and auditions'.[176] A more graphic example is the experience of Stephen (Acts 7.55-60). The provocation of this experience is Stephen's 'previous proclamation of an inspired message (6.3, 10)'.[177] In this experience, Stephen is enraptured so that he sees Jesus (the Son of man) at the right hand

---

173 Aune, *The Cultic Setting of Realized Eschatology*, p 7.

174 Cullmann, *Early Christian Worship*, p. 16: 'The coming of Christ into the midst of the community gathered at the meal is an anticipation of his coming to the Messianic meal and looks back to the disciples eating with the risen Christ on the Easter day'.

175 Wilder, *Early Christian Rhetoric*, p. 8.

176 Aune, *The Cultic Setting of Realized Eschatology*, p. 91.

177 Aune, *The Cultic Setting of Realized Eschatology*, p. 92.

of God (vv. 55, 56), and he experiences some sense of apocalyptic judgement in his committing of his own spirit to the 'Lord, Jesus' and in his intercession against the judgement of his persecutors (vv. 59, 60). The formal characteristics of this pericope point 'to the origin of this prophetic vision in a cultic setting'.[178]

We judge, then, that Word and cult are as much interrelated as Sacrament and cult.[179] 'Within the context of worship, the proclamation of the Word of God through the agency of prophetic personalities ..., the cultic hieros logos, is one of the vehicles through [*sic* – which?] both eschatological life and eschatological judgement are communicated'.[180]

One of the forms of the Word in the early Christian community was the narrative used as an agent of worship. The OT use of narrative is an appropriate analogy in this consideration because of the influence of the OT on the early Christian community. This is especially appropriate to Luke because he has shaped much of his material under the influence of the Septuagint.

Von Rad has given extensive treatment to the narrative form in the OT. He distinguishes several sub-categories of narrative – saga, episodes, poetic stories, and legends. The basic functions of narrative are served by each. The narratives are designed to connect a place with God or a revelation, to establish continuity from the old to the new and to provide festival reconstruction.[181]

These purposes are integral to Israel's use of her history. Israel's history was a 'direct expression of her faith'[182] and was the product of 'diverse cultic traditions'.[183] The narrative was an instrument for bringing the events of Israel's history to the level of contemporary experience. A special characteristic of the narratives is their 'openness to the future' which von Rad defines to mean that the narrative

178 Aune, *The Cultic Setting of Realized Eschatology*, p. 93: This is compatible with expectations gathered from the OT as well: Aubrey R. Johnson, *The Cultic Prophet in Ancient Israel* (Cardiff, Wales: University of Wales Press Board, 1944), pp. 25, 26.

179 Karl Ludwig Schmidt, *Der Rahmen der Geschichte Jesu* (Darmstadt: Wissenschaftliche, 1964), p. vi.

180 Aune, *The Cultic Setting of Realized Eschatology*, p. 23.

181 von Rad, *Old Testament Theology*, I, pp. 44, 45.

182 von Rad, *Old Testament Theology*, I, p. 50.

183 von Rad, *Old Testament Theology*, II, p. 418.

expects a future event wrought by God in fulfillment of the event narrated.[184]

The continuing use of the narrative is to be found in its religious function. The narrative (in what von Rad designates as saga) places the event narrated 'within the horizon of the narrator's own faith ... The narrator attests not only the once-for-all act done by God at a particular point in history, but also an act which has meaning for himself since in a sense that is contemporary'.[185] These narratives are 'confessional utterances'.[186] As a confessional statement, they are conceived as authoritative word, not just as history, but as the proclamation of the faith and the actualization of religious experience. The event becomes fused with its faith, and the telling of the event becomes the proclamation and propagation of the faith. The narrative is the Word.

The link between the OT materials and the NT lies in the understanding of the nature of God. This is an understanding that 'comes to expression in a story as it does in dialogue and in drama'.[187]

The NT story has become more stylized than the OT. Of particular note in the Transfiguration account is the word of promise attached to the story (Lk. 9.27). This word enables the story to be repeated under the expectation of future fulfillment. The same device is in evidence in the ascension account, though here the promise comes at the end (Acts 1.11).

The story repeated in a cultic setting provided the worshipper (or worshipping community) the three elements of experience designated earlier: the look back, the look forward and the existential perception. 'Within the context of worship the final goal of history is proleptically present to the worshipper; past and future merge into present cultic experience.'[188]

The repetition of the narrative provides a means of continuing the experience of worship identified with and provoked by the narrative, especially if that narrative contains a promise and a fulfillment. A narrative used in this manner is a 'cultic narrative'. 'A cultic motif

---

[184] von Rad, *Old Testament Theology*, II, p. 422.
[185] von Rad, *Old Testament Theology*, II, p. 421.
[186] von Rad, *Old Testament Theology*, I, p. 111.
[187] Wilder, *Early Christian Rhetoric*, p. 63.
[188] Aune, *The Cultic Setting of Realized Eschatology*, p. 14

arises when the cult participant historicises some element of his religious experience'.[189]

The cultic community is an effective instrument for the present realization of the kingdom of God without implying that time and history are complete.[190] The observation which we seek to make here is that the repetition of stories provided the community with a means to re-experience what was recorded or to pre-experience what was promised (or anticipated): 'One function of narrative is to so engage the reader or hearer that he experiences himself an experience similar to the one narrated and that he identifies with the characters'.[191] The narrative used in this fashion is so used because the worshipping community conceived of it as Word of God. Worship in the early church differed from the worship of God in the synagogue. The latter is worship by word separated from existential experience and it centers in forensic identification with what is proclaimed. A form of worship which permits the cultic body to experience the word proclaimed (such as by Sacrament, prayer and ecstasy [as in the Spirit]) allows the individual and the corporate body to become present and proleptic participants in the kingdom of God.

The designation of these experiences as 'in the Spirit' represents the essentiality of the Holy Spirit to the experience. As Jesus' presence was essential to the experience of the kingdom in the gospel of Luke, the Spirit's presence is essential to the experience of the kingdom in Acts. 'It is clear ... that St. Luke brings the ideas of the power

---

189 John R. Donahue, *Are You the Christ? The Trial Narrative in The Gospel of Mark* (SBL Dissertation Series 10; Missoula, MT: University of Montana, 1973), pp. 26, 27. This conclusion does not necessarily answer the question of the historicity of the event relate in the episode recited. It does imply, however, that the reason for the perpetuation of the account is the religious experience to which it is attached in the faith and consciousness of the community in which it is preserved.

190 Aune, *The Cultic Setting of Realized Eschatology*, pp. 12, 13:

> Within the history of early Christianity, whenever the final goal of history is regarded as somehow being capable of provisional realization within time and history, that realization always occurs within a communal or cultic setting, or else extends into the life of the individual believer through his organic relationship to a particular Christian Community.

Aune goes on to assert that such experience cannot be individualized. His evidence does not seem to warrant such a conclusion.

191 Donahue, *Are You the Christ?*, p. 231; von Rad, *Old Testament Theology*, I, p. 420: The characters in the story become types so that they 'possess a coefficient of present-day relevance'.

of the Kingdom and the working of the Spirit of God into very close relationship with each other; they are virtually identical'.[192]

In Acts, prayer is normally associated with being in the Spirit; it is related to the coming of the Holy Spirit, to ecstatic experience and to revelatory experiences. 'Prayer is, in fact, complementary to the Spirit's activity since it is the point at which the communication of divine influence becomes effective for its recipients.'[193]

The primary question that remains for this inquiry is this: What is the place of the Transfiguration in the preceding interpretation of cult? A secondary and related question concerns the ascension: How does the ascension relate to this interpretation of cult and what is its distinction from the Transfiguration?

The first and most obvious function is common to both: instructional. Luke had as one of his intentions the preservation of the records of two events which he considered a part of the gospel story. He also considered these events to be integral to his own theology. So, the Transfiguration and the ascension are preserved for this instructional value.

The instruction alone is not characteristic of Luke's presentation of Christ or of the church's life and witness. There is a dynamic about his presentation of these records; this dynamic is designed to involve the 'instructed' in an emotional experience; hence, one of 'ecstasy'. It recalls the experience of revelation.

If we can apply the term ecstasy to the experience of Peter, John, and James, the Transfiguration embodies two hypotheses. First, the Transfiguration shows an experience by which the three intimates may have an experience with the Transfigured Jesus without implying their transfiguration. They can see the kingdom, and be embraced within it, but remain in the mortal state.[194] We have attempted to make a case for this hypothesis in the exegesis.

Such an experience is specifically illustrated in the vision of Stephen (Acts 7.55, 56). Whatever may be said of the nearness of

---

192 Lampe, 'The Holy Spirit in the Writings of St. Luke', pp. 171, 172.

193 Lampe, 'The Holy Spirit in the Writings of St. Luke', p. 169.

194 Aune, *The Cultic Setting of Realized Eschatology*, pp. 4, 6: 'The ideational correlative of the rise and development of the "Christ-cult" is a presupposition which underlies all early Christian literature: the conviction that the eschaton has been enacted, but in such a way as to permit the continuation of time and history'. Cf. W.A. Whitehouse, 'The Modern Discussion of Eschatology' (*Scottish Journal of Theology Occasional Papers, 2*; Edinburgh and London: Oliver Boyd, 1953), p. 68

Stephen's death, this fact in itself shows that he was (though enraptured in the vision of the Son of man) of this world order. Stephen realized his identity with the glorified Jesus before his death, and the fact of the stoning and impending death showed his continued identification with this world order.

Second, it provides a vehicle by which the same experience can be conveyed to others. In this way we have a possible insight into the manner in which the Transfiguration was used in the worship of the early church. The Transfiguration story was the divine word by which believers experienced the glory of the kingdom in consummation.

In support of this hypothesis, I offer the following considerations. First, there is evidence that the Transfiguration account in its same basic form and context lies at a very early level of tradition.[195] This indicates the significance of this account in the early Christian community.

Second, the instances of allusions to the Transfiguration in other canonical records imply its significance to the early Christian community (Jn 1.14; Hebrews 2.6-10; 2 Peter 1.16-18). The manner in which the Transfiguration is presented in these passages is related to the heavenly and kingdom glory of Jesus. Cultic influences appear to be in all of the passages cited above. This would seem to confirm our opinion that the Transfiguration was in rather widespread circulation in the early Christian community. In these instances, the Transfiguration is consistently related to the glory of Christ.

Third, as has been shown, narrative is an appropriate instrument of worship. It would appear also that such an instrument of worship lies at the earliest level of tradition.[196]

In line with this point, we repeat our earlier observation that the Transfiguration account provided an effective instrument for the

---

195 Ellis, 'Present and Future Eschatology', p. 31 n. 4.

196 Aune, *The Cultic Setting of Realized Eschatology*, p. 5 n. 1 cites and translates Karl Ludwig Schmidt, *Der Rahmen der Geschichte Jesu* (Darmstadt: Wissenschaftliche, 1964), p. vi:

> If the rise of Christianity is the development of a cult – this recognition has prevailed more and more during recent years – then it is clear that the rise of early Christian literature must be understood on the basis of the cult. As far as I am concerned the significance of the early Christian cult and the exercise of divine worship for the development of gospel literature cannot be too highly regarded. The oldest traditions about Jesus are cult-oriented.

proleptic realization of the kingdom of God. This observation should now be expanded.

We have attempted earlier to show that what is shown in the Transfiguration in Luke is the kingdom of God in consummation; hence, what is experienced in the telling and hearing of this story is participation in the kingdom. It is to see Jesus in glory, to see him with the prophets (Moses and Elijah), to experience his 'exodus' and to be enveloped in the Shekinah with him as the three apostles were. 'There is a sense in which the Transfiguration (and the resurrection and the ascension) is a manifestation of the future apocalyptic kingdom of God in the present.'[197] The early Christian community lived in the non-apocalyptic manifestation of the kingdom actualized by the activity of Jesus through the Holy Spirit. They needed an experience of the future apocalyptic kingdom. This experience is provided in the narrative of the Transfiguration.

There are two elements here that are essential to the function of worship that we are describing: the divine Word and the divine presence. The Transfiguration is pictured as occurring in fulfillment of Lk. 9.27. The Transfiguration is the story of a singular revelation of the divine presence – the exalted Jesus, the Shekinah and the divine voice. The Transfiguration could occur only by the reality of these two elements: the divine promise and the divine presence. If such an experience is to occur after the departure of Jesus, it must do so by two commitments in the early Christian consciousness. The first is the acceptance of the Holy Spirit as Jesus' agent of action and presence in the world following the ascension. The Transfiguration is pictured as occurring in fulfillment of the divine promise of Lk. 9.27. In the repetition of the story, the Transfiguration is still redactionally and cultically the fulfillment of the divine promise.

There are two movements (corresponding to the two elements) in the Transfiguration story and its context that are particularly significant for cultic application: promise (Lk. 9.27) and fulfillment (Lk. 9.28-36). This is the order in which Luke presents the Transfiguration; this order represented for Luke the original order of events. The retelling of the story recapitulated this order in order to do for the hearing group what Luke understood to have been done for Peter, John, and James.

---

197 Farrell, 'The Eschatological Perspective of Luke–Acts', p. 46.

When the Transfiguration was retold in the early Christian community as an act of worship in the cultic body, Jesus' word (Lk. 9.27) promised a seeing (ἰδεῖν) of the kingdom. The story itself repeated the happenings in the Mt. of Transfiguration. The worshipping community by the Holy Spirit is translated 'in the Spirit' into the age to come.[198] These believers were enveloped with Jesus and Peter, John, and James into the Shekinah.[199]

This act renewed for the early church the order of promise and fulfillment and renewed the elements of divine Word and divine presence. The worshipping community reenacted the past, looked into the future and was translated into the realm of apocalyptic experience.

The particular apocalyptic scene to which they were translated by the Transfiguration story was the kingdom of God in consummation – the redeemed gathered in the presence of their exalted King-Messiah. It is the kingdom consummated.

This interpretation and application of the Transfiguration account is not precisely parallel with the kerygma in Acts. There is a contrast (though not an incompatible contrast) between Luke's aim in the gospel and his aim in Acts. The gospel forms the fountainhead of the tradition, but 'Luke's Gospel is not kerygmatic'.[200] The book of Acts presents that tradition in kerygmatic fashion.

---

198 In a summary of the work of Heinz-Wolfgang Schultz (*Enderwartung und gegenwartiges Heile Untersuchugen zu den Gemeindeliedern von Qumran* (Studien zur Umwelt des Neuen Testaments, Dd 4; Göttingen: Vandenhoech and Ruprecht, 1961); Aune (*The Cultic Setting of Realized Eschatology*, pp. 31-37) has shown that a similar consciousness existed in the cultic activity at Qumran.

> On the basis of 1QH 11.3-14 and 1QH 3.19-36 Kuhn enumerates five eschatological acts which are actualized and appropriated in the present age by those who have become members of the community: (1) resurrection (11.12), (2) new creation (3.21; 11.13), (3) communion with angels (3.21-23; 11.13f), (4) deliverance from the final power of the realm of death (3.19), and (5) proleptic eschatological transference to heaven (3.20).

A significant distinction between the worship at Qumran was the concept of the presence of the Holy Spirit. For Qumran the expectation of the eschatological gift of the Holy Spirit is still a future expectation. For the Christian community the Holy Spirit is already present.

199 This imagery (though not the symbolic vocabulary) is suggested by Acts 2.2-4. Verse 2, the whole house was filled with the sound of wind out of heaven; vv. 3, 4, the 'cloven tongues' sat upon each of the worshippers.

200 Talbert, 'Redaction Critical Quest', p. 212.

In the ascension we have a relationship between Word, Spirit and worshipping community that is analogous to the situation described above relative to the Transfiguration.

We may observe first that the ascension scene itself is as much capable of receiving the descriptive word 'ecstatic' as the Transfiguration. It is a spiritual experience dominated by God's presence and provides a revelation of which the apostles were naturally incapable.

This account was preserved in at least one tradition of worship consciousness in the early Christian community. Luke used this tradition to explain Jesus' physical absence and to show his continued personal presence by the gift of the Holy Spirit. There is yet another reason for its preservation; it was preserved in order to teach that Jesus was coming again and to show the manner in which he would come, as Acts 1.11 shows.

In this pericope, we have the two agents of religious experience operative: the Holy Spirit and the Word. The Holy Spirit is operative by Jesus' promise, and the Spirit's function is the manifestation of Jesus' presence and power in the Christian community. The Word is operative not only in the narrative itself, but also in the forward look of the promise in v. 11. For the early Christian community this was a divine promise; hence, it is Word of God. The repetition of the story is inseparable from the repetition of the promise which climaxes it.

The ascension narrative historicises that event as the Transfiguration narrative does that event. Both narratives, however, provide for the repetition of the religious experience commemorated in the respective narratives. They also provide for the pre-experiencing of the promise of the narrative which in each case is encapsulated in a single verse associated with the pericope (Lk. 9.27 for the Transfiguration; Acts 1.11 for the ascension).

The promise of Acts 1.11 is to see the Parousia; hence, this cultic narrative provides for the proleptic translation to the apocalyptic event of Jesus' return.

It is clear that the tradition from which Luke drew contained these two accounts and made a distinction between the Transfiguration and the ascension. Luke distinguished between them historically. One occurred prior to the crucifixion and the other occurred after the crucifixion and resurrection. We have noted the theological distinctions, but what were the worship distinctions between these two narratives?

The two accounts before us serve these two apocalyptic distinctions. The ascension anticipates Parousia. The Transfiguration anticipates the redeemed gathered around the Messiah in the kingdom of God established. The ascension as cultic narrative translates the worshippers into the experiencing and hope of the Parousia. The Transfiguration as cultic narrative translates the worshippers into the experiencing and hope of the kingdom in its final consummation.

5

CONCLUSIONS

In the statement of the problem which established the thesis of this study, the following hypotheses were set forth. The tradition of the Transfiguration was preserved and transmitted in the early Christian community as an event distinct from the resurrection. The Lukan Transfiguration account is designed to present a historical event in the life of Jesus; it is an event that presents the nature of the kingdom of God. Luke's Transfiguration narrative has special affinities with the ascension accounts. These two traditions were preserved in early Christian worship as 'cult narratives'. In the process of this study, I have attempted to show that each of these hypotheses is a correct assessment of Luke's theology and of his redaction of the Transfiguration account.

In Chapter 1, our review of the literature on this subject and the biblical accounts showed that most scholarly attention has been given to the Markan account of the Transfiguration. So, there is a need for more particular attention to the Lukan account of the Transfiguration, and there is a need for specialized studies along the lines of the hypotheses submitted earlier.

Chapter 2 represents a study of the text of Luke's Transfiguration account; the specific text chosen is Lk. 9.27-36. A review of Luke's account in comparison with Mark's shows adequately the priority of Mark, and it shows that Luke worked within the framework of the first gospel. The differences between Mark and Luke have led to the following conclusions on the question of Luke's sources. Mark is the basic document before Luke in the process of his writing. Though there is no evidence of specific Q citations in this pericope, it is clear that Luke did work from this source as well. The differences that make Luke stand out most prominently from Mark are to be attributed to the use of an L tradition (though I have made no conclusion whether this was a formal written tradition or an oral tradition) and to his own editorialization (which was strongly influenced by the Septuagint).

The redactional stance of Luke is shown in the Transfiguration especially by the significant divergences of Luke from Mark. The most prominent of these divergencies are Luke's association of prayer with Jesus' Transfiguration, the use which he makes of 'glory' in the account, the anticipation of Jesus' 'exodus', and the presentation of the Shekinah and the word of witness from the Shekinah. These differences serve the specific theological aims of the author.

From the standpoint of form-critical studies, the Transfiguration is not easily designated, except by the general designation as legend. There are similarities to the epiphany form in evidence in the Transfiguration scene. This study has also suggested the form of the 'cultic narrative' as an appropriate designation of the Transfiguration.

The aim of Chapter 3 is to present an exegetical basis for the conclusions drawn in the subsequent study of Lukan theology in the Transfiguration. The first problem addressed here was to show that Lk. 9.27 was intended by Luke to be a prediction of the Transfiguration experience. Our conclusion here is that this verse is not a Parousia prediction. It is a prediction that was to be fulfilled within the literary context in which it appears in Luke. It is a prediction of the seeing of the kingdom in consummation.

In the account of the Transfiguration itself, this study has reached the following conclusions. Luke establishes a causative relationship between Jesus' praying and his Transfiguration. This is appropriate for Luke's use of prayer in the life of Jesus and in the life of the early Christian community. The glory in which Jesus is seen in this scene is the eschatological glory of the Son of man. It is the glory in which he appears after the ascension and the glory in which he appears in Parousia. This scene serves to combine the general eschatological concept with the specific apocalyptic concept of the final glory of the kingdom of God. Moses and Elijah appear as eschatological messengers to the Transfigured Jesus. They are participants with him in the kingdom as is evidenced by their appearance in glory. In Moses the law and the prophets (divine mandate and divine promise) are represented. In Elijah eschatological fulfillment is represented in his role as precursor of the kingdom. Together they discuss with Jesus his coming 'exodus' in Jerusalem. They thus bring together the themes of suffering and glory in the person of Jesus and in his accomplishment of the kingdom of God. The cloud which descends over the Transfiguration scene is the Shekinah. It is eschatological and it fulfills the kingdom concept by overshadowing (tabernacling over) the entire company – Jesus, Moses and Elijah (all appearing in glory) and Peter, John, and James. They are all incorporated in the kingdom identified by the tabernacling of the Shekinah over them. The cloud is the origin of the voice of witness; hence the divine sonship of Jesus is proclaimed. Luke's peculiar form of witness ('chosen Son' rather than 'beloved Son') probably represents one of two streams of tradition developing from Isa. 42.1. Luke's expression brings together the themes of election and sonship. It is a quasi-technical designation of sonship and represents a title of the Jewish messianic king. The proclamation of sonship is an enthronement proclamation. The command 'Hear him' which follows this proclamation joins the role of messianic King to the role of eschatological prophet.

Chapter 4 seeks to bring the special themes of Luke's Transfiguration account into the single thesis that the Transfiguration is a presentation of the kingdom of God in consummation.

Luke makes three distinctions in the presentation of the kingdom of God. The first is the present manifestation of the kingdom; it is manifested in the presence of Jesus or through the activity of the Holy Spirit. The second is the manifestation of the kingdom in the Parousia. This is the public presentation of the Son of man in his glory. Its occurrence is the apocalyptic realization of the kingdom of God. The third distinction is the kingdom in consummation. This appears after and is dependent on the prior Parousia. It is characterized by the gathering of the redeemed around the Messiah. The Transfiguration is an episodic presentation of the kingdom of God in this last sense. It is a foreview of the kingdom in consummation. It is a proleptic experiencing of that kingdom stage by Peter, John, and James.

Prayer is a special thematic concern of Luke. The most consistently recurring association which he makes with prayer is eschatology. This is evident in the relation of prayer to the opening of the heavens at Jesus' baptism, to the choosing of the twelve, to the confession of

Peter, to the Transfiguration, and to the cross. Jesus' teaching about prayer is eschatological. The relationship of prayer to the work and gift of the Holy Spirit is eschatological. Prayer has a special relationship to experiences of revelation both in the life of Jesus and in the experience of the early Christian community. Prayer is the route into the Transfiguration and the realization of the kingdom of God.

Glory is the chief symbol of the transfigured Jesus. By this term, Luke refers to the apocalyptic concept of glory, which is consistently manifested in Jesus' post-ascension manifestations. It is particularly the form in which the Son of man appears at the end of the age and in the fulfillment of the kingdom of God. Three themes consistently appear in the concept of glory: revelation, redemption, and eschatology. The Transfiguration brings these together in the appearance of Jesus.

The term 'exodus' embraces all the events that were to take place in Jerusalem. In approaching the culmination at Jerusalem, Luke presents the journey to Jerusalem in the typology of the first exodus. He thus combines the redemptive motif of the OT exodus with the redemptive aims of the 'exodus of Jesus'. Exodus in representing the cross, resurrection and ascension includes both suffering and glory; it also represents the deliverance of both Jesus and those who follow him. By anticipation, the ascension represents the Parousia. The interpretative statement of Acts 1.11 specifically claims this for the ascension; the pattern of the ascension is the pattern of the return of Jesus. Herein lies the distinction between the ascension and the Transfiguration. The ascension anticipates the Parousia, which is prior to and essential to the consummation of the kingdom. The Transfiguration represents the kingdom as it is consummated in glory.

We have asserted that the Transfiguration and the ascension are cultic narratives. In order to support this thesis, we have set forth an interpretation of certain phases of worship in the early Christian community as Luke knew it and wished it to be normalized.

Ecstasy was a significant aspect and expectation of worship in this community. In this usage it refers to the enrapturement of the worshipper in his consciousness of the divine presence. Such experiences are used in Luke–Acts for special revelations and religious experiences.

The cultic pattern in Luke–Acts rests on four essential agents: the Holy Spirit, the Word, the sacraments, and prayer. This worship was also distinctively eschatological in its outlook.

The early Christian community worshipped with three perspectives: the backward look, the forward look, and the existential experience. In these three perspectives, their worship brought together the remembrance of Jesus' presence among the disciples, the hope of his return and the establishment of the apocalyptic kingdom, and the proleptical experiencing of that kingdom – a true 'realized eschatology'.

This eschatology is the reality of 'experiencing the kingdom' by an experience in the Holy Spirit. The worshipper is translated into an apocalyptic fulfillment proleptically.

The narrative form of the Word was a significant instrument of worship in early Christianity. In a cultic setting the narrative provided reenactment of the past, anticipation of what is promised or anticipated by the narrative, and spiritual identification with the events of the narrative itself.

It is within this concept of worship that the stories of Transfiguration and the ascension were told in early Christian worship. Associated with each pericope, there is an interpretive promise: Lk. 9.27 for the Transfiguration and Acts 1.11 for the ascension. Each pericope is conceived as a relating of the divine Word. Divine promise and divine fulfillment are thus combined.

The narrative of the Transfiguration kept before the worshipping community the consciousness of what the kingdom of God was to be like. By this story, they were drawn into it and experienced it.

The narrative of the ascension kept before the worshipping community the consciousness of the Parousia. By this story they maintained their hope in the return of Christ.

SELECTED BIBLIOGRAPHY

Books

Aune, David Edward, *The Cultic Setting of Realized Eschatology* (Leiden: Brill, 1972).

Baltensweiler, Heinrich, *Die Verklärung Jesu* (Zurich: Zeingliverlag, 1959).

Beardslee, William A., *Literary Criticism of the New Testament* (Philadelphia: Fortress, 1970).

Beare, Francis Wright, *The Earliest Records of Jesus* (Nashville and New York: Abingdon Press, 1962).

Black, Matthew, *An Aramaic Approach to the Gospels and Acts* (Oxford: Clarendon Press, 1946).

Blinzler, Joseph, *Die neutestamentlichen Berichte über die Verklärung Jesu* (Munster: Verlag der Aschendorfischem Verlagbuchhandlung, 1937).

Boobyer, G.H., *St. Mark and the Transfiguration Story* (Edinburgh: T & T Clark, 1942).

Borsch, Frederick H., *The Son of Man in Myth and History* (Philadelphia: Westminster, 1967).

Bousset, Wilhelm, *Jesus* (trans. J.P. Trevelyan; ed. W.D. Morrison; New York: G.P. Putnam's Sons, 1906).

Bowman, John, *The Gospel of Mark* (Leiden: Brill, 1965).

Branscomb, B.H., *The Gospel of Mark* (London: Hodder & Stoughton, 1937).

Brockington, L.H., 'The Septuagintal Background to the New Testament Use of Δόξα', in D.E. Nineham (ed.), *Studies in Luke–Acts* (Oxford: Basil Blackwell, 1955), pp. 1-8.

Brown, Raymond E., *The Gospel According to St. John I-XII* (The Anchor Bible; Garden City, NY: Doubleday, 1966).

Browning, W.R.F., *The Gospel According to St. Luke* (New York: Macmillan, 1960).

Bruce. F.F., *The Acts of the Apostles* (London: Tyndale, 1951).

Buchanan, George Wesley, *Hebrews* (The Anchor Bible; Garden City: NY: Doubleday, 1972).

Bultmann, Rudolf, *The History of the Synoptic Tradition* (trans. John Marsh; New York and Evanston: Harper and Row, 1963).

—*Theology of the New Testament* (trans. K.K. Grobel; New York: Scribner, 1951).

Burkill, T.A. *Mysterious Revelation* (Ithaca, NY: Cornell, 1963).

Burton, Ernst Dewitt, *Principles of Literary Criticism and the Synoptic Problem* (Chicago: University of Chicago Press, 1904).

Cadbury, Henry J., *The Making of Luke–Acts* (London: Society for the Preservation of Christian Knowledge, 1968).

—*The Style and Literary Method of Luke* (Harvard Theological Studies 6; Cambridge: Harvard University Press, 1970).

Caird, G.B., *The Gospel According to St. Luke* (Baltimore MD: Penguin, 1963).

Cole, R.A., *The Gospel According to St. Mark* (Tyndale New Testament Commentaries; Grand Rapids: Eerdmans, 1961).

Conzelmann, Hans, *An Outline of the Theology of the New Testament* (trans. John Bowden; New York and Evanston: Harper & Row, 1968).

—*The Theology of St. Luke* (trans. G. Buswell; London: Faber and Faber, 1960).

Creed, John Martin, *The Gospel According to St. Luke* (London: Macmillan and Co., 1957).

Cullmann, Oscar, *Early Christian Worship* (trans. A.S. Todd and J.B. Torrance; Chicago: Henry Regnery Co., 1953).

Davies, J.G., he *Ascended into Heaven* (London: Lutterworth Press, 1958).

Dibelius, Martin, *A Fresh Approach to the New Testament and Early Christian Literature* (trans. D.S. Noel and G. Abbott; New York: Scribner, 1936).

—*From Tradition to Gospel* (trans. B.L. Woolf; New York: Scribner, n.d).

Dillersberger, Joseph, *The Gospel of St. Luke* (Westminster, MD: Newman Press, 1958).

Donahue, John R., *Are You the Christ? The Trial Narrative in the Gospel of Mark* (Society of Biblical Literature Dissertation Series 10; Missoula, MT: University of Montana, 1973).

Dupont, Jacques, *The Sources of Acts* (trans. Kathleen Pond; New York: Herder & Herder, 1964).

Easton, Burton Scott, *The Gospel According to St. Luke* (New York: Scribner, 1926).

Ellis, E. Earle, *The Gospel of Luke* (London and Edinburgh: Nelson, 1966).

Evans, C.F., 'The Central Section of Luke's Gospel', in D.E. Nineham (ed.), *Studies in Luke–Acts* (Oxford: Basil Blackwell, 1955).

Flender, Helmut, *St. Luke, Theologian of Redemptive History* (trans. Reginald H. and Ilse Fuller; Philadelphia: Fortress, 1967).

Geldenhuys, Norman, *Commentary on the Gospel of St. Luke* (New International Commentary on the New Testament; Grand Rapids: Eerdmans, 1951).

Godet, Frédéric Louis, *Commentary on the Gospel of St. Luke* (trans. E.W. Shalders, 4th edn of the translation from the 2nd, French edn, 1887; reprint edn, Grand Rapids: Zondervan, n.d).

Goetz, Karl Gerhold, *Petrus* (Leipzig: J.C. Hinrichs'she Buchhandlung, 1927).

Gollwitzer, Helmut, *La Joie de Dieu* (Neuchatel et Paris: Editions Delachaux et Niesté S.A., 1966).

Grundmann, Waiter, *Das Evangelium nach Lukas* (Berlin: Evangelische Verlagsanstalt, 1934).

Haenchen, Ernst, *The Acts of the Apostles* (trans. Basil Blackwell; Philadelphia: Westminster, 1971).

Hahn, Ferdinand, *The Titles of Jesus in Christology* (trans. H. Knight and G. Ogg; London: Lutterworth Press, 1963).

Hughes, Philip E., *Paul's Second Epistle to the Corinthians* (New International Commentary on the New Testament; Grand Rapids: Eerdmans, 1962).

Jackson, F.S. Foakes, and Kirsopp Lake, *The Beginnings of Christianity: The Acts of the Apostles* (London: Macmillan, 1932; reprint ed., Grand Rapids: Baker, 1965).

Jeremias, Joachim, *The Parables of Jesus* (trans. S.H. Hooke; New York: Scribner, 6th edn, 1962).

—*The Prayers of Jesus* (trans. John Bowde *et al.*; London: SCM Press, 1967).

Jervell, Jacob, *Luke and the People of God: A New Look at Luke–Acts* (Minneapolis: Augsburg Press, 1972).

Johnson, Aubrey R., *The Cultic Prophet in Ancient Israel* (Cardiff, Wales: University of Wales Press Board, 1944).

Kee, Howard Clark, 'The Transfiguration in Mark: Epiphany or Apocalyptic Vision?', in John Reumann (ed.), *Understanding the Sacred Text* (Valley Forge, PA: Judson Press, 1972), pp. 135-52.

Kirk, Kenneth E., *The Vision of God* (New York: Harper & Row, 1966).

Klausner, Joseph, *The Messianic Idea in Israel* (trans. W.F. Stinespring; New York: Macmillan, 1955).

Kümmel, Werner Georg, *Promise and Fulfillment* (trans. Dorothea M. Barton; London: SCM Press, 1957).

LaGrange, P.M.J., *Evangile Selon Saint Luc* (Paris: Librarie Victor Le Coffre, 1921).

Lampe, G.W.H., 'The Holy Spirit in the Writings of St. Luke', in D.E. Nineham (ed.), *Studies in Luke–Acts* (Oxford: Basil Blackwell, 1955), pp. 159-200).

—'The Reasonableness of Typology', in T.W. Manson *et al.* (eds.), *Essays on Typology* (Naperville, IL: Alec R. Allenson, 1957), pp. 9-38.

Leaney, A.R.C., *A Commentary on the Gospel of St. Luke* (New York: Harper, 1958).

Lindsay, Thomas M., *The Gospel According to St. Luke* (New York: Scribner & Welford, 1887).

Linneman, Eta, *Parables of Jesus* (London: Society for the Preservation of Christian Knowledge, 1966).

Lohmeyer, Ernst, 'Our Father' (trans. John Bowden; New York: Harper & Row, 1952).

Loisy, Alfred, *The Birth of the Christian Religion* (trans. L.P. Jacks; New Hyde Park: University Books, 1962).
—*L'Evangile Selon Luc* (Paris: Emile Nourry, 1924).
Marshall, I. Howard, *Luke: Historian and Theologian* (Grand Rapids: Zondervan, 1970).
Marxsen, Wills, *Mark The Evangelist* (trans. James Boyce, *et. al*; Nashville and New York: Abingdon Press, 1969).
Mayor, Joseph B., *The Epistles of Jude and II Peter* (London: Macmillan, 1907; Grand Rapids: Baker, reprint edn, 1965).
Meeks, Wayne A., *The Prophet-King* (Leiden: Brill, 1967).
Meyer, Eduard, *Ursprung und Anfange des Christentums* (Stuttgart and Berlin: J.B. Cotta, 1923).
Moffat, James, *The General Epistles: New Testament Commentary* (New: York and London: Harper and Bros., n.d).
Montefiore, G.C., *The Synoptic Gospels* (London: Macmillan and Co., 1927).
Moore, A.L., *The Parousia of the New Testament* (Leiden: Brill, 1966).
Moule, C.F.D., 'The Christology of Acts', in D.E. Nineham (ed.), *Studies in Luke–Acts* (Oxford: Basil Blackwell, 1955), pp. 159-85.
—*The Gospel According to Mark* (Cambridge: The University Press, 1965).
Olshausen, Hermann, *Biblical Commentary on the New Testament* (6 vols.; trans. David Fosdick, Jr.; New York: Blakeman and Co., 1857-1858).
Otto, Rudolf, *Mysticism East and West* (trans. B.L. Bracey and R.C. Payne, New York: Macmillan, 1932).
Perrin, Norman, *The Kingdom of God in the Teachings of Jesus* (Philadelphia: Westminster, 1963).
Plummer, Alfred, *The Gospel According to St. Luke* (International Critical Commentary; New York: Scribner, 1896).
Rad, Gerhard von, *Old Testament Theology* (2 vols.; trans. D.M.G. Stalker; New York:. Harper & Bros., 1962).
Ramsey, Arthur Michael, *The Glory of God and the Transfiguration of Christ* (London: Longmans, Green and Co., 1949).
Redlich, Edwin Basil, *Form Criticism* (New York: Scribner, 1939).
Reicke, Bo, *The Gospel of Luke* (trans. R. MacKenzie; Richmond: John Knox Press, 1964).
Reiling, J., and J.L. Swellengrebel, *A Translator's Handbook on the Gospel of Luke* (Leiden: Brill, 1971).
Reumann, John, *Jesus in the Church's Gospels* (Philadelphia: Fortress, 1968).
Riesenfeld, Harald, *Jésus Transfiguré*: Copenhagen: Ejwar Munksgaard, 1947).
Robinson, James M., *The Problem of History in Mark* (Naperville, IL: Alec R. Allenson, 1957).
Rollins, Wallace Eugene, and Marion Benedict Rollins, *Jesus and his Ministry* (New York: Seabury Press, 1954).

Sanders, E.P., *The Tendencies of the Synoptic Tradition* (Cambridge: The University Press, 1969).
Schmidt, Karl Ludwig, *Der Rahmen der Geschicte Jesu* (Darmstadt: Wissenschaftliche, 1964).
Schniewind, Julius, *Das Evangelium nach Markus* (Göttingen: n.p., 1949).
Schweitzer, Albert, *The Quest of the Historical Jesus* (trans. W. Montgomery; New York: Macmillan, 1968).
Schweizer, Eduard, *The Good News According to Mark* (trans. Donald H. Madvig; Richmond: John Knox Press, 1970).
Soden von, Herman Freiherr, *Die wichtigsten Fragen im Leben Jesu* (Berlin: n.p., 1904).
Stonehouse, N.B., *The Witness of Luke to Christ* (London: Tyndale, 1951).
Strack, H.L., and Paul Billerbeck, *Commentar zum neuen Testament* (2 vols.; Munchen: Beck'she Verlangsbuchhandlung, 1924.
Strauss, David Friedrich, *The Life of Jesus Critically Examined* (trans. George Eliot; ed. Peter C. Hodgson; Lives of Jesus Series; Philadelphia: Fortress, 1972).
Streeter, Burnett Hillman, *The Four Gospels* (London: Macmillan, 1951).
Talbert, Charles H., *Literary Patterns, Theological Themes and the Genre of Luke–Acts* (Society of Biblical Literature Monograph Series 20; Missoula, MT: Scholars Press, 1974).
—*Luke and the Gnostics* (Nashville and New York: Abingdon Press, 1966).
Taylor, Vincent, *Behind the Third Gospel* (Oxford: Clarendon Press, 1926).
—*The Formation of the Gospel Tradition* (London: Macmillan, 1949).
—*The Gospels* (London: Epworth Press, 1939).
—*The Passion Narrative of St. Luke* (Cambridge: The University Press, 1972).
Teeple, Howard M., *The Mosaic Eschatological Prophet* (JBL monograph series 10; Philadelphia: Society of Biblical Literature, 1957).
Tinsley, E.J., *The Gospel According to Luke: The Cambridge Bible Commentary* (Cambridge: University Press, 1965).
Tödt, H.E., *The Son of Man in the Synoptic Tradition* (trans. Dorothea M. Barton; London: SCM Press, 1973).
Wand, J.W.C., *Transfiguration* (London: Faith Press, 1967).
Weiss, Bernard, *A Commentary on the New Testament* (trans. G.H. Schodde and E. Wilson; New York: Funk & Wagnalls, 1906).
Whitehouse, W.A., 'The Modern Discussion of Eschatology' (*Scottish Journal of Theology Occasional Papers, 2*; Edinburgh and London: Oliver Boyd, 1953).
Wilder, Amos N., *Early Christian Rhetoric* (Cambridge, MA: Harvard University Press, 1971).
Wrede, William, *The Messianic Secret* (trans. J.C.G. Greig; Cambridge and London: James Clark & Co., 1971).

Reference Works

Aland, Kurt, *et al.*, *The Greek New Testament* (New York: American Bible Society, 1966).

Bauer, Walter, *A Greek-English Lexicon of the New Testament* (trans. William F. Arndt and F. Wilbur Gingrich; Chicago: University of Chicago Press, 1957).

Blass, Friedrick W., Albert Debrunner, and Robert W. Funk, *A Greek Grammar of the New Testament* (Chicago: University of Chicago Press, 1961).

Delling, Gerhard, 'πληρόω' in Gerhard Kittel, Geoffrey William Bromiley, and Gerhard Friedrich, *Theological Dictionary of the New Testament* (trans. G. Bromiley; 10 vols.; Grand Rapids, MI: Eerdmans, 1964-).

Kittel, Gerhard, and Gerhard von Rad, 'δόξα', in Gerhard Kittel, Geoffrey William Bromiley, and Gerhard Friedrich, *Theological Dictionary of the New Testament* (trans. G. Bromiley; 10 vols.; Grand Rapids, MI: Eerdmans, 1964-).

Foerster, Werner, 'ἀστραπή', in Gerhard Kittel, Geoffrey William Bromiley, and Gerhard Friedrich, *Theological Dictionary of the New Testament* (trans. G. Bromiley; 10 vols.; Grand Rapids, MI: Eerdmans, 1964-).

Jeremias, Joachim, 'εὔχομαι', in Gerhard Kittel, Geoffrey William Bromiley, and Gerhard Friedrich, *Theological Dictionary of the New Testament* (trans. G. Bromiley; 10 vols.; Grand Rapids, MI: Eerdmans, 1964-).

—'Ἡλ(ε)ίας', in Gerhard Kittel, Geoffrey William Bromiley, and Gerhard Friedrich, *Theological Dictionary of the New Testament* (trans. G. Bromiley; 10 vols.; Grand Rapids, MI: Eerdmans, 1964-).

—'Μωυσῆς', in Gerhard Kittel, Geoffrey William Bromiley, and Gerhard Friedrich, *Theological Dictionary of the New Testament* (trans. G. Bromiley; 10 vols.; Grand Rapids, MI: Eerdmans, 1964-).

Kautsch, E., 'Theophany', in *The New Schaff-Herzog Encyclopedia of Religious Knowledge* (New York: Funk and Wagnalls, 1911), II, pp. 403-405.

Metzger, Bruce M., *A Textual Commentary on the Greek New Testament* (London and New York: United Bible Societies, 1971).

Michaelis, Wilhelm, 'ὁδός', in Gerhard Kittel, Geoffrey William Bromiley, and Gerhard Friedrich, Theological Dictionary of the New Testament (trans. G. Bromiley; 10 vols.; Grand Rapids, MI: Eerdmans, 1964-).

—'σκηνή', in Gerhard Kittel, Geoffrey William Bromiley, and Gerhard Friedrich, Theological Dictionary of the New Testament (trans. G. Bromiley; 10 vols.; Grand Rapids, MI: Eerdmans, 1964-).

Moulton, James Hope, *A Grammar of New Testament Greek* (3 vols.; Edinburgh: T & T Clark, 3rd reprint edn, 1957).

Oepke, Albrecht, 'ἐπιστάρης', in Gerhard Kittel, Geoffrey William Bromiley, and Gerhard Friedrich, *Theological Dictionary of the New Testament* (trans. G. Bromiley; 10 vols.; Grand Rapids, MI: Eerdmans, 1964-).
—'νεφέλη', in Gerhard Kittel, Geoffrey William Bromiley, and Gerhard Friedrich, *Theological Dictionary of the New Testament* (trans. G. Bromiley; 10 vols.; Grand Rapids, MI: Eerdmans, 1964-).
Zimmerli, Walther, and Joachim Jeremias, 'παῖς θεοῦ', in Gerhard Kittel, Geoffrey William Bromiley, and Gerhard Friedrich, *Theological Dictionary of the New Testament* (trans. G. Bromiley; 10 vols.; Grand Rapids, MI: Eerdmans, 1964-).

Dissertations

Best, Thomas F., 'Transfiguration and Discipleship in Matthew' (PhD dissertation, Graduate Theological Union, 1974).
Boomershine, Thomas Eugene, 'Mark, the Storyteller: A Rhetorical-Critical Investigation of Mark's Passion and Resurrection Narrative' (PhD dissertation, Union Theological Seminary, 1974).
Carruth, T.R. 'The Jesus-as-Prophet Motif in Luke–Acts' (PhD Dissertation, Baylor University, 1973).
Farrell, Hobert Kenneth, 'The Eschatological Perspective of Luke–Acts' (PhD dissertation, Boston University, 1972).
Harris, Oscar Gerald, 'Prayer in Luke–Acts: A Study in the Theology of Luke' (PhD dissertation, Vanderbilt University, 1966).
Pilgrim, Walter E. 'The Death of Christ in Lukan Soteriology' (PhD dissertation, Princeton Theological Seminary, 1971).

Periodicals

Allegro, J.M., 'Further Messianic References in Qumran Literature', *Journal of Biblical Literature* 75 (1956), pp. 174-87.
Babcock, F.J., 'The Transfiguration', *Journal of Theological Studies* 22 (1921), pp. 321-26.
Bacon, Benjamin W., 'After 6 Days: A New Clue For Gospel Critics', *Harvard Theological Review* 8 (1915), pp. 94-121.
—'The Transfiguration Story', *American Journal of Theology* 6 (1903), pp. 230-65.
Beardslee, William A., 'The Casting of Lots at Qumran and in the Book of Acts', *Novum Testamentum* 4 (1960), pp. 245-52.
Bernardin, Joseph B., 'The Transfiguration', *Journal of Biblical Literature* 52-(1933), pp. 181-89.

Braithwaite, William C., 'The Teaching of the Transfiguration', *Expository Times* 17 (1905-06), pp. 372-75.

Bretscher, Paul G., 'Exodus 4.22-23 and the Voice from Heaven', *Journal of Biblical Literature* 30 (1968), pp. 301-11.

Burn, A.E., 'The Transfiguration', *Expository Times* 14 (1902-03), pp. 442-47.

Carlston, Charles Edwin, 'The Transfiguration and Resurrection', *Journal of Biblical Literature* 80 (1961), pp. 233-40.

Davies, J.G., 'The Prefigurement of the Ascension in the Third Gospel', *Journal of Theological Studies*, n. s. 6 (1955), pp. 229-33.

Denis, A.M., 'Une theologie de la vie Chretiene chez saint Marc', *Vie Spirituelle* 41 (1959), pp. 416-27.

Dodd, C.H., 'The Kingdom of God Has Come', *Expository Times* 48 (1936), pp. 138-42.

Easton, Burton Scott, 'Linguistic Evidence for the Lukan Source L', *Journal of Biblical Literature* 29 (1910), pp. 139-80.

Ellis, E. Earle, 'Present and Future Eschatology in Luke', *New Testament Studies* 12 (1965-66), pp. 27-41.

Evans, Edward, 'The Transfiguration of Jesus', *Evangelical Quarterly* 26 (1954), pp. 97-104.

Feuillet, A., 'Les perspectives proposés á chague évangéliste', *Biblica* 39 (1958), pp. 281-301.

Forsom, J. Hathieson, 'The Transfiguration', *Expository Times* 17 (1905-06), pp. 140-41.

Fryer, A.T., 'The Purpose of the Transfiguration', *Journal of Theological Studies* 5 (1904), pp. 214-17.

Groves, William L., 'The Significance of the Transfiguration of Our Lord', *Theology 11* (1925), pp. 86-92.

Harnack, Adolf von, *Die Verklärungsgeschichte Jesu, der Bericht des Paulus (1 Kor. 15, 3ff) und die beiden Christusvisionen des Petrus* (Sitzungsberichte der Königlich Preussischen Akademie der Wissenschaften zu Berlin 7; Berlin: Walter de Gruyter, 1922).

Harrison, E.F., 'The Transfiguration', *Bibliotheca Sacra* 93 (1936), pp. 315-23.

Holmes, R., 'The Purpose of the Transfiguration of Our Lord', *Theology* 11 (1925), pp. 86-92.

Jensen, Peter, 'Die Verklärungsberg-Szene und Nachbarepisoden in einem chinesichen Märchen?' *Theologische Studien und Kritiken* 104 (1932), pp. 229-37; 105 (1933), pp. 330-36.

Johnson, S. Lewis, Jr., 'The Transfiguration of Christ', *Bibliotheca Sacra* 124 (1967), pp. 133-44.

Kennedy, H.A.A., 'The Purpose of the Transfiguration', *Journal of Theological Studies* 4 (1903), pp. 270-73.

Lohmeyer, Ernst, 'Die Verklärung Jesu nach dem Markus Evangelium', *Zeitschrift für Neutestamentliche Wissenschaft* 21 (1922), pp. 185-215

McCurley, Foster R., Jr., '"And After Six Days" (Mk 9.2): A Semitic Literary Device', *Journal of Biblical Literature* 93 (1974), pp. 67-81.

MacMillan, Hugh, 'Water-Marks in the Narratives of Our Lord's Transfiguration', *Expository Times* 7 (1895-96), pp. 25-27.

Martin, E.J., 'The Transfiguration', *Expository Times* 38 (1926-27), pp. 89.

Masson, D., 'La Transfiguration de Jésus (Marc 9.2-13)', *Revue de Theologie et Philosophie* 97 (1964), pp. 1-14.

Müller, Hans-Peter, 'Die Verklärung Jesu, Eine motivgeschichtliche Studie', *Zeitschrift für Neutestamentliche Wissenschaft* 51 (1960), pp. 56-64.

Ramsay, W.M., 'The Time of the Transfiguration', *Expositor* 7 (1908), pp. 557-62.

Rivera, L.F., 'El misterio del Hijo del Hombre en la transfiguración', *Revista Biblica* 28 (1966), pp. 19-34.

Roehrs, Walter, 'God's Tabernacles Among Men: A Study of the Transfiguration', *Concordia Theological Monthly* 35 (1965), pp. 18-25.

Rowe, G. Stringer, 'The Transfiguration', *Expository Times* 15 (1903-04), pp. 336.

Stein, Robert H., 'What is *Redaktionsgeschichte*?' *Journal of Biblical Literature* (1969), pp. 45-56.

Talbert, Charles H., 'The Redaction Critical Quest for Luke the Theologian', *Perspective* 11 (1970), pp. 171-222.

Thrall, Margaret E., 'Elijah and Moses in Mark's Account of the Transfiguration', *New Testament Studies* 16 (1970), pp. 305-17.

Ziesler, J.A., 'The Transfiguration Story and the Markan Soteriology', *Expository Times* 81 (1970), pp. 263-69.

Index of Biblical (and Other Ancient) References

Index of Authors

www.ingramcontent.com/pod-product-compliance
Lightning Source LLC
Chambersburg PA
CBHW072141090426
42739CB00013B/3247
9781953358035